S0-DTQ-950

National Urban Policy

Problems and Prospects

National Urban Policy

Problems and Prospects

●A15047 403840

Edited by

Harold L. Wolman

and

Elizabeth J. Agius

HT
123
.N333
1996
West

 WAYNE STATE UNIVERSITY PRESS • DETROIT

Copyright 1996 by Wayne State University Press, Detroit, Michigan 48201. All rights reserved. No part of this book may be reproduced without formal permission. Manufactured in the United State of America.

99   98   97   96   5   4   3   2   1

Library of Congress Cataloging-in-Publication Data

National urban policy : problems and prospects / edited by Harold L.
    Wolman and Elizabeth J. Agius
            p.   cm.
    Papers presented at a conference held Mar. 1994, Wayne State
University.
    Includes bibliographical references.
    ISBN   0–8143–2543–2 (pbk. : alk. paper)
    1. Urban policy—United States—Congresses.   2. United States.
Dept. of Housing and Urban Development. President's national urban
policy report—Congresses.   I. Wolman, Harold.   II. Agius,
Elizabeth J.
HT123.N333   1996
307.76'0973—dc20   95–39194

Contents

Preface

The president is charged by Congress with preparing and presenting a national urban policy report to Congress and the nation every second year. The first report was issued in 1972 and a report has been prepared and published approximately every two years since. Initially the report was intended to serve as a forum for policy recommendations and to evaluate current approaches to urban problems. In time, though, the report has primarily been used to set forth the administration's "point of view" toward urban areas and urban problems and to provide descriptions of the major programs directed toward urban areas. Though they vary widely in form, quality and impact, the reports are nonetheless important, for they are virtually the only vehicle that forces the government to focus comprehensively on urban areas and their problems.

In March 1994, the College of Urban, Labor and Metropolitan Affairs at Wayne State University sponsored a conference designed to examine national urban policy and the role of the national urban policy report. The conference was funded by the college and held on the campus of Wayne State University in Detroit. This book is a result of that conference and draws upon papers, commentaries, and discussion from it.

The conference was a two-day working seminar, and its focus was twofold: to identify the critical problems and concerns facing the nation's urban areas and to consider the role and function of the national urban policy report in the public policy-making process. The conference was therefore concerned with identifying and conceptualizing the most important urban problems that a national urban policy report should address, the nature, extent, and intensity of these problems, and the most promising approaches for dealing with them. At the same time it grappled with the question of how the report could be improved, altered, and/or restructured to more effectively contribute to understanding, informed debate, and public policy.

The conference format consisted of four parts. It began with a general background paper, presenting a history and analysis of the national urban policy reports. This was followed by the presentation of the major conceptual questions involved in preparing a national urban policy report.

These issues include such concerns as: What is meant by urban? What should the focus of the analysis be? And what are some alternatives for organizing the categories presented? We used these questions to stimulate a discussion and create a framework for viewing the remaining sessions. Five papers were then presented, reflecting the core areas of the urban system: labor markets, households and residents, social institutions, physical systems, and the public sector. The papers explored the problems a national urban policy report should address, provided data on conditions and trends with respect to these problems, and suggested promising policy responses. The final session was devoted to the report. In this discussion the participants focused on the issues they felt needed to be included, and engaged in substantial discussion about the report's nature, function, and format.

The Introduction brings together the main themes of the conference papers, discussant comments, and the ensuing discussions. This is followed by a background paper on the national urban policy report and then by the five substantive papers, each followed by the discussant's response.

The editors would like to thank the participants listed below for their contributions to a highly stimulating conference and to this book. They would also like to thank Sue Marx Smock, Dean of the College of Urban, Labor and Metropolitan Affairs at Wayne State University for support, both intellectual and financial, that made the conference and therefore this book possible.

Harold L. Wolman
Elizabeth J. Agius

Conference Participants

Elizabeth J. Agius is a graduate research assistant in the College of Urban, Labor and Metropolitan Affairs and a doctoral student in the Department of Political Science at Wayne State University.

William R. Barnes is Director of the Center for Research and Program Development at the National League of Cities in Washington, DC.

Robin Boyle is the Chairman of the Department of Geography and Urban Planning at Wayne State University.

Phillip L. Clay is Professor and Department Chair in the Department of Urban Studies and Planning at Massachusetts Institute of Technology.

Sheldon Danziger is Professor of Social Work and Public Policy, Faculty Associate in Population Studies, and Director of the Research and Training Program on Poverty, the Underclass and Public Policy at the University of Michigan.

Randall W. Eberts is Executive Director of the W. E. Upjohn Institute for Employment Research in Kalamazoo, Michigan.

Peter Eisinger is Professor of Political Science and Public Policy and Director of the LaFollette Institute of Public Affairs at the University of Wisconsin.

Coit C. Ford, III is graduate research assistant in the College of Urban, Labor and Metropolitan Affairs and a doctoral candidate in the Department of Political Science at Wayne State University.

Royce Hanson is Dean and Professor of Political Economy, School of Social Sciences at the University of Texas at Dallas.

Edward W. Hill is Professor of Urban Studies and Public Administration at the Maxine Goodman Levin College of Urban Affairs of Cleveland State University and editor of *Economic Development Quarterly.*

Harry J. Holzer is Professor in the Department of Economics at Michigan State University.

Helen F. Ladd is Professor of Public Policy Studies and Economics at Duke University, where she is also Director of Graduate Studies in Public Policy.

Larry Ledebur is Director of the Center for Urban Studies and Professor in the College of Urban, Labor and Metropolitan Affairs at Wayne State University.

Charles J. Orlebeke is Professor and Director, School of Urban Planning and Policy at the University of Illinois at Chicago.

Robert D. Plotnick is Professor of Public Affairs and Social Work at the University of Washington and Associate Dean of the Graduate School of Public Affairs.

Sue Marx Smock is Dean of the College of Urban, Labor and Metropolitan Affairs at Wayne State University.

Anita A. Summers is Professor Emeritus of Public Policy and Management in the Wharton School of the University of Pennsylvania and a Senior Research Fellow in the Wharton Real Estate Center.

Lyke Thompson is Associate Professor in the College of Urban, Labor and Metropolitan Affairs at Wayne State University.

Margaret Wilder is Professor in the Department of Geography and Planning at the State University of New York at Albany.

Harold L. Wolman is Associate Dean of the College of Urban, Labor and Metropolitan Affairs and Professor of Political Science at Wayne State University.

Introduction

Harold L. Wolman

The problems of America's urban areas, intertwined as they are with problems of race and class, have been widely acknowledged over the past several decades as serious national concerns, even if public policy has not always addressed them as such. In the early 1970s Congress recognized this by mandating the president to prepare and present to Congress a national urban policy report every second year. Initially the report was intended to serve as a forum for policy recommendations and for evaluating current approaches to urban problems. In time, however, the report has come to be used primarily to set forth the administration's "point of view" toward urban areas and urban problems and to provide descriptions of the major programs and/or proposed administration policy initiatives directed toward them. The reports serve as virtually the only vehicle that forces the federal government to focus comprehensively on urban areas and their problems.

In March 1994 the College of Urban, Labor and Metropolitan Affairs at Wayne State University sponsored and funded a conference designed to examine national urban policy and the national urban policy report. The purpose was both to ask whether and how the report could be made into a more useful document and to discuss the kinds of urban problems, issues, and policy approaches that such a document might concern itself with.

Participants were asked to address themselves to a set of questions about urban policy and the national urban policy report, including (for a complete discussion outline, see Appendix 1):

- Should the federal government have an explicit and articulated "urban policy"?
- Should there be a national urban policy report? What functions can or should such a report serve?
- What should a national urban policy report consist of? Should it focus on conditions, trends and indicators, identification of the most critical problems, program description, evaluation of public policies and programs, policy recommendations, or some combination of these?
- What should be the geographic focus of urban policy and of the report, i.e., what do we mean by urban?
- Should urban policy and the urban policy report be people-based, place-based, or some combination thereof?
- How can the national urban policy report be changed and improved?

Papers were commissioned for the conference on five topics:

- The urban economy and labor markets.
- Urban households, residents, and their well-being.
- Urban social institutions.
- Urban physical systems.
- The urban public sector.

For each of these topic areas, authors were asked to address the most important problem with which a national urban policy and a national urban policy report should be concerned, to present data on conditions and trends with respect to these problems, and to discuss possible approaches for solving these problems.

In this introduction, the main themes of the conference are summarized as reflected in the conference papers, the discussants' responses, and the ensuing discussion by the participants, which was recorded and transcribed.

As Peter Eisinger noted in his remarks at the concluding session, much of the conference—not only the discussion, but the papers themselves—was preoccupied with the question of "why should there be a national concern for cities" and what the federal role should be.

Peter Eisinger: I believe there is a federal interest in cities. I think the case has to be made more powerfully, though. In some ways I think the responsibility is on the federal government to make the case. It is more convincing from that angle than it is, say, from the cities'. For cities to argue that there ought to be a federal interest is too self-serving.

Royce Hanson argued powerfully, both in his paper and in discussion, that national concern for cities must be rooted in functions that cities and the urban system perform for the nation as a whole. In discussing the federal role in urban physical systems, Hanson wrote:

> The first step is to come to terms with just what the national interest is in the physical networks, facilities, capital stock, and spaces of urban regions. Not all of the physical system of every city is of national concern. In our federal system, a definition of national interest requires more than the mere presence of a problem somewhere in the nation. It requires a nationally shared interest in it and a judgment that intervention by the national government is an appropriate use of its power and resources.
>
> In this light, I argue that there is a national interest in four aspects of the urban physical system:
>
> 1. The elements of national infrastructure that support the urban base for U.S. participation in an advanced international economy.
>
> 2. The facilities and environment that attract and sustain the institutional capacity needed to provide world leadership in value added through knowledge in products and services produced in American cities.
>
> 3. The regional planning and governance capacity to guide the development of a physical environment that allows American cities to compete successfully as the locations of the leading sectors of the world economy.
>
> 4. Investments in physical systems and regulatory policies that support domestic social policies. (p. 151)

Randy Eberts took the same approach in his article on labor markets, arguing that, "As the core structure of cities deteriorates and the advantages of close proximity diminish, businesses and households have left inner cities for outlying areas. This shift . . . has helped to diminish the nation's capacity to spawn high-productivity, high-growth activities." Anita Summers summed up much of this discussion at the last session:

Anita Summers: Why is there a federal interest in cities? Why should there be? It seems to me, around the table, we have suggested several ways. One is because markets don't work smoothly in evening out labor markets. That is why we've got high fixed unemployment rates in some places, relative to others, for forty to fifty years. So the market does not iron these wrinkles out very smoothly.

Second, because there are national policies, such as the federal housing policies we have been talking about, that impose costs on particular jurisdictions. Those jurisdictions should be compensated. And third, because there are huge infrastructure investments in cities that will get lost; these investments are declining in value as cities decline.

However, this formulation of the national interest in cities was challenged. Responding to Royce Hanson's argument:

Hal Wolman: Let me play devil's advocate. You won't have much trouble convincing anybody that it is important for the United States to have the research and development capacity needed to provide world leadership in value added through knowledge or that it has the physical capacity to compete successfully in the world economy.

But, why does that capacity have to be in cities? Or does it have to be? Are you arguing that if those institutions and physical facilities we now have in cities decline, they will not occur elsewhere, and we will be diminished in our international capacity?

Or are you suggesting that the cost of replicating that capacity outside the cities would be so expensive and so much greater than incremental aid to restore existing capacity in cities that it would be uneconomic to do so. What is the link that says these things must occur in cities?

Royce Hanson: I think there are two levels of response. One is that more than likely they will occur in cities, and the question is which cites. Another is whether they will be in U.S. cities or other cities, because it seems to me the competition for not all but most of these kinds of activities is a competition among cities in economically advanced countries.

The second level of the argument is that while clearly some of these things don't absolutely have to be in cities, the agglomeration economies that support these kinds of activities, and which encourage their joint location, is urban in character. It is often not urban in the scale or intensity of land use of the traditional city, but it is still very urban. And in addition to just the economic activity that still tends to cluster, in spite of all the wonders of telecommunications, the systems of soft infrastructure, education systems, cultural systems, and various kinds of community systems that are necessary for the full development of a competitive international economy, also tend to be urban.

Nor were all of the participants comfortable with the implications of Hanson's formulation for the national interest in providing federal aid, as the following exchange illustrates:

Bill Barnes: Go back to the choice you posed, which is what do we do if we have a dollar to spend on the physical environment. Shouldn't we spend it on "local" needs instead of these so-called "national" investments in urban areas?

Royce Hanson: No, here I would say that the federal government should not spend it on planting trees or fixing curbs. I think that in looking at this in the context of the federal system, that local government—and particularly state government—ought to be spending a lot more on its physical capital than it is spending.

Peter Eisinger: I want to follow up on the same general point in terms of what Royce said about transportation subsidies. You suggest that the place where we ought to be putting our federal dollars in the inner city is in transportation facilities, airports, interurban highways, rather than operating or even construction subsidies for mass transit facilities in cities. I am wondering how else such systems could survive without federal aid? I can't imagine that they would, that they are sustainable without outside money. I have never seen any indication that cities, or even metropolitan areas, can generate the user revenues or tax revenues to build and sustain mass transit systems.

And I would suggest that there is a federal interest in viable mass transit systems, reducing automobile use, facilitating economic efficiency.

Royce Hanson: It seems to me that a great deal of the federal money in mass transportation systems is not a good economic investment in mobility. In many cases there are better ways of moving people about than the use of rail systems.

What I am trying to say in the paper is not that mass transportation of cities is not important, but that in terms of federal investment there are better places to put the money.

The conferees also continually came back to the question of whether urban policy should be place-based or people-based (although most were unwilling to reduce this to an either/or choice) and the related question of whether it should focus on cities, metropolitan areas, or all urban places.

Peter Eisinger: When you talk about urban labor markets, it is natural in the place-versus-people choice to end up with a people policy. But I want to suggest that we need to be cautious about that. You can't throw out the place. You have to do both at the same time. Place-based strategies, I think, are still politically important. Lots of people are stuck in a place, or they choose not to leave it, and when we talk about a people-based strategy, you're talking about omitting the place's capacity to serve those people.

Helen Ladd: In the work I have done on enterprise zones I identified three categories: people-oriented strategies, pure place strategies, and place-based people strategies. I put the Clinton empowerment zones in the place-based people strategy. The English enterprise zones were actually not people oriented, directly; they were pure place strategies. Ultimately they were meant to help people, but they were oriented toward vacant land areas; the idea was that you get new development there, and things take off. The goal was not to help people who currently lived in that zone, but rather to help people in a broader area. The goal was new economic development.

But I think it is important to keep bearing in mind what we are trying to do. Are we trying to just use the place-based strategy to improve the quality of life for the people who are there now, because they are stuck there, at least in the short run? That's a legitimate thing to do, I think. Or are we thinking about it in a more dynamic sense as an economic development strategy where we do things to bring some firms into the area in an effort to promote economic development.

I think it is important to think separately about those two. We might argue for place-based strategies for the first reason, to help the people there and provide social services in a place-based manner. But I think we oversell the economic development component of the place-based strategy.

Phillip Clay: I would like to raise a question that we all can use on our final exam. If we were in the position of writing the urban policy report, would we write a report that addresses the issues faced by urban residents, central-city residents who have massive needs, and would we write it in response to their needs? Or would we write a more universal report about urban places? We could make the political case with a lot more acceptance if we included both people and place concerns.

Randy Eberts: Maybe I would say what Phil said in a slightly different way. I see two questions. In focusing on the people problems, I would ask: are there aspects of the traditional city that we want to preserve or promote in dealing with people problems? And the other question would be from the other end: how would we better be able to address problems of people if we took place concerns scale, externalities, urban spatial structure into account?

Anita Summers: We are interested in people, ultimately, but if your are going to help people, one of the ways in which you have to do it is to change some of the institutional structures. They exist in jurisdictions, and people versus place isn't a choice. We need to help people directly, *and* we need to reframe some of the institutions that are imposing and sustaining these problems for people. I don't think it is either/or. We need policies that address both.

The people-versus-place debate was also played out in another interesting way. If a mobility strategy succeeded and poor people, particularly poor minorities, were successful in moving from areas of high poverty concentration ("underclass areas") to non-poverty concentration areas, what would be the impact on those left behind and on the community institutions and fabric? In his chapter, Phil Clay notes that those who have been labeled the "underclass" constitute no more than 20 percent of inner-city residents and goes on to add:

> A comparable if not larger number of their brethren is doing better than ever before. These more prosperous young people are moving in even larger numbers to the suburbs or to areas away from crisis communities. Even the poor peers who move out seem to do better in a different environment. The latter point underscores the power of place for transmission of opportunity. The flight is part of the problem in that the low-income area is worse off for their leaving. Those who leave are part of the solution in that they are often going to an area where their children will have more opportunities, face fewer risks, and enjoy a more supportive environment. (pp. 166–67)

The concern for the fate of these inner-city areas and their residents was particularly expressed by Margaret Wilder in her reaction to Royce Hanson's paper and presentation:

Margaret Wilder: As you talked about ways in which the feds could have a role, and suggested investments in things like transportation and so forth, all those things struck me as the part of regionalism that worries me the most. These investments are not going to do anything about the disinvestment, loss of economic activity, and viability of those inner-city areas. And it strikes me that these very investments, if I think about airports in particular, have a tendency to increase dispersal, and increase disinvestment, increase concentration in the new suburban nodes.

I am struggling with how we reconcile those two things. Or can we ever reconcile them?

Royce Hanson: I don't know that you can fully reconcile them. I think you have to say that indeed Emerson was right, it is important to be able to hold, simultaneously, two contradictory ideas. A number of the things that we will do in terms of investments will accelerate trends toward dispersement.

When we were working on urban policy at the National Academy a few years ago, we came up with a neat, slippery formulation of this, which is that you have to invest in the mainstream, but you cannot forget the people in places that are left behind. Therefore you have a second-tier policy that is ameliorative policy, aimed at reducing the burden on the most disadvantaged as a result of the movement of the more successful into the mainstream of economic activity. I'm not sure that this quite answers your question.

Margaret Wilder: That bothers me more. It strikes me that you are exacerbating the problem and sort of saying, "Well, we'll try to do something about it, but I'm not sure what."

Royce Hanson: Strategically, what you want to do is try to move more and more people into that mainstream of economic activity, and that relates to some of the things we were talking about yesterday, such as improving the operation of the labor market and investments in human capital. And it seems to me that investments in the physical capital of the city go along with this.

In identifying the main problems facing urban areas and setting forth appropriate federal government roles for dealing with these, the authors of the articles took a wide variety of approaches, as might be expected, given the diversity of the topics they were addressing. However, there was widespread agreement that, while an activist federal role and federal assistance were necessary, some of the problems facing urban areas were due to (or exacerbated by) previous federal programs that had inadvertently contributed to urban decline. In her article, for example, Anita Summers writes:

There are a large number of federal policies that have the worthy objectives of helping the low-income population, improving the nation's transportation network, facilitating home ownership for veterans, and encouraging capital investment, but which inadvertently have contributed to the distress of the nation's largest cities. It is important to underscore the fact that these policies were designed to contribute to the well-being of various groups but that their potential impact on cities was ignored. The concentration of low-income housing in cities warrants particular attention. It was destructive to cities and to housing-development residents. The expanded transportation network helped to empty cities; the criteria for VA mortgage encouraged the move to the suburbs; and the requirement for many years that lower investment tax rates be applicable only to new investments meant that investments in places other than old cities were subsidized. (p. 127)

In addition, there was widespread agreement that any new federal initiative or assistance must take place within very severe resource constraints. Summers indicates that her proposals are intended to be expenditure-neutral, noting that, "Fiscal constraints are severe at all levels of government, and fiscal restraint is a requirement for political acceptability and for sharpening the real choices" (p. 130). Hanson echoes the same theme in his article: "For the foreseeable future, federal resources will be scarce. We cannot provide an indiscriminate array of fiscal transfers for a wide set of undeniable needs for local public works" (p. 151). And Clay sets forth as one of five criteria for developing policies toward neighborhoods and communities that they "should be within the resource constraints of the federal government" (p. 179).

It is within this context that most conferees described the critical urban problems and set forth their preferred solutions. In his article, Randy Eberts identified a series of problems in urban labor markets:

For individuals, these issues include slow wage growth, increased earnings inequality, persistent earnings gap between whites and minorities, disparity in job opportunities and earnings between inner cities and suburbs, the spatial mismatch of jobs, and the increased isolation of many inner-city residents. For the nation, the issues are the social fallout from growing income disparities and reduced income mobility and the economy's diminished growth capacity as the physical and social infrastructure supporting urban area markets deteriorates. (p. 53)

He also points to a series of "intellectual barriers of poor education and inadequate support groups and referral networks" (p. 61) and emphasizes that "The growing gap between skill requirements of the workplace and skills of inner-city residents deters many workers from participating in urban labor markets." Eberts refers to a lack of "workplace competencies" for many low-skilled persons and particularly blacks. He cites research indicating that:

> many disadvantaged individuals have difficulty finding or holding jobs because they do not understand what employers expect of them, such as proper dress, getting to work on time, coming to work every day, working well with fellow employees and management. They also lack other basic skills necessary to perform any job, such as problem solving, resource and time management, and organization. (p. 62)

However, in his discussion of Ebert's paper, Harry Holzer stresses recent evidence that the primary problem is the lack of *basic cognitive skills*—i.e. reading and math—and that these may underlie some of the deficiencies in other "workplace competencies" that Ebert notes.

Holzer also notes that, while mentioned in Eberts's paper, employer discrimination against blacks does not receive the emphasis it deserves. According to Holzer:

> Employers clearly *perceive* lower skills, poor attitudes, and worse job performance among blacks, especially males. To the extent that these perceptions are correct *on average*, we may still have a problem of "statistical discrimination," in which these characteristics are attributed to *all* blacks by employers whose ability to accurately screen across different individuals is very limited. To the extent that employers exaggerate these differences, or cater to the prejudices of their customers and employees as well as their own, we may have "pure discrimination" as well. Either way, the results of recent audit studies by the Urban Institute and others suggest these employer perceptions are major additional barriers. (p. 70)

Eberts's policy suggestions begin with the need to address the underlying economic and social causes of the slowdown in national productivity growth that he holds responsible for both the sluggish growth in real income and widening income disparities that now characterize the condition of urban labor markets. At the urban level, widening gaps between cities and suburbs with respect to earnings, employment, and quality of life should be addressed through a national urban policy "promoting the establishment of regional governments, sharing of tax bases, and coordinating metropolitan provision of government services" (p. 64). He argues for improving the quality of education and work-related training as a means of overcoming the intellectual barriers to employment referred to above. In particular he urges a more intensive case-management effort to establish workplace competencies and attach disadvantaged individuals to the workforce:

> Establishing support groups and supplying appropriate role models through mentoring and employment advocacy programs will provide access to the labor market and ensure that workers remain in the labor force. Assigning workers to case managers on a long-term basis, at least until the person has been on the same job for six months, would keep individuals from getting lost within the system and keep them attached to the workforce. (p. 65)

Finally, Eberts advocates programs to that will increase workforce experience and attach disadvantaged workers to the labor force. In particular, he suggests wage supplements and public service employment programs as desirable means to these ends.

In his article, Robert Plotnick develops a series of indicators to assess the well-being of urban households and residents and then applies these to compare, first, metropolitan areas to non-metropolitan areas, and then central cities to suburbs. He concludes:

> Metropolitan areas have higher median income, less poverty, and better health-care coverage than non-metropolitan areas, and so score better in terms of material well-being and economic security. Indicators of physical security show that metropolitan areas are far worse off than non-metropolitan areas. Measures of health status mostly show the same thing. Because crime reduces the ability to take part in community life, this aspect of well-being is lower in metropolitan areas. However, another indicator of this

functioning—income inequality—shows parity between metropolitan and non-metropolitan areas. The very incomplete indicators of family life presented here suggest that this component of well-being is lower in metropolitan areas as well. The well-being of metropolitan-area residents in general therefore compares unfavorably to that of non-metropolitan residents, unless one weights material well-being strongly.

Within metropolitan areas it is clear that central cities have lower levels of well-being than their surrounding smaller cities and suburbs, and often substantially so. Most of the nation's largest cities are also worse off than average on most of the indicators presented here, but there is considerable variation among these cities on every indicator. (p. 98)

Commenting on Plotnick's paper, Sheldon Danziger stresses the last point and cautions those who utilize such indicators not to focus solely on differences between categories such as metropolitan and non-metropolitan areas or cities and suburbs, but instead on the "large and growing extent of within-group inequality. . . . By calling attention to a set of spatial categories, it leads Plotnick and the rest of us to derive conclusions based on *between-group* comparisons even though these differences are smaller than the *within-group* differences in every locale."

Plotnick recommends a comprehensive approach to deal with the problems of low levels of average well-being for residents of cities:

The generally low performance of central cities across a wide range of indicators suggests that no single policy intervention can hope to raise the average well-being of city dwellers up to national levels. Rather, a comprehensive policy strategy embracing labor-market performance, income support programs, health care, crime prevention, and supportive family services will be necessary. At the same time, the clear differences among cities and metropolitan areas on every indicator mean it would make little sense to apply a uniform mix of policies to all. Policies tailored to each city's or area's particular problems and strengths would hold greater promise. (p. 98)

Anita Summers identifies the primary problem for the urban public sector quite succinctly in her article: "cities are being assigned an increasing share of the *nation's* poverty-related burdens, without being allocated resources to deal with these burdens" (p. 107). Furthermore, she adds, cities cannot in general control the expenditures that result from this poverty burden, many of which result from national-level policy decisions (such as immigration policy) that are outside of the scope of city government influence. As a consequence, she argues:

> The growing level and density of poverty in central cities lead to a fiscal burden that many central cities cannot continue to bear for the nation without proper recompense. Poverty clearly is a national problem. The size and allocation of the welfare safety net is determined primarily at the national level. Moreover, while poor local-service delivery has stimulated the migration of the middle class to the suburbs, cities did not invite the poor to concentrate within their borders. A complex web of socioeconomic factors and the dynamic of historical demographics helped produce the current location patterns. (p. 111)

Summers articulates both short- and long-term strategies to address the urban fiscal problems facing cities. In the short term she calls for new allocational formulas for the flow of federal (and state) funds to cities that "reflect the extra social cost, economic and fiscal costs of the dense concentrations of the poor and immigrants." In the long run she stresses the importance of policies that reduce the concentration of the poor now living in central cities. Like Eberts, she believes this requires a "macro-policy that emphasizes high levels of employment," as a necessary but not sufficient condition. She also argues for federal and state legislation (including subsidies) to facilitate the formation of regional tax and service institutions and changes in federal policies (particularly housing) that inadvertently concentrate poverty within cities.

Summers also contends that there are institutional problems in city government that contribute to urban fiscal problems, commenting that "the political structure in many of the largest cities contributes to the relatively inefficient management of the limited local resources that are available" (p. 107). She believes that strong, centralized municipal government structure is to be preferred to decentralized, neighborhood-based forms in order to bring about efficient delivery of public services:

> The consequences of the increased empowerment of individual constituencies and sharply delineated geographical parts of municipalities may be very counterproductive to local government's efforts to improve the economy. When

elected officials from their constituencies and neighborhoods vote on the allocation of a city's resources, they typically do so to maximize the welfare of their political base,
rather than to achieve what is best for the city as a whole.
Inefficient expenditures are the result. (p. 126)

Accordingly, Summers recommends that federal grant fund allocation criteria allocate more resources to cities that have "efficiency-driven"
organizational structures as a way to encourage structural reform at the
municipal level.

In her comments, Helen Ladd largely agrees with and elaborates
on Summers's main theme of the fiscal mismatch between city poverty-related burdens and available resources, but expresses skepticism about her
inefficiency theme, noting that, "The concept of inefficient provision is
complex, and it is not obvious how the federal government would promote
it even if promoting efficiency were deemed an appropriate role for the
federal government" (p. 140).

Comments by participants during the discussion also questioned
Summers's call for centralized municipal government:

Hal Wolman: I wanted to comment on Anita's plea for a more
highly centralized structure of local government. There is no
area in the urban political science literature that has been the
subject of more research, discussion, and commentary, than
the question of what is the proper structure of local government, and for what purpose. You are buying into a debate that
stems from the progressive era, which suggests that cities
ought to be run like businesses. It's a corporate model. The
argument is "We ought not to worry about divisive neighborhood concerns or effects. We ought to look at the good of the
city as a whole."

Research comparing these more centralized "reform" structures to the more traditional "unreformed ones" indicate that
businesses and the middle class benefit, and the diverse, heterogeneous neighborhoods and ethnic groups are losers. So I
am suggesting that there are distributional questions, as well as
efficiency questions, that you need to be aware of.

Royce Hanson: I agree wholeheartedly with Hal on that. I think
there is an awful snare there. In fact, as cities have decentralized politically, in response to the Voting Rights Act, to allow
minorities to get into the action, there is beginning to be some
redistribution within local government in the way in which
money is being spent in the city, because minority neighbor-

hoods are now getting some voice in the distribution of those funds.

Royce Hanson argues in his article that past federal policy toward urban physical systems has not only had inadvert perverse effects, but that its conceptual premise no longer is relevant. Past federal policy:

> has been designed to revitalize the monocentric industrial city. It has been premised on the economic centrality of the central business district and the radial transportation patterns that support it. The city, for the most part, was seen as the center of a metropolitan settlement and a hinterland that was progressively less densely settled. (p. 148)

However, Hanson observes, a new urban system that is significantly different from that described above has taken its place:

> Urban space has continued to be transformed. The restructuring of the national economy in the last two decades has led to an ever greater dispersion of urban housing and environment. It is now rare for a central business district to contain more than a sixth of an important urban region's employment or income generation. . . . As a consequence of the rapid dispersion of employment, "polycentric" is no longer an adequate description of the extent of dispersion of economic activity in many urban regions. . . . The economic trends that have changed both the functions and forms of major cities have also produced a new system or hierarchy of cities that is international in scope. Some cities have become nerve centers of the new international economy built around the transactions of multinational corporations and the international specialization of labor. . . . Many cities are undergoing a process of simultaneous diversification of their economies and social functions. A new hierarchy of cities has emerged, with a few functioning as command and control centers in the international economy and the remaining cities performing subordinate and specialized functions. (pp. 148–49)

In this context, Hanson argues that although there are a vast array of infrastructure needs at the local level, federal infrastructure investments, in the context of constrained federal resources, should be directed where a substantial return can be expected in the form of private investments and increased gross national product. Given the new and still evolving urban system described above, Hanson suggests that this means that "the national government should give its highest priority to investments in facilities that help create an integrated and efficient national urban system that can advance international competitiveness" (p. 151).

Hanson cites several examples: aid in the development of an advanced computing/telecommunications network connecting the system of cities and their principal public and private institutions, which he calls "essential if the United States is to remain the world's economic leader"; assistance in the continuing development and maintenance of a high quality inter-city transportation system; aid in the construction of international transportation centers such as international airports and regional transportation terminals that serve the needs of international trade and commerce; and investment in infrastructure and amenities that will permit "American cities to be attractive places for the leading industries of a knowledge-based economy to locate and grow," including "facilities and amenities that sustain the research and development capacity in urban areas" (p. 152). Hanson also urges that federal infrastructure aid for these purposes to states and localities should encourage the development of an enhanced regional planning and governance capacity so that recipients of federal infrastructure investment will be able to "function effectively and capitalize on their investment."

In commenting on Hanson's paper, Charles Orlebeke endorses his call for a policy of federal infrastructure aid for places and projects that have the highest potential for generating a return in terms of enhancing the performance of America's urban system in the international political economy. However, he questions how such a system would or could be implemented:

> Who would make these complex and fateful investment decisions, and on what basis? Drawing up the criteria for national or international significance as opposed to merely local benefit is a nightmarish task, and whatever the outcome, almost any self-respecting urban lobbyist could make a compelling, or at least plausible, case for *his* city's pet project." (p. 162)

Others questioned Hanson's formulation of the national interest in providing federal assistance, citing various important urban needs that would not be met if his criteria were accepted. The flavor of this discussion has already been presented (see above).

In his article Phillip Clay addresses the role of neighborhoods, institutions, and families in a national urban policy. His concern is with:

> a growing number of urban neighborhoods that seem unable to frame or reframe the social contract, set and enforce community standards, or maintain the basic institutional infrastructure. In short, they lack a social fabric. . . . The evidence clearly documents that we are creating an increasingly concentrated population that seems outside our economic, social, and political markets and institutions. There is a negative connotation associated with the label "underclass," which is often used to describe this group. . . . The young people in these communities in crisis have not been presented with a set of values, venues, and opportunities to conform to the American mainstream or the more traditional working-class urban versions that worked for previous generations of low-income people. (pp. 165–66)

Clay notes that the causes of this distressing phenomenon are much the same as have been discussed in other articles: low job growth, loss of high-paying low-skilled jobs in the manufacturing sector, poor public education, and the legacy of past and present federal programs, some of which have made things worse: "Welfare policy systematically discourages intact families; urban renewal and public works projects divided or disestablished neighborhoods with highways and other projects. Programs that force the creation of special boundaries set up artificial neighborhoods and undermine rather than build social fabric" (p. 177).

Clay calls for a national urban policy toward neighborhoods, institutions, and families that has the goals of "strengthening neighborhoods, empowering people, and supporting community-based organizations" (p. 178). Such a policy should include additional assistance for housing, community development, and related programs; assistance for the development and dissemination of "best practices" in local communities and institutions; support for partnerships and collaborations that leverage resources from the federal government and engage charitable, corporate, and private resources in urban communities; empowerment of community-based and resident organizations; and requirement of a neighborhood impact statement for proposed projects or policies that might affect urban neighborhoods.

In her comments on Clay's paper, Margaret Wilder cautions against placing too much of the blame for the atrophy of informal social institutions (e.g. neighborhoods, families, churches) on past federal policy. She comments that:

Since the 1970s, declining urban conditions have been blamed on ineffectual policy at best and wasteful initiatives at worst. This critique is overdrawn. The nature of urban ills suggests that formal and informal institutions have been affected by social change, economic restructuring, political and spatial reorganization, technological innovation, *and* past policies. (p. 184)

Discussion focused on two aspects of Clay's presentation. First, Margaret Wilder questioned the significance of the *concentration* of poor people described in Clay's paper, setting off a vigorous discussion.

Margaret Wilder: I have read some of the poverty concentration literature, and I think it makes a compelling case that the concentration of poverty makes it that much harder to resolve the poverty problem. I think that is a valid point to make.

But to then make the policy leap that by deconcentrating the poor, you are somehow going to solve the poverty problem, I think is a misdiagnosis of the problem. The problem is that these people are poor. The problem is not that they all live together. That is aside from the fact of the basis problem. I am convinced that our lack of shared visions or assumptions about the root causes of the problem makes us stumble when we try to have these kinds of discussions.

Peter Eisinger: That masks the argument that it is the concentration of poor, not just poverty in varied amounts, that generates the problems. And deconcentration is critical.

Margaret Wilder: I disagree with that, fundamentally. If those people were concentrated and not poor, there would be no problem. That's my point. So while concentration has a lot of side effects, it is the fact that the people are poor in the first place that means that you now have an increased ripple effect from that poverty, because it is concentrated.

Bob Plotnick: There really is no research consensus on the effects of neighborhood concentration of poverty. And I think we would be very poorly advised to make this the centerpiece of a national policy effort. That is a very important point. If you deconcentrate poverty, but the level of poverty has linear effects on the extent of other social problems, like teen pregnancy, it would just spread the problems around, without reducing their levels in the whole Metropolitan Statistical Area (MSA). So I agree that poverty itself is a problem that stands all on its own regardless of neighborhood concentration.

Others questioned the nature of the federal role in addressing the problem of informal institutions such as neighborhoods, communities, and families:

Hal Wolman: I very much liked Phil's paper and how he sets this up. But I don't get the punch line. Is there a federal role, and can there conceivably be a federal role in dealing with this problem of community fraying, particularly in terms of the informal institutions Margaret talks about. Is this something that a national urban policy, or federal government activity can really have an impact on? If so, how?

Margaret Wilder: I would say that in an urban policy per se, probably not. But there are functional areas such as welfare and education policy, where there are opportunities to address, very directly, some of the issues I was raising, about the roles and the expectations of these institutions.

If you decide that you're going to provide child care and health care, as part of a welfare package, and you make those reasonable and accessible, then you create the ability of that new changed family institution to accommodate its new role by providing all of its needs.

This is a very different family structure than what we assumed thirty years ago. And policy ought not to respond by saying, "there's something wrong with this structure, and we need to somehow change the structure of that family unit." Instead, I think we need to recognize this as a new family structure, and ask how we can facilitate the survival and the viability of that structure.

Phillip Clay: I don't really have an answer to Hal's question except through some illustrations that are encouraging. In terms of the federal role, I would only say that we need to figure out a way to make federal policy encourage experimentation and demonstration projects.

In the opening and concluding sessions, conferees addressed the role and nature of a national urban policy report in the context of the kinds of urban problems and proposed solutions discussed above.

The first article, by Elizabeth Agius and Harold Wolman, presents the historical development of the national urban policy report and analyzes the reports' contents, summarizing the main themes of each report, the types of material covered, organizational format, kinds of data and analysis used, and policy recommendations made. It also discusses the processes by which these reports have been put together, the audience(s) to which they have been addressed, and their utilization.

Wolman and Agius conclude that the reports have been disappointing. They observe that the reports:

> have fallen short of expectations; observers agree that they
> have not generally driven or been a part of a coherent national urban policy process, nor indeed have they contributed in most cases to the administration's ongoing process of domestic policy-making. The quality of analysis and presentation has been spotty. And the reports have not stimulated a national public (or indeed congressional) debate about urban problems, neither have they achieved even a modest level of public visibility. (p. 30)

They cite others who are equally critical:

> For example, Royce Hanson in a paper for this conference, writes "the biennial reports have been late, vague, self-serving, and fortunately obscure. There is no evidence that they have had any discernible effect on federal policy, much less on actual urban development." Marshall Kaplan concurs, noting "the reports have been little more than a summary of trends . . . and self-serving analysis." And one interview source stated "they are of little use, there is no inherent value in their work, and no intellectual attractiveness to using them." As these comments suggest, the report seems to have provided only limited use as a policy document or starting point for an urban policy debate. (p. 45)

The conference participants in general concurred with this harsh evaluation. Indeed, Ned Hill asked whether the report was "so insignificant and trivial in the policy-making process that we ought to ask whether it should even exist in the first place." Nonetheless, in his comment on the paper by Agius and Wolman, Peter Eisinger observed, "I think it is useful to read these national urban policy reports all together, *ad seriatim*. If you do, you come to see, that the sum of the parts is in fact more interesting than the individual reports." Eisinger feels the reports constitute a running debate about political economy in the United States and the proper relationship of the federal government to the market. They reflect, sometimes quite explicitly and directly, each administration's view of the appropriate relationship of state to market in addressing the nation's urban problems.

The discussion focused primarily on how the report could be reshaped to make it a more useful document. Several models were suggested. (1) The report should focus on urban conditions and trends, developing a set of urban indicators that would be tracked over time. (2) The report should focus intensively on analysis of a small number of critical urban issues and that these issues would vary from one report to another (modeled after the economic report of the president). (3) The report should be concerned with evaluating current policies as they affect urban areas. (4) The report should set forth the president's policy recommendations for addressing the problems of urban areas. (5) The report should make the case to Congress and the public for the importance of urban areas and the necessity of aggressively addressing the problems of these areas. There was substantial agreement that the report should be recast so that, at a minimum, it presents consistent data on urban trends and conditions, but less agreement on whether it should include policy recommendations.

> **Larry Ledebur:** It seems to me that the urban policy report exists, but its purpose is unclear. What is the report's goal? Is it to monitor? Is it to inform the policy process? Is it to develop policy options? The general question is, "what purpose do you want the report to serve." Then work back from that and ask how to meet the goal.
>
> **Anita Summers:** What the report really needs to do is to demonstrate what functions cities are performing on behalf of the nation. Then people will see the stake they have in them. In addition, we have had a repeated discussion of the importance of having measurements of the state and cities. I think that is one function the report can serve.
>
> **Coit Ford:** It seems to me that you could have a report that is a descriptive report, and then you could have one that is a prescriptive report. In other words, here are these sets of facts, how do we evaluate them subjectively?
>
> **Bob Plotnick:** We need to institutionalize this as a national urban conditions report.
>
> **Peter Eisinger:** If we develop a consensus on what indicators should be included, the report could include longitudinal tables.
>
> **Helen Ladd:** But we don't have good data in many cases. And in some cases data are available only in census year—like poverty rates by city, which is frustrating. Perhaps we can use this as a means of generating better, more regular data.
>
> **Royce Hanson:** Suppose the report were in two phases. The first phase could be a report on the status of problems of cities. If it were organized around such indicators as are available and repeated biannually, reporting on the status of human capital,

physical capital, institutional capital, and information capital for cities, and were simply produced in that form, it could be publicly released and could serve as the basis of congressional hearings, or a meeting of the governor's conference, or the National League of Cities (NLC), or whatever. It could then be followed by a short statement, the president's policy or the federal policy on cities, which would be whatever it would be. Preferably, in a perfect world, it would respond to the status report, which could in turn be prefaced with a statement about why the national government should care about cities.

And, ultimately, then the president would say, "I care, and this is the best way I care about it, and this is what we're going to do in terms of any federal initiatives that we follow."

Bill Barnes: The options that you just laid out did not include, at least as I understood it, the model of the Council of Economic Advisers' report we discussed earlier, where you do an analysis on topics of interest, as opposed to a standard data report.

Royce Hanson: I see no reason not to include that. In fact, I see every reason as the report matures to include it. To say not only produce the data, but interpret it, and maybe focus on one topic or a small number of different topics each time. I like the idea of not having it do everything, every time—although I also like having some things done all the time, so that you get a clear sense.

Bob Plotnick: I do want to echo some of these thoughts. I strongly agree that the report should not become a policy platform or a kind of political document. That would really eliminate a lot of its usefulness. As a starting point, it should focus on the data and the trend issues.

Chuck Orlebeke: The original point and purpose of the report's requirement was to put the president on the spot. It seems to me that's a good purpose, and I think it applies now, as it applied originally. The idea that it should not be a policy document is absurd. Of course it should be a policy document.

Participants also discussed what the proper focus of a national urban policy report (and of national urban policy) ought to be. Should it focus squarely on the central city, on the metropolitan area as a whole (perhaps breaking out the problems of central cities and suburbs within that context) or on *problems* that are *national* in scope (e.g. unemployment, poverty, crime), but disproportionately present in urban settings? Anita Summers was particularly forceful in urging that the focus be on central cities, but there was substantial disagreement:

Anita Summers: But what should be the focus of the report? It must be cities because that is where the problems are. And the city economy is completely different from the suburban economy. Why should we focus on the cities as a place rather than on problems that are national in scope? I think the one-line answer is that concentrations of poverty are different than poverty, and that it is not linear. If you had all the poor in the country distributed evenly over the acreage, the nature of the resultant problems would be very different than when they are concentrated in a small central-city area.

Peter Eisinger: I wanted to follow up on what Anita said. I am a little concerned about making such a sharp distinction between city and suburb, because in fact many of the so-called urban problems are spilling over into the suburbs. Also, this masks an enormous variation in suburban characteristics even in your own area. Isn't Camden a suburb of Philadelphia? The poverty rate in suburbs is nationally about half of what it is in a central city. It is 8 or 9 percent, I think, which is pretty damned high. The black out-migration rate, from central cities to suburbs, is much higher right now than the white out-migration rate, in percentage terms. And what African Americans are finding when they get to the suburbs is that they are resegregating, or they are resegregated.

I think lots and lots of the central-city problems are in fact being reproduced in the suburbs.

Hal Wolman: In functional terms it is the metropolitan area, not the central city, that is the real economy, so in an economy sense "urban" means "metropolitan."

This discussion led, perhaps inevitably, to the question of whether there was a political constituency for the national urban policy report and for urban policy in general, and, if not, whether such a constituency could be created.

Hal Wolman: We have a political problem in focusing on the central city, in that city residents constitute only 30 percent of the nation's people, and their representatives constitute only 30 percent of Congress.

Bill Barnes: I think it is even more complex than that. Some of that 30 percent who live in central cities, statistically defined, are not "central city" in terms of dealing with the kind of problems with substantial poverty and social and racial issues you have in mind. They would not get in the line behind "Philadelphia" if you asked them to divide up in a room. They would be in another line. So the subset here is even substantially smaller politically.

Helen Ladd: I fully agree with Hal that there is a political problem here, but it is even worse than the one he stated in terms of numbers. There is a racial dimension, as well. And the sorts of people who are living in the big cities are not politically powerful people at the national level.

Anita Summers: The notion is that we are interested in trying to develop the political constituency by showing suburbanites that they are distinct beneficiaries of the fact that the cities take care of the poor for them.

The other way to put it is this: if you vote to concentrate low-income housing in cities through the federal housing policies in which we have engaged in the past, then you have to understand that there are costs associated with that vote that inadvertently fall on city areas,. And these costs were not understood to be associated with that legislation. If you reviewed all the federal housing legislation, you would not find any discussion of the fiscal costs and extended poverty costs imposed on cities by that policy.

Chuck Orlebeke: Remember why they were advocating low-income housing? It was because there were terrible slum conditions where the existing poor people were living, and what they were advocating was for structures that were "decent, safe, and sanitary."

Somebody mentioned the immigration argument as well. National policy did not mandate that the immigrants go to the big cities, that they locate there specifically.

Anita Summers: The purpose here is not to say what the right immigration policy is. It is simply to say that when we decide what is right for the United States as an appropriate immigration policy, we need to know who is bearing the costs. That's the only question. And whoever is bearing the cost has to be compensated, because the total volume of immigrants is a national decision.

Bob Plotnick: I think identifying these unfair cost burdens is very valuable, and if it can be made trenchant and convincing in a policy report, I think it would be very useful to have data laying out the true cost to cities of concentrating poor people there. I know it looks like a real tough one because a suburbanite might say, "Great, the state has voted just what we want, me and my suburb residents." But some people might feel guilty about it, and sometimes data get people to think about whether this is the right way to do business.

Coit Ford: I am going to take your argument as gospel—that concentration of poverty in cities is in fact the problem, and that cities are bearing the cost that the remainder of the region is not paying for. But I would like to think about it from a different perspective. Assume that you can compute these payments and costs, and then present them to the suburban constituencies that are not currently paying them. You then present them with a rational decision on whether (a) to pay some sort of subsidy back to the city in exchange for the burden the city bears, or (b) bear some of the costs themselves in terms of the direct decentralization of poverty to the suburbs. Why do you assume they will somehow choose the latter instead of the former? Aren't they more likely to say, "Fine, we'll pay some costs to keep the locus and concentration of poverty in the city; we will keep the problem where it is."

Anita Summers: I think that is a fully justifiable remark. You are absolutely right that the concentration of poverty could remain. But it is an improvement in the situation if the burden is being financially reduced. That's all that can be said.

Coit Ford: I agree with you that it is an improvement, but here is the problem I foresee. It is an improvement at the cost of a legitimation of the system (i.e. concentration of poverty localized in the city) that you now say is unpalatable.

Margaret Wilder: Isn't there a third possibility—that the suburbs basically say, "so what?" Why presume that they would argue for a redistribution or taking on some of the burden of poverty through a deconcentration of the poor, what if they simply say we like it the way it is?

Maybe I am being cynical here, but I think the choice that would seem rational, from the suburbanites' point of view, would be not only not to contribute, but to begin to try to cut back on those expenditures, period. To not pay in every sense of the word.

Royce Hanson: I think Margaret's point is exactly right. The suburbs do not look on themselves as beneficiaries; if they think of it at all, they are free riders.

Although the conference participants made no effort to come to an explicit consensus on the nature of urban problems, appropriate urban policy, or the way in which a national urban policy report should be revised and restructured, there was a substantial degree of agreement (as the above summary indicates) in several important areas. The most important urban problems revolve around the increasing inability of lower-skilled workers to gain employment at decent wages in the labor market, the increasing disparity in income, employment, and quality of life between city and suburban residents and between majority and minority populations, the concentration of poverty in central cities and the lack of city fiscal resources to respond to the resultant service needs, and the fraying of traditional social and community institutions, particularly in areas characterized by concentrated poverty.

There was also substantial agreement on some of the most appropriate responses: greater emphasis on education and job training, efforts to attach the poor and unemployed to the labor market through employment subsidies and public service employment, targeted federal assistance to cities, and increased regional planning, service delivery, and tax-base sharing. And there was near consensus that a restructured national urban policy report should include a longitudinal set of urban indicators, both to track urban conditions and to focus public attention on the plight of urban areas.

On one important issue, however, there was an ominous lack of consensus: how to create a viable political strategy to persuade the majority of Americans who are not poor and do not reside in cities to respond to the needs of these areas, which now constitute only 30 percent of the American population. The debate swung between those who argued that the public could be swayed either by enlightened self-interest (the well-being of the nation as a whole and even of suburbs is inextricably bound up with the well-being of cities) or by moral suasion and those who contended that this was ultimately a losing strategy. Instead, the latter argued that policy should be focused not on cities but on problems that are national in scope (but happen to be concentrated in cities) or on people who are in need regardless of where they live (though people in need are likely to live disproportionately in cities).

The President's National Urban Policy Report as a Policy Document: A History and Analysis of the First Twenty Years

Elizabeth J. Agius

and

Harold L. Wolman

The 1960s were a period of growing interest and concern among national policy makers about urban areas. This interest was reflected in Title VII of the Housing and Urban Development Act of 1970, the Urban Growth and New Communities Development Act. The act called for the development of a national urban growth policy and also required the president to produce a biennial report on national growth and development. The legislation was amended in 1977 to call for the development of a national urban policy (rather than a national urban growth policy) and the production of a national urban policy report. While the interest in urban policy as the object of national concern subsided significantly during the 1970s and 1980s, the legislative requirement still stands. Although no administration (except for the Carter administration in its initial years) has taken seriously the mandate to develop a national urban (or urban growth) policy, the called-for report, first issued in 1972, has been published for every even-numbered year (although frequently considerably late) until 1990. In 1992, the legislation was amended to require the report every odd-numbered year. There was no 1992 report; the 1993 report will be published in 1995. In this paper we will examine the history and provide an analysis of the president's national urban policy reports.

History and Background

The 1970 legislation calling for a national urban growth policy report required the merger of separate interests. Urban activists and proponents of growth management competed for attention, using social turmoil and rising growth projections to plead their case for a more coherent policy.

The history leading up to the legislation begins a few years before its passage. With the creation of the Department of Housing and Urban Development (HUD), urban affairs found a new voice in the federal government. During the 1960s cities were the beneficiaries of a wide range of federal categorical programs. From urban renewal to antipoverty programs and the model cities plan, urban policy was squarely placed on the decision agenda. Collectively, however, the programs lacked consistency and at times worked at cross purposes with one another (Kaplan 1990: 175). In addition, the riots of the late 1960s focused attention on the problems of cities. Questions about how to address urban problems and the appropriate federal role were prominent on the policy agenda.

However, the initial calls for a national policy came from those more concerned with urban growth than with urban decline. Demographers had predicted a rapidly rising population, most of whom would be crowded into large cities. Mayors and governors were joined by groups of home builders, developers, and environmentalists in the call for policies to promote a balanced distribution of people to prevent overcrowding (Orlebeke 1990: 187–8). In 1968 two reports were published, one by the Advisory Commission on Intergovernmental Relations and one by a group called the National Committee on Urban Growth Policy. Each displayed an interest in the trends toward growing cities and supported the idea of building new towns to alleviate the stress (Eisinger 1983: 6–7).

There were thus two sets of goals for a national urban policy, one more closely related to traditional urban needs and one interested in the growth issue. The bill passed by Congress embodied some elements of both concerns, but appeared more heavily weighted toward the issues of urban growth. The act itself was very broadly worded. It declared that:

> the rapid growth of urban population and uneven expansion of urban development in the United States, together with a decline in farm population, slower growth in rural areas, and migration to the cities, has created an imbalance between the Nation's needs and resources and seriously threatens our physical environment, and that the economic and social development of the Nation, the proper conservation of our natural resources, and the achievement of satisfactory living standards depend upon the sound, orderly, and more balanced development of all areas of the Nation.

It concluded that the "Federal government, consistent with the responsibilities of state and local government and the private sector, must assume responsibility for the development of a national urban growth policy" and "shall transmit to Congress a report on urban growth every even-numbered year" (see Appendix 1 for the complete text). In describing the biennial report requested of the president, Congress stated that it should include:

1. information and statistics describing characteristics of urban growth and stabilization and identifying significant trends and developments;

2. a summary of significant problems facing the United States as a result of urban growth trends and developments;

3. an evaluation of the progress and effectiveness of federal efforts designed to meet such problems and carry out the national urban growth policy;

4. an assessment of the policies and structure of existing and proposed interstate planning and developments affecting such policy;

5. a review of state, local, and private policies, plans, and programs relevant to such policy;

6. current and foreseeable needs in the areas served by policies, plans, and programs designed to carry out such policy, and the steps being taken to meet such needs; and

7. recommendations for programs and policies for carrying out such policy, including such legislation and administrative actions as may be deemed necessary and desirable.

As the Carter administration took office, it became clear that the urban problems discussed no longer referred to vague notions of growth, but to the more specific conditions facing cities. In 1977 Title VII was amended to drop the word "growth" from the name so that the legislation called for a national urban policy report rather than a national urban growth report. In 1992, new amendments further emphasized the need to focus both the "national urban policy" and the report on core urban problems. The previous urban policy objective calling for coordination of "Federal programs so as to encourage desirable patterns of urban development" (Title VII 1977) was amended to read:

increase coordination among Federal programs that seek to promote job opportunities and skills, decent and affordable housing, public safety, access to health care, educational opportunities, and fiscal soundness for urban communities and their residents.

Further the 1992 amendment changed the provision that policy recommendations in the report shall include such legislative and administrative actions "as may be deemed necessary and desirable" to carry out a national urban policy and substituted a long list of concerns the report should address in its recommendations. This list includes:

a. to promote coordination among federal programs to assist urban areas;

b. to enhance the fiscal capacity of fiscally distressed urban areas;

c. to promote job opportunities in economically distressed urban areas and to enhance the job skills of residents of such areas;

d. to generate decent and affordable housing;

e. to reduce racial tensions and to combat racial and ethnic violence in urban areas;

f. to combat urban drug abuse and drug-related crime and violence;

g. to promote the delivery of health care to low-income communities in urban areas;

h. to expand educational opportunities in urban areas; and

i. to achieve the goals of the national urban policy.

Finally, the due date was changed from February of even-numbered years to 1 June of every odd-numbered year beginning with 1993.

Analysis of Reports

The ten reports themselves have fallen short of expectations; observers agree that they have not generally driven or been a part of a coherent national urban policy process, nor have they contributed in most cases to the administration's ongoing process of domestic policy-making. The quality of analysis and presentation has been spotty. And the reports have not stimulated a national public (or indeed congressional) debate about urban problems, nor have they achieved even a modest level of public visibility.

Nonetheless, the reports are worthy of some attention and analysis. While most of them may not have been important policy documents, they do provide the only opportunity for the federal government to address in a focused and comprehensive fashion the problems of America's urban areas. Most policy-making is functional in nature (e.g. housing, agriculture); it is usually not organized around spatial or geographic concerns. The report provides an opportunity to view how the administration thinks about and approaches urban problems and the appropriate government role with

Table 1

Main Themes of National Urban Policy Reports

report	president	main themes
1972	Nixon	balanced and orderly growth
1974	Nixon	quality of life
1976	Ford	resource constraints and conservation
1978–1980	Carter	problems of distressed central cities
1982–1988	Reagan	healthy national economy leads to healthy cities
		need to decentralize
		need to involve private sector
1990	Bush	empower the poor

respect to them. It provides some illumination on an important but usually shady area.

In the following section we review and analyze the ten existing reports published prior to the Clinton administration. We begin by examining the main themes of each report, then turn to its focus, the coverage and organization, the different types of data and analysis provided, the issues and problems discussed, the nature of policy recommendations made, and how each administration viewed the role of the federal government.

Main Themes

In this section we attempt to identify the main substantive themes characterizing each report, the "capsule headlines" it attempts to convey (see Table 1 for a summary). In the first three reports the main themes revolved primarily around managing the problems of growth. The first report, delivered in 1972 by the Nixon administration, subtly but clearly redefined the purpose of the report from a report on urban growth, which it deemed too "narrow," to a report on national growth policy, including rural as well as urban growth. Indeed the report noted that "citizens residing in our rural areas are confronted with problems no less pressing and no less deserving of national attention than those of our citizens who are afflicted by what is generally described as the 'urban crisis'" (National Urban Policy Report 1972: ix—hereafter NUPR).[1] Urban concerns were thus deemphasized (though not ignored) and achieving the twin objectives of "balanced and orderly growth" became the main theme. The report also

---

[1] For convenience, the reports are all referred to as national urban policy reports, regardless of their actual title.

made clear that the aim of the statute was to "assist in the development of national policy—not to 'enunciate' such policy." The report stressed that indeed no single policy could accomplish the objectives of "balanced and orderly growth," "meeting these objectives will require stimulating and channeling private initiative . . . it will also require strengthening the capacity of government at all levels to respond to growth challenges."

The 1974 report, retitled "Report on National Growth and Development," refocused its main theme from the 1972 report's emphasis on "balanced and orderly growth" to "quality of life." It justified this shift by noting that "growth is not something which affects the quality of our lives; it is the measure of that effect" (NUPR 1974: 1). The report noted that government policy had important impacts on a wide range of quality-of-life issues and reasserted that a single national policy was not desirable or possible. It stressed, as its main theme, the need for sorting out the roles of the various levels of government and for improving policy and program coordination within and among them.

The 1976 report of the Ford administration moved its concern from growth and quality of life to that of resource constraints, particularly energy, and the environment. As the report observed:

> Developments in the country since 1974 have shaped the character and formed the themes of this Report. Economic Recession coupled with increased concerns about resource scarcity have brought into question sustained levels of economic growth and expansive physical development as the bases for future planning. In all specific policy areas of national growth examined in this Report, there is a growing recognition of the limited nature of both fiscal and natural resources. (NUPR 1976: ii)

Throughout, the report is concerned with resource scarcity, fiscal limits, the need for better management, priority setting, efficiency, and conservation. There is a substantial concern with the problem of cities, primarily within the context of resource conservation. "The appearance of resource shortages and cost increases argues for more intensive use of the tremendous fixed capital investment represented by our existing cities and towns" (NUPR 1976: xii). In addition, the report deals directly for the first time with problems of poverty and poor housing.

As a result of both the 1977 amendments changing the report from national growth and development policy to national urban policy, and of the political constituency of the new Carter administration, the main theme of the 1978 report shifted from the impact of growth and development to problems of urban areas and particularly of older cities. This shift represented an ideological and political commitment to a more active federal government. The concept of a national urban policy was taken seriously and the report was used as a vehicle for developing and articulating it. The report enunciated a policy that was targeted to distressed areas, and to a lesser extent distressed individuals. It called for an active federal government providing "fiscal relief to the most hard pressed communities," "incentives to attract private investment to distressed communities," and "provision of employment opportunities, primarily in the private sector, to the long term unemployed and disadvantaged in urban areas." In an effort to create a comprehensive policy, the report stressed the need to create partnerships among government, business, labor, and neighborhood groups. The partnership idea was enunciated fully in a report by the Urban and Regional Policy Group entitled *New Partnerships to Conserve America's Communities.* Carter's second report in 1980 repeated these themes, remarking that the set strategy was valid and needed only to be strengthened.

> The basic principles guiding the 1978 urban policy will remain of paramount importance during the 1980s. Federal leadership will be required to sustain a coordinated public and private response to the nation's deep-seated problems. (NUPR 1980: chap. 13, p. 3)

The needs of older central cities and the neediest people were a constant in both reports.

The reports of the Reagan administration, beginning in 1982, while retaining the focus on urban areas, rejected the Carter administration's support of a comprehensive national urban policy or of an activist federal role in addressing urban problems. The most pervasive themes of the four reports of the Reagan administration were the need to assure a healthy national economy as a means of bringing about healthy cities, to redefine government roles and to decentralize decision-making, and to encourage private-sector involvement. While all of these themes were expressed in the 1982 report, their clearest expression was in the 1984 report, which set forth three strategies for the Reagan administration's urban policy:

> 1. Maintaining sustained noninflationary economic growth, recognizing that a healthy economy is our most powerful tool for revitalizing our cities and improving their fiscal position.
>
> 2. Strengthening State and local governments by giving them increased authority and flexibility to manage their own resources and returning decision-making closer to the people.

    3. Stimulating public and private cooperation to main-
tain and improve the social and physical conditions in our
Nation's cities. (NUPR 1984: vi)

In 1986, a fourth objective, that of encouraging self-sufficiency
among those able to work, was added. With respect to aiding cities, the
federal government could not reverse trends, but could assist in adjustments to structural economic change and in special areas such as crime and
civil rights. However, in general, the role of federal programs was deemphasized and denigrated. Referring to past programs, the 1982 report
bluntly stated that "the programs were unsuccessful—sometimes spectacu-
larly so" (NUPR 1982: 46). In contrast to the Carter years, the reports
during the Reagan presidency focused more on problems of people and
less on problems of places and jurisdictions.

    Another theme sounded from 1984 to 1986 was one of success.
The 1986 report boldly states, for example, that the "Urban Renaissance in
the 1980s is directly linked to the Administration's economic policies"
(NUPR 1986: 1). While their policies were generally viewed as successful,
the final Reagan report in 1988 did sound a slightly different theme. In
reviewing urban policy it noted that social problems, such as drugs and
crime, persist and have not been solved by emphasizing people aid over
place aid, despite overall improvements in urban conditions.

    While retaining some of the previous administration's emphasis on
economic growth, the Bush administration sounded a new approach, one
it called the "New War on Poverty." The anti-poverty measures set forth
in the 1990 national urban policy report were directed at those who had
not benefited from the growing national economy. However, unlike the
poverty programs of the Great Society, poverty was to be attacked through
efforts to "empower" the poor and to remove barriers rather than through
programs involving substantial public expenditures. Secretary Kemp's introduction set forth the goals of independence, encouraging self-sufficiency among the able-bodied, and building public–private partnerships to
manage urban conditions. By widening the scope of opportunities available to the poor, and reducing barriers to individual potential, the administration felt the poor would be able to share in the nation's prosperity.
This theme of a shared responsibility in reducing urban problems is a
carry-over from the last report of the Reagan years.

Coverage

    The range of areas covered and the type of material presented in
the national urban growth/urban policy reports have lacked consistency
over the years. The publications have provided, to varying degrees, information related to conditions and trends characterizing urban areas, the

Table 2

Level of Coverage

coverage of	72	74	76	78	80	82	84	86	88	90
conditions and trends	M	M	S	S	S	M	M	M	M	L
problems	L	L	M	M	M	M	M	M	M	L
review of broad sectors	L	L	S	S	S	M	M	M	M	L
functional areas	L	M	S	M	M	M	M	M	M	L
current /past federal policies	L	M	M	M	M	S	S	S	S	M
administration's rationale	M	M	M	S	S	M	M	M	M	S
policy recommendations	M	M	L	S	S	L	L	L	M	M

S = Substantial coverage   M = Moderate coverage   L = Little or no coverage

causes of these conditions and trends, problems resulting from these trends, a review of broad sectors (e.g. the urban economy, social problems, physical problems), and/or specific functional areas (e.g. housing, crime, energy, environment), a description and/or evaluation of current and past federal policies affecting urban growth or urban areas, a prescription and rationale for the current administration's own efforts, and/or an offering of policy recommendations. Not every report has covered each of these items, and some have put much greater emphasis on specific topics relative to others (see Table 2).

Similarly there has been no fixed organizational format for the reports; the placement of topics has followed no pattern as evidenced by the tables of contents of the various reports (see appendix). With both the coverage and organization, the report is designed to showcase the concerns or policies that the current administration feels are important.

Most of the ten reports spent a significant amount of effort describing the conditions and trends influencing, first, national growth, and later urban areas. Compared to the Carter reports, which expounded on conditions affecting central cities, the Reagan reports moved slightly away from being conditions-oriented. The 1990 Bush report differed from the others by self-consciously omitting "detailed presentations of statistics on urban poverty and other aspects of urban conditions" (NUPR 1990: 10).

Efforts to explain the causes of these conditions were briefly mentioned in each of the reports, although some (and especially the one from the Ford administration) devoted more concern to their implications than to causes. The Carter administration, which produced the lengthiest reports, devoted the most attention to the causes of conditions in central cities. The first (1972) report was particularly concerned with trends and causes, but not "problems." Coverage of individual functional areas and problems peaked in the reports of the Carter administration, but received notable attention in the Ford report as well. The reports during the Reagan years bundled problems into broader economic, social, and physical categories. The 1990 report of the Bush administration confined its coverage almost completely to housing, and to a lesser degree economic development.

In accordance with the letter of the legislation, the reports not only reviewed federal policies, but those of state and local governments as well. While the 1978 and 1980 reports spent more time on federal actions, reports produced under the Reagan administration provided extensive examples of state and local involvement. Additionally these reports were used to point out what steps had been taken previously to address a particular condition.

Nearly all the growth and development and urban policy reports dedicated considerable time and attention to describing the policies and activities of the administration in terms of their contribution to addressing the problems set forth. However (and perhaps not surprisingly), the reports have been conspicuously lacking in serious evaluation of the administration's own policies and how they have worked. Evaluations of policies pursued by previous administrations are more frequent, particularly after a partisan change in the White House. When critiques are forwarded they are generally done in a positive manner. The Carter administration began its 1980 report with an evaluation of the national urban policy set forth in 1978, announcing its intent to stay with this comprehensive approach. During the Reagan administration reports, especially the second in 1984 and the last in 1988, evaluations pronounced the success of policies in meeting their urban objectives.

From the beginning, the reports rejected the concept of a single "national urban policy"; only the 1978 Carter administration report (reinforced by the 1980 report) consciously recommended a national urban policy, but this consisted of a variety of specific policies, sometimes related, sometimes not, rather than a single overarching policy. Nonetheless, individual policy recommendations were set forth as requested in the first two reports, although they were largely absent from the 1976 Ford administration report, which preferred to present many options for consideration. As noted, President Carter's two reports changed course by fully itemizing a particular set of recommendations in the form of an explicit urban policy. The Reagan administration declined to use the report as a format to present many recommendations, but did enunciate a social agenda in its final report of 1988. The 1990 report simply reiterated the legislative initiatives of the Bush administration.

Type of Data and Analysis

For the most part the type of data and the analytic tools used in all of the presidents' national urban policy reports are fairly similar. The most common type of data, used to some degree in each report, are statistical trends related to population growth and movement and the economy. Each report, of course, picks and chooses its trend data with care, using them to draw attention to the particular interests of the administration. For example, early reports placed heavy emphasis on population trends and resource consumption, which was in line with the concerns over managing national growth (see Table 3).

In general the reports are light on analysis and evaluation and heavier on descriptions and examples of what the administration believes to be the central elements of its urban policy. Rather than analyze the policies—in place or proposed—the reports provide descriptions of the current programs and proposals. Some reports, such as those of 1976 and 1978, analyze the effects of changing conditions on urban areas and use this to explore the variety of options available to policy makers. Some reports (e.g. 1974, 1978) explicitly address the impact of present or past federal policies on urban areas. However, in general, critical evaluations of past policies can be found only after a partisan change in leadership, and they do little more than provide the rationale for current measures. When evaluations of current policies are made, as in the 1984 and 1986 reports, they are of a self-congratulatory nature. As Hanson notes, the quality of the analysis is diminished when the publication requirement coincides with an election year (Hanson 1982: 91).

The initial report provided both a fairly comprehensive look at the changes in population, its growth and movements, and an examination of the state role in growth policy. The second report undertook the task of evaluating the impact of federal policies on urban areas. In addition it explored and analyzed the major growth issues of the day (NUPR 1974: ii). By 1976 the report had added many topics and expanded its use of tables and charts. Instead of a heavy focus on population trends, this report emphasized land use and resource trends. Compared to past reports, it was considered to be more substantive, due in part to the use of consultants (Hanson 1982: 32). The reports produced by the Carter administration also furnished an evaluation of the effects of federal policies. The 1978 and 1980 reports used trends in employment, manufacturing, and changes in households to underscore the problems of central cities. These two reports differed from the others in both their heavy use of descriptive trends and their focus on creating a measure of community needs and distress levels. The reports of the Reagan years contained less information on specific central-city problems and more on the general trends facing the nation. More recently, the Reagan reports used statistics on income

Table 3

Common Types of Data

data types	72	74	76	78	80	82	84	86	88	90
population changes										
national	✓	✓	✓	✓	✓	✓	✓	✓	✓	
metro		✓	✓	✓	✓	✓	✓	✓	✓	
central city			✓	✓	✓	✓	✓	✓	✓	
unemployment rates										
national			✓	✓	✓	✓	✓	✓	✓	
metro			✓							
central city			✓	✓					✓	
employment changes										
national		✓			✓		✓	✓	✓	
metro		✓	✓	✓	✓	✓		✓	✓	
central city			✓	✓	✓	✓				
poverty rates										
national	✓		✓			✓	✓	✓	✓	✓
metro			✓	✓	✓		✓			
central city			✓	✓	✓		✓			
household income										
metro				✓	✓	✓	✓		✓	
central city			✓	✓	✓	✓	✓		✓	
national inflation rates							✓	✓	✓	
crime rates						✓		✓	✓	
federal grants in aid			✓	✓	✓	✓	✓		✓	
housing availability			✓	✓	✓	✓	✓	✓	✓	✓
housing affordability						✓	✓	✓	✓	✓

Note: There are many differences in the depth of information provided in these Reports, for example, some reports list only the level of employment, while others provide information on changes in various sectors of employment.

growth and inflation and unemployment declines to show improvements in urban conditions. From 1984 to 1988 descriptions of state and local activities added to the analysis. The 1990 report provided more prescriptive analysis, succinctly describing the administration's policy preference. This report contained very little by way of statistics, citing that trends and conditions could be gathered from other documents.

Policy Recommendations Made

The original Title VII legislation specifies that the report:

> shall contribute to the formulation of such a [national urban] policy and in addition shall include . . . recommendations for programs and policies for carrying out such policy, including such legislation and administrative actions as may be deemed necessary and desirable.

Perhaps not unexpectedly, the extent to which this injunction has been taken seriously has varied substantially from report to report. Recommendations have been sporadically offered; some reports have provided special chapters or sections to highlight proposals, while some have incorporated them into the general text. The recommendations vary from specific legislative and/or administrative recommendations to broad policy directions and strategies.

The first biennial report devoted its last chapter to making policy recommendations. In general these proposals reflected the Nixon administration's desire to reform the federal government structure. The eight proposals were: government reorganization (including the establishment of a department of community development), revenue sharing, expanded rural credit, institution of planning and management assistance, national land use policy, a power plant siting act, welfare reform, and tax changes.

In their second report the Nixon administration also reserved the concluding section to setting forth its recommendations. Unlike the previous report, however, this set of proposals spanned various levels of government; federal, multistate, state, local, and substate levels. The focus of these recommendations was "to suggest ways to improve the ability of federal, state and local governments to assess the overall effects of present and proposed governmental actions" (NUPR 1974: iii). Specific policy suggestions with respect to growth and development were replaced by calls for better management techniques, policy coordination, and improved service delivery.

The Ford administration's 1976 report deviated from the course set by previous reports by refraining from making policy recommendations. In doing so the administration noted that the "principle recommendations can be found in the Budget Message, the State of the Union Message and legislative proposals now before the Congress" (NUPR 1976: ii).

During the Carter administration, policy recommendations were more tightly woven and called for a comprehensive national urban policy for the first time. In the 1978 report's final chapter, President Carter's explicit urban policy was set forth. It began with a set of principles and criteria upon which to base policy, followed by nine policy objectives and implementation strategies:

1. Encourage and support efforts to improve local planning and management capacity and the effectiveness of existing Federal programs.

2. Encourage states to become partners in assisting urban areas.

3. Stimulate greater involvement by neighborhood organizations and voluntary associations.

4. Provide fiscal relief to the most hard-pressed communities.

5. Provide for strong incentives to attract private investment to distressed communities.

6. Provide employment opportunities, primarily in the private sector, to the long-term unemployed and disadvantaged in urban areas.

7. Increase access to opportunity for those disadvantaged by a history of discrimination.

8. Expand and improve social and health services to disadvantaged people in cities, counties, and other communities.

9. Improve the urban physical environment and the cultural and aesthetic aspects of urban life and reduce urban sprawl. (NUPR 1978: 123–26)

The Carter administration also noted (as had the Ford administration) that other recommendations "are treated in separate reports—notably the Economic Report, the Report of the Council on Environmental Quality" (NUPR 1978: 1). In addition to the plans in the section on urban policy, the report proposed such measures as a national water policy, recreational policy, and a new transportation policy.

The Carter administration's second report maintained an explicit urban policy, but reduced its scope somewhat. Based on the same policy principles as the 1978 report, it enunciated five policy recommendations: strengthening urban economies, expanding job opportunities, promoting fiscal stability, expanding opportunity for those disadvantaged by discrimination and low income, and encouraging energy-efficient urban development patterns. Following these broad statements were more specific action statements related to achieving these goals. These included revising tax policies that inadvertently harm urban areas, expanding federal facility location and procurement in distressed communities, enacting the Targeted Fiscal Assistance Program, encouraging neighborhood revitalization, and refining regulations impacting urban development.

Unlike previous reports, the Reagan reports were used more to review current and past policies, rather that to propose new ones. Recommendations for policy actions were curtailed in the four Reagan administration reports. With the exception of the 1988 report, which contained a section entitled "Urban Social Policy Agenda, none of these reports provided a separate recommendations section. The first document in 1982 made few new policy proposals but presented various administration initiatives in place as a part of its urban policy. The foundation of the urban policy was the Economic Recovery Program, but the report also included proposals for a federalism initiative and new anti-crime legislation.

The 1984 report set forth a three-part strategy for "prosperity and stability in our nation's cities" (NUPR 1984: 2). Among the few suggestions offered were plans to target assistance to the needy, Project Self-Sufficiency to reduce welfare dependency, and enterprise zones to aid struggling cities. Reagan's third report also began with the statement of goals and the focus on economic growth as the basis for urban policy. Four major recommendations were included: enterprise zones, a new fair-housing policy, welfare reforms, and a restructuring of transportation programs. The administration's final report in 1988 ventured further with its policy recommendations. In addition to current activity it presented a normative social agenda for the future. This list flowed from a "recognition of problems" and a look at the changes affecting the nation. Rather than proposing specific programs, the recommendations were broad and general (combat drug use, break welfare dependency, more demanding requirements from schools) (p. 6).

The 1990 report of the Bush administration furnished a number of recommendations, but its scope was much narrower than previous reports. All proposals were focused on poverty reduction and were programs of the Department of Housing and Urban Development (HUD). Centered around housing programs, the proposals dealt with increasing home ownership, funding for modernization projects, and the institution of resident manager programs. The Bush administration also offered a modified version of enterprise zones to revitalize urban areas.

Role of the Federal Government

Not surprisingly, the question of the appropriate role of the federal government in urban policy receives a great deal of attention and thought in most of the reports. Every administration acknowledges that the federal government has an important part to play, but the scope of this role has been debated.

The Nixon administration's report in 1972 regarded the proper role of the federal government as limited. In its view the federal reaction to urban growth and development issues had been the creation of narrow programs that often conflicted with other programs. More importantly, it argued that the majority of decisions concerning the nation's growth were not of national significance—they affected only a single state or jurisdiction (NUPR 1972: 65). For this reason, decisions would be better made at those levels; that is, state and local governments are best suited to address their own needs. As for the federal government, it would benefit from restructuring to mitigate the "undesirable consequences" of too many programs (ibid.).

In the 1974 report this theme was extended. While the federal government was seen as having a role to play in growth policy, its efforts often added confusion. "Federal programs often have conflicting objectives," which interfere with their intentions (NUPR 1974: 3). Instead, the Nixon administration asserted that "states are uniquely suited to managing growth and development processes because of the constitutional powers they enjoy and their relationship to local governments" (NUPR 1974: 31).

President Ford's 1976 report envisioned a more active federal government role. In spite of the preeminent role of state and local governments and the private sector in growth management, the federal government was still an actor in this arena. In addition, the federal government was responsible for such activities as redressing inequities in the distribution of benefits to citizens and units of government, promoting equality of opportunity, and compensating for extreme inequities in standards of living (NUPR 1976: 144).

Under the Carter administration the magnitude of the federal role was expansive as spelled out in principle number six: "National urban policy must reflect the commitment of the Federal government to play a central role" (NUPR 1980: 120). The federal government would provide more active support to state and local governments and take a more active role in direct assistance measures. This represented a major shift in thought regarding the role of government. The 1980 report maintained the broader view of the federal role. It stressed the importance of the federal government's leadership abilities to sustain a coordinated response to urban problems. The Carter administration's reports did point out the importance of partnerships with state, local, and private sectors to meet the needs of urban communities; federal assistance alone would be insufficient (NUPR 1980: 13–1).

The scope of the federal government's role narrowed once again in the reports of the Reagan administration. Similar to the views of the Nixon administration, Reagan sought to reduce the federal role in favor of greater participation by state and local governments. In both 1982 and 1984 the reports contained chapters related to the "restoration of balance" on the federal system. This meant providing state and local governments with information and technical assistance to help them meet their responsibility for urban affairs. The primary federal role was to ensure a healthy national economy. The 1984 report also cited the continuation of such programs as the community development block grants, urban action development grants, and general revenue sharing as evidence of the federal role of helping cities "having difficulty adjusting to economic changes" (NUPR 1984: 5).

President Reagan's third report showed no sign of change except to note that reductions in federal spending necessitated the shifting responsibilities. The final report was much the same. It clearly stated that the federal role should be limited and should directly assist people, encourage personal responsibility, and break the cycle of welfare dependency. It also encouraged state and local cooperation to reduce their dependence on the federal government.

Process: How the Reports Were Put Together

A variety of methods have been used to assemble the national urban (growth) policy reports. As part of our research we conducted a series of ten interviews. These interviews included academics specializing in urban policy and civil servants who had participated in formulating the reports, as well as others with a strong interest in urban policy. Several pointed out that the political nature of the process generated obstacles for those actually writing the piece. As a presidential report it needs White House approval; this prompts those in HUD responsible for the report to energize the White House or someone in the domestic policy office for input. Disagreements between the secretary of HUD and the White House occurred causing delays in the document's release. Final approval of the finished product must come from the White House and the Office of Management and Budget; the former to see that it fits the agenda and the latter to review the financial implications of any policy recommendations.

The reports have generally been pieced together by various agencies, with HUD providing the leadership. HUD prepares an initial draft and requests input from other agencies, a process that has often generated interagency competition for leverage and has been open to some criticism. First, HUD's ability to lead the process is hampered by what one person referred to as its status as a "minor player" among federal agencies. In addition, as another respondent noted, the report is not closely related to other projects in which HUD staffers are involved. Many even commented that the writers are given little leeway with respect to the substance of the report and are discouraged by the prospect of having to take part in the process. One person went so far as to say that it is "despised by all who work on it." While the primary writing has been done by the Office of the Assistant Secretary for Policy Development and Research of HUD, in some cases academics and think tanks have been used as consultants to provide background information on specific topics.

While the process described above reflects many general themes, variations occur within each administration. The first report produced by the Nixon administration started out in a domestic council subcommittee until HUD was assigned to take over. Upon rejecting the first document, the domestic council made several revisions to the next draft before releasing it (Hanson 1982: 16–17). Hanson also describes how the second report, formulated through greater interagency consultations and HUD leadership, was still characterized by many White House restrictions. President Ford's report began with a summary of the formulation process, noting the use of an interagency task force, regional seminars on growth and development, and public forums. As one source noted, unlike previous reports, this report involved less White House input, but did utilize outside consultants. The two reports of the Carter administration were characterized by a somewhat different approach. In addition to a more prominent White House role, these reports were produced by another unit in HUD. Initially assigned to Policy Development and Research, in a much publicized change it was moved to Community Planning and Development, which coordinated the activities of the newly created Urban and Regional Policy Group (URPG) (Wolman and Merget 1980: 406). The URPG was an interagency body that, according to the 1978 report, formed numerous task forces, held forums, interviewed civic groups, business leaders, and state and local officials (NUPR 1978, pp. 114–16). During the Reagan years, both in an effort to simplify the process and as a sign of some disinterest, the reports borrowed heavily from the previous documents in style and language. According to one familiar with the subject, the Bush report in 1990 generated less White House involvement than previous reports and was essentially the work of the secretary of HUD, Jack Kemp.

Audience and Usage

At the time of its enactment, Congress had a number of reasons for requesting the reports. According to Royce Hanson, in addition to addressing the urban crisis and urban growth problems, it was envisioned that the report would promote the leadership necessary for sustained policy action, reduce the level of conflict among federal policies and eventually create a staff of urban experts to generate information (Hanson 1982: 15). One purpose of the report was to provide Congress, as the primary audience, with knowledge about the state of relations between the federal government and America's cities. It was to provide an opportunity for Congress to receive the administration's views about urban problems as well as its responsibility in these areas. In its ideal form, the report would present a direction for policy and a foundation upon which to move forward. According to one source close to the process, the report would reveal how important cities were to the current administration and what actions would be appropriate.

By nearly all accounts, the report has fallen far short of these expectations. For example, in his paper for this conference, Royce Hanson writes "the biennial reports have been late, vague, self-serving, and fortunately obscure. There is no evidence that they have had any discernible effect on federal policy, much less on actual urban development." Marshall Kaplan concurs, noting "the reports have been little more than a summary of trends . . . and self-serving analysis" (1990: 182). Another participant has suggested that "the irrelevance of the president's report is a fitting metaphor for the state of explicit urban policy" (Orlebeke 1990: 185). And one interview source stated "they are of little use, there is no inherent value in their work, and no intellectual attractiveness to using them." As these comments suggest, the report seems to have provided only limited use as a policy document or starting point for an urban policy debate.

Respondents provided many reasons to support their contention that the reports have little appeal. The chief complaint is that the level of substance has decreased over the years; there is little by way of new and useful information in the documents. There is a perception that neither the administration nor the Congress it is written for is sincere about their role in the creation of the reports. The lack of sincerity can be evidenced by the failure of Congress to hold hearings on the report and the executive branch's unwillingness or inability to produce the report in a timely manner. Many felt that its limited use as a point of departure for policy-making reduces the amount of favorable attention the report would gather.

During the interview process a few key problems continually arose. First, the reports are not tied to any ongoing policy action beyond the array of programs in separate departments. HUD, the lead agency behind the reports, lacks the power and interest to push for coherent urban policy (Kaplan 1990: 182). Next, according to one source, the reports "are not written with a particular constituency in mind." This is a concern because congressional and interest-group activity is built around servicing more discrete units than the urban policy report does. As time has passed, there has been a growing sense of confusion about what these reports are meant to do. It is difficult for an instrument that is so imprecise, sparsely backed, and little understood to stir much interest among policy makers.

Other factors add to the limitations of the president's report as a potentially meaningful policy document. First is the change in administrations and accompanying philosophy; with each shift the nature and importance of the report alter. Each report takes on its own set of characteristics, depending on who is in charge and the attitudes of those working on the document. These changes mean that, for the most part, successive reports do not build upon each other, and they do not lead to further policy development. The building process and the report's usefulness are further limited by the lack of consensus on definitions of and goals for urban policy. Finally, the report is supposed to reflect a "national urban policy" that does not exist except to the (very limited) extent it is devised for purposes of the report. Here, as elsewhere, efforts to devise a coherent and effective policy (or policies) are constrained by lack of available budgetary resources, public support, and political will.

Finally, as Kaplan observed, it would seem that urban policy is a hazardous topic for policy makers and politicians to expend their energy on (1990: 184). Several of those interviewed concurred with Kaplan's assessment, noting that everyone from the administration to the agencies involved are "wary" of the report. The cautious approach from the administration's standpoint is due in part to what one respondent referred to as the "vulnerability" it creates. People are reluctant to make negative statements and are concerned about the ability to fund program recommendations. The usefulness of this device is related, it seems, to the interest of Congress. The White House will comply and produce a document, but the burden is on the legislature to react to it and use it. And in general,Congress has not found it useful or indeed paid much attention to it.

Of course, Congress is not the only group the report is of interest to. While the stated audience is restricted, each administration knows that a variety of interests look to the report as a signal for the direction that urban policy will take. According to one source, an important part of what the reports do is to spell out the administration's "vision" for urban areas. As the vision of the administration narrows, the prospective audience narrows as well. The reports of Nixon, Ford, and Carter provided a fairly broad vision of where cities were heading. The first three reports affected anyone concerned with growth, especially housing groups. Carter's audience targeted those concerned with older cities experiencing the effects of economic change. Under Ronald Reagan a vision for the future of urban areas was not clearly enunciated. This had the effect of reducing the potential audience and usefulness of the documents.

The national urban policy reports do not appear to be an important work for most interest groups active in the area of urban policy. The information in these reports is not directed to any particular interest group. Mayors, housing groups, realtors and the like probably find their use limited by the summary nature of the information in them. Those who are interested in urban policy, or more accurately in some area of policy, generally are conversant with relevant trends and the administration's response to problems through other means. The fact that few interest groups exert much influence, or even attempt to influence the process, is a sign that, as one person close to the process stated, "the report is a yawn."

At least two other groups have been identified as potential users of the reports. State and local governments, as well as academics, have been able to reap small benefits from them. While the reports revolve around the federal role, state and local governments have played an increasing role as each administration has sought to stimulate its activity on urban policy. These units look to the report as another source for understanding what the federal government will expect them to be responsible for. For scholars, the reports as a base of information are of little value. Many note that they lack substance and provide only summary information; this is a particular criticism of those reports which utilize the "laundry list" of programs and activities or "suspender snapper" self-congratulatory style. For some, though, they are a point of departure to discuss the current state of federal urban policy. This has been the case when the reports have made substantive policy statements. Aside from these few episodes, their use by academics has primarily been as a subject for articles and conferences and as teaching devices.

For all of the reasons mentioned above, the president's report has suffered a lack of credibility over the years. Our informal survey of informed academics and bureaucrats reveals a general consensus that these reports, with a few exceptions, have not been taken too seriously. Reports issued prior to 1982 garnered more interest because they put forth a clearer policy direction. As interest in urban policy has waned, and the documents have come to serve as snapshots of ongoing activity rather than as a blueprint for action, the response to its issuance has turned to indifference. One respondent sees the report as an extension of domestic policy, and as such it is taken seriously only if domestic policy has a high priority on the agenda.

In fact, publicity of the reports has been very limited because of the lack of interest in and debate over an explicit urban policy. In general, the first report of each new administration tends to be the recipient of the most attention as the interested parties await the new strategy. The 1972 document received substantial attention, since expectations were high for the first report and the topic still had a strong following. Nixon's and Ford's remaining reports failed to obtain the same attention as the interest in a comprehensive policy faded. The Carter reports received a fair amount of publicity for several reasons. From his days as a candidate, Jimmy Carter made urban policy an important part of his agenda and he signaled this commitment during a campaign speech to mayors (Stegman 1993: 1755). Both reports are recognized by those familiar with them as more policy-oriented than others. Their publicity in part reflects their connection to actual policies; conversely, the lack of attention to forthcoming reports represents their detachment from policy. From 1982 forward, the national urban policy reports were seldom the topic of attention. As some suggest, this move was purposive, to send a message that explicit urban policy was not a high priority for this president. These reports were often delayed and released when Congress was out of session, undercutting their ability to respond.

Conclusion

The president's national urban policy report has been envisioned by many of its proponents as a vehicle for the federal government to examine the nation's urban problems in a comprehensive manner and to articulate a response to them. As we have demonstrated, the reports have usually fallen far short of these expectations. Indeed, the very purpose of the reports—as well as their nature, structure, and coverage—must be rethought if they are to be reshaped into useful documents. At a minimum, the reports could present a consistent set of urban indicators, providing the ability to track changes in urban conditions and well-being over time (see Plotnick's article below). Beyond that, there are a variety of models that might provide a useful contribution (see the discussion in the introduction of this volume).

But if the reports are to be "useful," someone must be paying attention. At present the audience appears limited to a handful of academics. The reports, required by congressional legislation, should surely be the subject of congressional hearings and should be responded to by the major urban interest groups. In practice, a "useful" national urban policy report will require not only changes in the report itself, but changes in the political environment that will increase the visibility and importance of urban problems on the national policy agenda.

References

Domestic Council, Committee on Community Development. 1974. *National Growth and Development: Second Biennial Report to the Congress* (Washington, DC: U.S. Government Printing Office).

Domestic Council, Committee on Community Development 1976. *1976 Report on National Growth and Development* (Washington, DC: U.S. Government Printing Office).

Eisinger, Peter. 1983. "The Search for a National Urban Policy 1968–1980," *Journal of Urban History* 12 (1): 3–23.

Executive Office of the President, Domestic Council. 1972. *Report on National Growth 1972* (Washington, DC: U.S. Government Printing Office).

Hanson, Royce. 1982. *The Evolution of National Urban Policy 1970–1980: Lessons from the Past* (National Academy Press: Washington, DC).

Kaplan, Marshall. 1990. "National Urban Policy: Where Are We Now? Where Are We Going?" in Marshall Kaplan and Franklin James (eds.), *The Future of National Urban Policy* (Durham: Duke University Press).

Orlebeke, Charles. 1990. *Chasing Urban Policy: A Critical Retrospective,* in Marshall Kaplan and Franklin James (eds.), *The Future of National Urban Policy* (Durham: Duke University Press).

Sec. 921—Housing and Community Development Act of 1992, Pub.L.No. 102–550, 106 Stat. 3672 (1992).

Stegman, Michael A. 1993. "National Urban Policy Revisited," *North Carolina Law Review* 71 (5): 1737–77.

Title VII—Urban Growth and New Community Development Act of 1970, Pub.L.No. 91–609, 84 Stat. 1791 (1970).

Title VII—National Urban Policy and New Community Development Act, Pub.L.No. 95–128, 91 Stat. 1143–44 (1977).

U.S. Department of Housing and Urban Development. 1978. *The President's National Urban Policy Report 1978* (Washington, DC: U.S. Department of Housing and Urban Development).

_____. 1980. *The President's National Urban Policy Report 1980* (Washington, DC: U.S. Department of Housing and Urban Development).

_____. 1982. *The President's National Urban Policy Report 1982* (Washington, DC: U.S. Department of Housing and Urban Development).

_____. 1984. *The President's National Urban Policy Report 1984* (Washington, DC: U.S. Department of Housing and Urban Development).

_____. 1986. *The President's National Urban Policy Report 1986* (Washington, DC: U.S. Department of Housing and Urban Development).

_____. 1988. *The President's National Urban Policy Report 1988* (Washington, DC: U.S. Department of Housing and Urban Development).

_____. 1990. *The President's National Urban Policy Report 1990* (Washington, DC: U.S. Department of Housing and Urban Development).

Wolman, Harold, and Astrid Merget. 1980. "The Presidency and Policy Formulation: President Carter and the Urban Policy," *Presidential Studies Quarterly* X, no. 3.

Appendix A

National Urban Policy Reports

Tables of Contents

Urban Labor Markets

Randall W. Eberts

In every developed economy, cities are the center of economic activity and opportunity. They bring together businesses, workers, and customers into close physical proximity, thus offering firms and workers advantages that lead to more efficient markets, enhanced productivity, and greater economic success. These benefits come about in several ways. Large metropolitan areas allow firms and workers to specialize in activities in which they hold a comparative advantage. By being close to suppliers and customers, firms can build efficient supply networks that lower costs and enhance productivity. Also, dense urban environments enhance the flow of ideas and the transfer of technology through informational networks, which create growth-enhancing spillovers to firms. Workers also rely on informational networks to add to their general knowledge, establish support groups, enhance job-related skills, and gain access to job openings. Consequently, the physical and informational proximity of businesses and workers within metropolitan areas yields the nation's most productive activities, spawns technological and organizational innovations, and launches new business ventures.

For most urban residents, economic success is determined by the jobs and income generated by labor markets. A labor market rewards those people with the appropriate skills, energy, and ideas. Acquisition of these qualifications results from long-run decisions to invest in education and training, to choose work over leisure, and to be networked with people

I wish to thank Tim Bartik and Harry Holzer for helpful comments and suggestions and Ken Kline and Wei-Jang Huang for expert research assistance.

who been successful. Labor markets also provide the signals and incentives for individuals to make these decisions and to be in a position to take advantage of opportunities when they arise.

By offering the greatest opportunity for economic success, cities attract both the nation's most talented and successful individuals and the most disadvantaged. While people of all skills are important to generate the economic complementarities that enhance productivity, many of the least skilled people do not find the success they had hoped for. Therefore, cities stand as a stark dichotomy of those who have succeeded and those who have not. They generate a large proportion of the nation's wealth but also house much of the nation's poverty and homelessness.

Cities have always exhibited this stark contrast between those who have achieved economic success and those who have not. The ancient Greek philosopher Plato gave commentary to his times in observing that "there are two cities: one for the rich and one for the poor" (*The Republic*). The ability of urban labor markets to improve the quality of life for all groups of workers varies over time. In recent years, opportunities for economic advancement have diminished. Real earnings growth has slowed to a paltry 0.9 percent during the last decade. Worse yet, only those individuals with college degrees experienced improvements in real income; people with high school degrees or less saw their real earnings decline.

The slowdown in earnings and the rise in income inequality has placed considerable stress on cities. Many cities have been unable to make sufficient investments in the physical and human capital required for efficient markets and the easy flow of information. As the core structure of cities deteriorates and the advantages of close proximity diminish, businesses and households have left inner cities for outlying areas. This shift in location has left inner cities with fewer resources to devote to mounting social problems. This shift has also helped to diminish the nation's capacity to spawn high-productivity, high-growth activities.

The purpose of this chapter is to assess the current condition of urban labor markets and to suggest a national urban policy agenda that addresses these concerns. For individuals, these issues include slow wage growth, increased earnings inequality, persistent earnings gap between whites and minorities, disparity in job opportunities and earnings between inner cities and suburbs, the spatial mismatch of jobs, and the increased isolation of many inner-city residents. For the nation, the issues are the social fallout from growing income disparities and reduced income mobility and the economy's diminished growth capacity as the physical and social infrastructure supporting urban area markets deteriorates.

It is appropriate for the federal government to create and carry out a national urban policy for two reasons. First, many of the issues listed above are related to the redistribution of income, which is a traditional function of the federal government. Second, the close proximity of activities within metropolitan areas generates externalities that contribute more than proportionately to growth and which compound the many social problems facing cities. Therefore, to reflect the urban environment that generates these economic and social trends, a national urban policy must incorporate these externalities. The policy statement should emphasize the effect of physical and informational proximity on growth, the benefits of efficient urban markets, and the importance of the access of workers to urban labor markets. These characteristics distinguish a national *urban* policy from simply a national policy targeted at people who happen to live in cities.

The article is divided into sections that describe several major issues facing urban workers. Each discussion presents data on these trends and identifies current research that offers insights into the underlying causes. In addition, the discussion attempts to show these issues within the context of the urban environment and to identify how these externalities should be incorporated into a national urban policy.

I. Metropolitan Growth

The fiscal and social distress experienced by cities in recent years has been well documented. Yet, despite increased concern about urban crime, congestion, air quality, and high housing prices, metropolitan areas continue to grow and to offer their expanding populations greater job opportunities and higher income than the declining nonmetropolitan areas. Between 1980 and 1990, the number of metropolitan residents swelled by 13.7 percent, while the U.S. population grew 9.8 percent. Nonmetropolitan areas actually lost population. As a result, the share of the U.S. population residing in the 268 designated metropolitan areas rose from 74.8 percent in 1980 to 77.5 percent in 1990. In 1990, a greater proportion of working-age metropolitan residents were employed than nonmetropolitan residents, and the median income of a metropolitan worker was $4,000 higher than that of his or her nonmetropolitan counterparts (1990 Census). This ability to create relatively high-paying jobs attests to the advantages cities offer to firms through higher labor productivity and proximity to suppliers.

The economic performance of central cities and suburbs is strongly linked. Workers in both central cities and suburbs benefit to a large extent from the growth of the entire region. Several articles have shown the intrametropolitan linkage between earnings and employment. For example, Stanback and Knight (1976) found that 67 percent of suburban income was generated by central-city earnings in the mid 1970s. Ledebur and Barnes (1992) showed that suburban employment suffered when central city income growth lagged behind suburban income growth. In addi-

Figure 1

Profiles of Central City and Suburban Residents and Movers

	central city residents	movers	suburban residents	
median income	$27,796	$29,966	$40,204	median income
		38 %		
high school	34 %	15 %	39 %	high school
		6.9		
college	12.3 %	⇌	14 %	college
unemployment	5.7 %	$25,064	4.1 %	unemployment
		42 %		
		11 %		

Source: U.S. Department of Commerce, Bureau of Census, Geographic Mobility: March 1989 to March 1992. *Current Population Report*s. P20–473, November 1991

tion, job growth was markedly better for metropolitan areas with smaller disparities between central-city and suburban income. The linkages between the two entities continue to strengthen as a greater percentage of holders of central-city jobs reside in the suburbs. Savitch et al. (1993) show for a selected sample of ten metropolitan areas that suburbanites claimed a rising share of an expanding central-city economy.

Even with these linkages, considerable disparity exists between central cities and outlying suburbs. The median income of central-city residents is 40 percent lower than that of suburban residents (Figure 1). Also, central-city residents are less educated and have a significantly higher unemployment rate than suburbanites. Movements between central cities and surrounding areas have only worsened these disparities in recent years. From 1989 to 1990, the median income and educational attainment of households moving from central cities to suburbs were higher than those they left behind. The median income and education levels of households leaving the suburbs for the central city were not only lower than their former suburban neighbors, but also lower than central-city residents. Twice as many people moved from the central city to the suburbs than from the suburbs to the central city. This exodus from central cities and the persistent economic disparities heighten the physical and intellectual barriers between central cities and suburbs.

Despite the flow of people out of central cities, central-city population grew during the last decade, and at a slightly higher rate than urban fringe areas. The proportion of the U.S. population living in central cities rose from 30.0 percent in 1980 to 31.3 percent in 1990. Hispanics accounted for almost half the central-city population growth. Their share of central-city population increased from 10.8 percent in 1980 to 15.3 percent in 1990, and their share of total metropolitan growth increased from 7.5 percent to 10.5 percent. While this increase is most evident in southwestern cities, Hispanics' presence has increased in many cities throughout the country, as the total Hispanic population has increased 53 percent during the ten-year period.

The influx of Hispanics into central cities has shifted the composition of metropolitan populations toward more Hispanics and fewer whites. The proportion of blacks has remained about the same. White residents' share of central-city population has decreased from 69.7 percent in 1980 to 66.1 percent in 1990, while their share of total metropolitan population has declined from 81.9 percent to 78.3. Black residents' share of central-city and metropolitan population has remained constant at 22 percent and 13 percent, respectively. Since the median income of Hispanic households is $9,000 less than that of white households, the shift in the composition of central-city population from white to Hispanic has contributed to lower median income of central cities.

Central cities have also experienced a shift in industrial composition from manufacturing to service jobs, which has contributed significantly to the income differential between central cities and suburbs. The decline in the percentage of manufacturing jobs has had a large effect on low-skilled workers. Factory jobs traditionally offered low-skilled workers higher wages than they could find in other jobs. Bound and Holzer (1991) and Bluestone et al. (1991) find that metropolitan manufacturing employment substantially impacts the employment and earnings of young men, particularly young black men, with a high school education or less.

II. Slow Earnings Growth and Rising Income Dispersion

The traditional role of cities as a place to seek job opportunities and achieve income advancement has been eroded during the last two decades by historically low earnings growth for most groups of workers. The less-skilled workers have experienced a loss in real income, and consequently a decline in their living standards. While city dwellers on average have fared better than the national average, their earnings have followed the national trend of slower earnings growth. These trends stem from a complex assortment of economic, demographic, and social forces. Many of the factors are symptomatic of urban problems. Focusing on the more important factors offers perspective on how a national urban policy might prioritize the host of problems facing urban labor markets.

During the two decades following World War II, Americans became accustomed to income growth of nearly 3 percent per year, after adjusting for inflation. All income groups enjoyed such real-income gains. In fact, the lowest quintile registered the largest annual increase and the higher quintile the lowest. Only half a percentage point rate of growth separated the fastest- from the slowest-growing income groups (*Economic Report of the President* 1994).

However, starting around 1970, real income growth slowed dramatically. From 1973 to 1992, median family real income increased by only 0.1 percent per year. All income groups experienced a slowdown, but those at the lower end of the distribution were the most severely affected. The highest quintile of families enjoyed a 0.93 annual increase in median real income between 1973 and 1992, whereas the lowest quintile suffered a loss in real income of 0.69 percent annually.

Slower real-income growth is directly related to the slowdown in productivity growth. About the time that earnings growth slowed dramatically, productivity growth slowed from an average annual rate 2.8 percent from 1958 to 1973 to an annual rate of 0.9 percent thereafter. Many economic factors are responsible for slower productivity growth, including a decline in worker skills, lack of adequate investment in private and public capital, and decline in innovative activities. With cities traditionally at the forefront of the nation's productivity gains, the slowdown draws attention to urban concerns that may have contributed to this problem. Current urban problems of poor educational opportunities in inner cities, the movement of jobs away from the urban core, and the decline in investment in urban infrastructure may have contributed to the productivity slowdown. Urban social issues, such as low skills, lack of an adequate support structure, and lack of participation in the workforce have also prevented many urban workers from enjoying the benefits of productivity growth.

Changes in social characteristics also contributed to the change in household income. According to one study, social characteristics had an even greater effect than economic factors. Ryscavage, Green, and Welniak (1991) show that the decline in married-couple households as a percentage of all households and the increase in educational attainment had large offsetting effects on household income. Of seven factors considered (age, race, type of household, education, work experience and head of household, work experience of spouse, and industry of household head), type of household and education registered the largest effects. They estimate that as the percent of married-couple households declined from 70 percent in 1969 to 55 percent in 1989, median household income fell by $3,226, or 10 percent.

They also estimate that the increase in educational attainment boosted median household income by $3,010. Between 1969 and 1989, the percentage of persons age 25 and older with four or more years of college rose from 10.7 percent to 21.1 percent. The higher earnings from educational attainment resulted from two factors. The first was higher educational attainment. The second was the increase in the educational wage premium during the 1980s. During the 1970s, the earnings ratio between college and high school graduates remained constant at 1.4 for men and 1.8 for women. However, after around 1979, the education premium rose significantly, climbing to 1.7 for men and 2.1 for women by 1989, as demand for skilled workers outstripped supply. In fact, for young men, only those with four years of college or more enjoyed a real wage increase during the 1980s. Real income of high school graduates and dropouts declined during this period (*Economic Report of the President* 1994: 92).

These same factors which affected median income—household type, educational attainment, and industry mix—also shifted the income distribution. Had these factors not changed during the last twenty years, the income distribution would have been more equal. These two social factors affected the various income groups differently. Household type significantly affected the lower quintiles of the income distribution but not the higher quintiles. Educational attainment affected the high end of the distribution but not the low end. Industry mix affected the lowest quintiles, suggesting the heavy dependence of low-skilled workers on the rents they received from manufacturing jobs (Bartik, 1993).

III. Minority Earnings Gap

One of the most troubling and persistent concerns in the performance of urban labor markets, and one that a national urban policy must address, is the earnings gap between blacks and Hispanics and whites. Blacks and Hispanics earn considerably less than whites, and neither group has made any significant strides in narrowing this gap during the last decade. In 1980, black household median income was 58 percent of white household income. By 1991, the ratio stood at 60 percent. The ratio of the median income of Hispanic households to white households remained steady at 72 percent during this period. Even considering married-couple households, the gap, although not as large, has not narrowed appreciably since the mid 1970s. Before then, black married households advanced from 72 percent of white income to 80 percent.

When all households are considered, household type—married versus single head, usually female—plays a large role in explaining differences among the three major racial and ethnic groups. Between 1969 and 1989, the proportion of all black households that consisted of married couples dropped from 56.7 percent to 35.7 percent. By 1991, the percentage had fallen even further to 32.8 percent. In contrast, the proportion of all white households that were married couples shrank from 73 percent to 59 percent between 1969 and 1989, and stood at 57 percent in 1991.

The depressing effect of the rise in female-headed households can be seen by comparing the median income of female-headed households versus married-couple households. In 1991, the median income of a black female-headed household was $11,414 versus $33,307 for married-couple households. The income of single female parents was even lower—$9,417.

IV. Lack of Economic Progress of Black Men

With household type accounting for much of the black–white household income differential, it is tempting to place most of the blame on the deterioration of the married-couple family for the lack of progress in narrowing the gap between blacks and whites. However, while important, it detracts from the underlying reasons for family breakups and ignores the problems facing household heads, in particular black males.[1]

Since joblessness among black males leads to fewer marriages, the decline in black married couples is self-perpetuating (Welch 1990). In addressing the lack of economic progress among urban minority workers, a national urban policy must focus on the disadvantages minorities face in seeking employment and the increasing disenfranchisement of low-income black males.

The widening black–white earnings and employment gaps among young men cut across all education levels. Bound and Freeman (1992) show that the gap is most severe for college graduates and high school dropouts and that blacks in the Midwest experienced the largest decline. Bound and Freeman conclude that the black economic experience is too diverse to support a single-factor explanation. For college graduates, changed occupational composition, shifts in industry demand, and growth in relative supply are major contributors. For high school dropouts, the reduction in the real minimum wage lowers earnings and the increase in the proportion of young blacks with criminal records are major causes of reduced employment. For blacks in the Midwest, decline in manufacturing, changes in occupational composition of jobs, decline in unionism and the real minimum wage, and the growth of relative supply were major factors.

A more important factor in explaining the decline in real income of low-skilled men is a significant decline in their labor market participation

---

[1] Income of Hispanics is also lower on average than whites. With their increased presence in metropolitan areas, particularly central cities, factors leading to their earnings and employment gap should also be addressed. However, the literature on this topic is considerably less extensive and that which does exist reflects a great diversity within the Hispanic population and with respect to their employment issues. This topic will not be covered in this paper, although it is an issue that demands increased attention.

rate. For example, the employment-to-population ratio of white male high school dropouts fell fourteen percentage points, from 0.89 in 1967 to 0.75 in 1987. The decline was even greater for black male high school dropouts (Juhn 1992). Central-city black men are less likely to find work than their suburban counterparts. In 1990 when national unemployment was around 5.5 percent, the difference in unemployment rates between central-city and suburban residents was two percentage points.

The fall in employment is largely accounted for by a rise in the number of men who experienced long spells of labor-market inactivity, and not in more frequent spells (Juhn 1992). The increasing number of working-age males who are detached from the labor force has long-run economic and social consequences. Without more frequent work experience, a growing portion of the workforce loses valuable job skills, which is detrimental to the national economy in wasting valuable labor resources as well as to individuals who lose income. They also lose the job contacts necessary to retain employment or find better job prospects. Nonparticipants in the labor market contribute to social problems. Those who are unemployed and no longer actively look for employment are much less likely to marry and live with a spouse than labor-market participants (Welch 1990). As shown earlier, the increase in female-headed households has led to a decline in household income and contributes to a persistent cycle of welfare dependency.

V. Barriers to Economic Success

Urban workers benefit from metropolitan economic growth only if they have access to the urban labor market. For minorities and low-skill workers, this access is impeded by physical barriers of spatial isolation and intellectual barriers of poor education and inadequate support groups and referral networks. Therefore, in designing a national urban policy, efforts should also be made to increase access to the urban labor market.

The shifting industrial mix of central cities and suburbs has left some groups of workers isolated from decent-paying jobs. The movement of manufacturing jobs to the suburbs has made it increasingly difficult for many inner-city residents to finds jobs close by that offer the same wages as manufacturing jobs. Various types of service jobs have concentrated in central cities, but either the pay is lower or the skill requirements are higher than the qualifications of many residents.

Beginning with Kain (1968), several studies have proposed that physical distance between jobs and workers could be a major factor in the low employment rate and income levels of blacks, particularly black males. Kasarda (1989) found that black males without high school degrees who held full-time jobs spent ten minutes longer traveling to work than their white counterparts. Ihlanfeldt and Sjoquist (1990, 1991) presented convincing evidence that spatial mismatch has lowered the earnings of central-city non-college graduates significantly. Using more aggregate data, Price and Mills (1985) estimated that the concentration of blacks in central cities could explain as much as one third of the black–white earnings gap. Focusing on minority youths, Ihlanfeldt (1992) estimated that a five-minute reduction in commuting time would increase the probability of employment by 0.075, which would cause the mean employment rate of this group to rise by 26 percent.

Physical distance is not the only barrier that prevents low-income inner-city residents, particularly minorities, from gaining access to better-paying jobs. Intellectual barriers also play a major role. Intellectual barriers prevent people from participating in the formal and informal information networks through which people learn about job opportunities, are referred to employers, and gain appropriate role models and support groups. These barriers stem in part from physical isolation, such as the increasing concentration of poverty. But they also result from a growing gap in the ability of inner-city residents to meet the skill requirements of the workplace and to communicate and move comfortably within an increasingly sophisticated work environment. While distances may become effectively shorter because of better transportation, intellectual barriers may continue to grow as businesses demand higher skills than many inner-city workers can match.

The growing gap between skill requirements of the workplace and skills of inner-city residents deters many workers from participating in urban labor markets. Without appropriate skills and workplace knowhow, workers are shut out of many jobs, even entry-level ones. The lack of quality education for residents of inner-city areas has been blamed for the detachment from the workplace. However, focusing on education to explain the difference in economic success between black men and white men is somewhat controversial. One would expect a greater demand for high-skill workers to worsen the absolute and relative labor-market position of black men, since on average they have less educational attainment and less work experience. However, Bound and Freeman (1992) find strong evidence that interracial differences in measured educational attainment explain little or none of the deterioration in the labor-market position of black men.

Evidence of poor-quality inner-city schools compared to suburban schools raises the possibility that this difference is a significant factor in explaining black–white earnings differentials. Card and Krueger (1992) use state-level data on school attributes to show that improvement in school quality can narrow the black–white wage differential. Bound and Freeman (1992) are not as convinced that educational quality is a major factor and cite statistics that show standardized test scores of blacks rose modestly relative to whites during the 1980s.

A major barrier to low-skilled persons, particularly blacks, is the lack of basic workplace competencies. Detailed studies conducted in Cleveland (Hill, Rittenhouse, and Allison 1994) and in Michigan (Bartik and Erickcek 1992) found that many disadvantaged workers do not meet the basic requirements of entry-level jobs. Through interviews and focus groups, it became evident that many disadvantaged individuals have difficulty finding or holding jobs because they do not understand what employers expect of them, such as proper dress, getting to work on time, coming to work every day, and working well with fellow employees and management. They also lacked other basic skills necessary to perform any job, such as problem-solving, resource and time management, and organization. Many employers interviewed by the studies believed that schools were not preparing students with these competencies. If schools do not properly prepare students for viable jobs or prepare them to enter and succeed in college, their physical isolation in inner-city ghettos will be reinforced by intellectual isolation from networks that allow them to take advantage of the opportunities of the urban labor market.

Business hiring practices and informational and referral networks may also place blacks at a disadvantage. The move to more informal referral systems with the decline of unionism and the emerging importance of small businesses in job creation may have made this more of a factor in recent years. The majority of workers learn about job openings and obtain referrals through informal networks of friends and relatives (see Holzer 1991 for a literature review). Holzer (1988) found that the most frequently used methods of job search by youths are checking with friends and relatives and making direct applications without referrals. O'Regan and Quigley (1993) found that family networks of fathers, mothers, and siblings were most important in helping at-home youths gain access to jobs. Moreover, jobs obtained informally are generally associated with higher earnings and more prestigious occupations (Granovetter 1974).

Blacks also appear to have a disadvantage throughout much of the job process from interview to promotion. Black men fare worse than whites in interviews (Kerschenmann and Neckerman 1991) and are at a disadvantage with respect to specific employer practices and attitudes in recruiting, hiring, and promotion (Braddock and McPartland 1987).

Wilson (1987) suggests that geographic concentration of low-income households may lead to social isolation, further limiting the ability of residents to improve their economic situations. The spatial separation of households with different income and educational levels is more pervasive than simply between central cities and surrounding suburbs. Concentration of poverty, and thus the loss of networks of families and friends with positive work experience, has occurred within central cities. Studies have shown that low-income households have become increasing concentrated in central-city neighborhoods during the last several decades (Reischauer 1988). For example, a recent analysis of poverty in the Cleveland area by

Coulton et al. (1990) shows that it has become more geographically concentrated during the 1980s. In the city of Cleveland, between 28 and 47 percent of the population reside in high-poverty neighborhoods. The analysis uses 40 percent as the high-poverty threshold. The effects of concentrated poverty are more evident for the nonwhite population than the white population.

Migration of the non-poor out of neighborhoods contributes significantly to the rising spatial concentration of poverty. Coulton et al. (1990) estimated that migration of the non-poor from emerging poverty areas accounts for 60 percent of the increased concentration of poverty in Cleveland. Between 1980 and 1988, 23 percent of the non-poor moved, while only 1 percent of the poor moved out of these areas.

The effects of neighbors or members of a support group are critically important in the acquisition of skills, incentive and value structures, and tendencies toward various types of behavior. Crane (1991) finds that high school dropout and teenage pregnancy rates are significantly lower in neighborhoods with a higher proportion of adults holding management and professional jobs. Case and Katz (1991) find contagion effects among neighboring youths for several different outcomes: criminal activities, drug use, unemployment, gang membership, and church attendance. Therefore, the breakdown of informal networks as friends and relatives with jobs or job experience leave a neighborhood reduces the prospect of finding employment for those who remain.

Crime and the participation in illegal business activities are also detrimental to a young black man's employment prospects and earnings potential. Living in a crime-ridden area also indirectly affects a person's ability to function properly in the labor market. Bound and Freeman (1992) report that greater criminal activity may induce some young men to forego employment. Conversely, the deteriorated job market for the less skilled may make crime more attractive. Freeman (1992) underscores the long-term adverse consequences of involvement in crime on youth employment and argues that improvement of skills and increase in legitimate opportunities should be part of a crime reduction effort. Unfortunately, the tremendous increase in crime in inner-city neighborhoods may discourage the location of businesses, which reduces the number of jobs available to these residents.

VI. Policy Issues and Suggestions

An effective national urban policy must embody the unique characteristics of cities while addressing the trends that pervade the national economy. The distinguishing features of cities include the spatial proximity of businesses and households, the flow of information between these parties, and the linkages of markets within urban areas. These characteristics generate both positive and negative externalities, which give cities a prominent position in the economy. Consequently, government's role and the primary purpose of a national urban policy should be to design programs that promote growth, internalize externalities, improve market efficiency, and strive for a more acceptable income distribution. Current trends facing urban workers and the findings of a large body of research described in this article suggest the following policy directives.

Growth

The slowdown in productivity growth resulted in two major national issues: sluggish real-income growth and widening income dispersion. These trends directly affect the welfare of urban workers and indirectly alter the structure of metropolitan areas by promoting decentralization of businesses and households. Weakening the core structure of metropolitan areas may diminish the economic advantages of cities. A national urban policy should address the underlying economic and social causes of the productivity slowdown. Increased productivity is critical to boost earnings and create additional employment opportunities.

Long-term growth hinges on investment in physical and human capital. Consequently, a national urban policy should include provisions to increase the national savings rate and allocate resources to education, research and development, and a more efficient flow of technological information. Cities are the obvious place for this investment, as they offer the greatest return per dollar spent. However, in doing so, redistributing growth across metropolitan areas through favorable tax incentives or government subsidies for selected areas should be minimized.

Efficient Urban Markets

Growth policies should also focus on increasing the efficiency of urban markets. Cities provide businesses access to skilled labor, to supplier networks, to product markets, and to information. However, access has been impeded by congestion, the decentralization of employment, and deficiency in skills of some workers. Widening gaps between central cities and suburbs with respect to earnings, employment, and quality of life have also reduced the efficiency of urban markets and have impeded overall growth. In addition, inner-city residents benefit from overall growth of the metropolitan economy, not only in the neighborhoods in which they live.

A national urban policy should include measures to narrow these disparities through promoting the establishment of regional governments, sharing of tax bases, and coordinating metropolitan provision of government services. Urban externalities can be internalized by reducing fragmentation of metropolitan-area governments, which will enhance overall metropolitan growth. The benefits of the concentration of economic activities in the urban core as well as the costs of supporting social programs of urban areas can be shared throughout the metropolitan area. This would reduce the fiscal incentives to leave the inner cities and help revitalize these areas.

Increase Access to Urban Labor Markets

Increased economic growth benefits only those people with access to urban labor markets. A growing number of urban residents face physical and intellectual isolation from urban opportunities. Isolation deprives individuals of greater economic success and deprives the nation of potentially productive workers. It also breeds behavior that is burdensome to society, such as welfare dependency, the breakdown of support networks, the decline in traditional married-couple families, and involvement in criminal activity.

A national urban policy must address the disadvantages faced by minorities in qualifying for and obtaining jobs and the disenfranchisement of low-income urban minorities. These programs should strive to get people into jobs and keep them employed. Improving the quality of education and work-related training for inner-city residents will help to overcome intellectual barriers. Establishing support groups and supplying appropriate role models through mentoring and employment advocacy programs will provide access to the labor market and ensure that workers remain in the labor force. Assigning workers to case managers on a long-term basis, at least until the given worker has been on the same job for six months, would keep individuals from getting lost within the system and keep them attached to the workforce. Providing more convenient and affordable public transportation to people who must commute in directions and at times not typically served by mass transit will increase access to jobs. In addition, setting up an electronic job placement system that offers information on job seekers and job vacancies for the greater metropolitan region would give inner-city residents access to the broader labor market.

Finally, work experience is critical for economic success. Sustained employment offers benefits that go beyond a weekly paycheck. Workers benefit from on-the-job learning and from establishing a network and support system of economically successful people, which offer opportunities for future advancement. Programs such as wage supplements and public service employment have proven successful in getting disadvantaged workers into the workplace and on their way to more active involvement in the labor force.

References

Bartik, Timothy J., and George Erickcek. 1992. "An Economic Opportunity Concept for the Northside of the City of Kalamazoo," W. E. Upjohn Institute for Employment Research Report, December.

Bartik, Timothy J. 1993. "Economic Development and Black Economic Success," Upjohn Institute Technical Report No. 93–001, January.

Bluestone, Barry, Mary Stevenson, and Chris Tilly. 1991. "The Deterioration in Labor Market Prospects for Young Men with Limited Schooling: Assessing the Impact of 'Demand Side' Factors." Presented at the Eastern Economic Association Meetings, March.

Bound, John, and Harry J. Holzer. 1991. "Industrial Shifts, Skills Levels, and the Labor Market for White and Black Males." National Bureau of Economic Research Working Paper No. 3715, May.

Bound, John, and Richard B. Freeman. 1992 "What Went Wrong? The Erosion of Relative Earnings and Employment among Black Men in the 1980s," *Quarterly Journal of Economics* 107 (1) February: 201–232.

Braddock, Jomills H., and James M. McPartland. 1987. "How Minorities Continue To Be Excluded from Equal Employment Opportunities: Research on Labor Market and Institutional Barriers," *Journal of Social Issues* 43 (1): 5–39.

Card, David, and Alan B. Krueger. 1992. "School Quality and Black–White Relative Earnings: A Direct Assessment," *Quarterly Journal of Economics* 107(1) February: 151–200.

Case, A., and L. Katz. 1991. "The Company You Keep: The Effects of Family and Neighborhood on Disadvantaged Youth." NBER Working Paper No. 3705.

Coulton, Claudia J., Julian Chow, and Shanta Pandey. 1990. "An Analysis of Poverty and Related Conditions in Cleveland Area Neighborhoods." Technical Report, Center for Urban Poverty and Social Change, Case Western Reserve University, Cleveland, Ohio, January.

Crane, J. 1991 "The Epidemic Theory of Ghettos, and Neighborhood Effects on Dropping Out and Teenage Childbearing," *American Journal of Sociology*, 96: 1226–59.

Economic Report of the President. 1994. (Washington, DC: U.S. Government Printing Office), February.

Freeman, Richard F. 1992. "Crime and the Employment of Disadvantaged Youths." In George E. Peterson and Wayne Vroman (eds.), *Urban Labor Markets and Job Opportunity* (Washington, DC: The Urban Institute Press).

Granovetter, Mark S. 1974. *Getting a Job: A Study of Contacts and Careers* (Cambridge, MA: Harvard University Press).

Hill, Edward W., Julie Rittenhouse, and Rosalyn C. Allison. 1994. "Recommendations to the Minority Economic Opportunity Center and the Greater Cleveland Urban League on Improving Training and Employment Prospects for the Hard-to-Employ in Greater Cleveland." Report 94–7,

The Urban Center, College of Urban Affairs, Cleveland State University, Cleveland, Ohio, April.

Holzer, Harry J. 1988. "Search Method Use by Unemployed Youth," *Journal of Labor Economics* 6 (January): 1–20.

_____. 1991. "The Spatial Mismatch Hypothesis: What Has the Evidence Shown?" *Urban Studies* 28 (1): 105–22.

Ihlanfeldt, Keith R. 1992. *Job Accessibility and the Employment and School Enrollment of Teenagers.* Kalamazoo, MI: W. E. Upjohn Institute for Employment Research.

Ihlanfeldt, Keith R., and David L. Sjoquist. 1990. "Job Accessibility and Racial Differences in Youth Employment Rates." *American Economic Review* 80: 267–76.

_____. 1991. "The Effect of Job Access on Black and White Youth Employment: A Cross Sectional Analysis," *Urban Studies* 28 (2): 255–65.

Juhn, Chinhui. 1992. "Decline of Male Labor Market Participation: The Role of Declining Market Opportunities," *Quarterly Journal of Economics* 107 (1) February: 79–122.

Kain, John. 1968. "Housing Segregation, Negro Employment, and Metropolitan Decentralization," *Quarterly Journal of Economics* 82 (May): 175–197.

Kasarda, John D. 1989. "Urban Industrial Transition and the Underclass." *The Annals of the American Academy of Political and Social Science* 501: 26–47.

Kerschenman, Joleen, and Kathryn M. Neckerman. 1991. "'We'd Love to Hire Them, But . . .': The Meaning of Race for Employers," in Christopher Jencks and Paul Peterson (eds.), *The Urban Underclass* (Washington, DC: Brookings Institution).

Ledebur, Larry C., and William R. Barnes. 1992. *Metropolitan Disparities and Economic Growth* (National League of Cities).

O'Regan, Katherine M., and John M. Quigley. 1993. "Family Networks and Youth Access to Jobs," *Journal of Urban Economics* 34: 230–248.

Price, Richard, and Edwin Mills. 1985. "Race and Residence in Earnings Determination." *Journal of Urban Economics* 17: 1–18.

Reischauer, Robert D. 1988. *The Geographic Concentration of Poverty: What We Know* (Washington, DC: Brookings Institution).

Ryscavage, Paul, Gordon Green, and Edward Welniak. 1991. "The Impact of Demographic, Social, and Economic Change on the Distribution of Income." U.S. Bureau of the Census, Presented at the Annual Research Conference of the Association for Public Policy Analysis and Management.

Savitch, H. V., David Collins, Daniel Sanders, and John P. Markham. 1993. "Ties that Bind: Central Cities, Suburbs, and the New Metropolitan Region," *Economic Development Quarterly* 7 (4), November: 341–57.

Stanback, Thomas M., Jr., and Richard Knight. 1976. *Suburbanization and the City* (Montclair, NJ: Allanheld, Osmun & Co.).

Welch, Finis. 1990. "The Employment of Black Men," *Journal of Labor Economics*, 8: S26–75.

Wilson, Julius William. 1987 *The Truly Disadvantaged* (Chicago: University of Chicago Press).

U.S. Department of Commerce, Bureau of the Census. 1992. "1990 Census of Population, General Population Characteristics."

_____. 1991. "Geographic Mobility: March 1989 to March 1992," *Current Population Reports* P20–473, November.

Commentary
Urban Labor Markets

Harry J. Holzer

In his paper, Randy Eberts correctly argues that developments in urban labor markets largely reflect overall trends in the national labor market, especially the declining demand for less-skilled labor, growing earnings inequality, and the particular problems impeding the progress of minorities. He provides a good survey of the many factors that appear to contribute to these problems, and draws some appropriate conclusions for policy.

I would like to add to Eberts's discussion of black–white employment and earnings differences. With regard to the important issue of skills, Eberts leaves us unsure of exactly *which* skills are lacking among young blacks entering the labor force. But recently there has been quite clear evidence of rising returns to *basic cognitive skills* in the labor market, even after controlling for level of education. Apparently the effects of these reading and math skills (as measured by test scores) on earnings rose in the 1980s, and the continuing racial gaps in these scores accounted for large fractions of racial earnings and employment gaps.[1] Though Eberts correctly points out that the racial gap in test scores has narrowed, the magnitude of the relative improvement for blacks has been modest, and much smaller than the increase in labor-market demand for these skills.

Perhaps these cognitive skill differences partly underlie the perceived deficiencies in "workplace competencies" that Eberts notes. He puts more emphasis on what has come to be known as "soft skills," such as attitudes toward work and social/interactive skills.[2] No doubt, employers

---

[1] See Murnane et al. (1993); O'Neill (1990), and Rivera–Batiz (1992).

[2] See Moss and Tilly (1993) for evidence from interviews with employers on these issues.

seem to perceive deficiencies among prospective black workers in both areas, although more objective evidence on the latter is hard to come by.

I would also add somewhat to Eberts's discussion of urban spatial issues and "access" problems for blacks. By now it is clear that employer relocations led to substantially higher net employment growth in suburban areas relative to central cities in the 1980s, and especially to those parts of suburban areas which are located furthest away from black populations. Furthermore, the continuing problem of residential housing segregation, along with transportation costs for those without cars, limited information and social contacts, as well as perceived hostility among suburban whites, all tend to reduce the tendency of inner-city workers to seek and gain employment in these growing suburban labor markets. These factors appear to underlie the evidence of "spatial mismatch" that Eberts notes in his paper.[3] Furthermore, housing segregation and rising poverty rates can account for much more of the rising concentration of poverty in central-city neighborhoods than does the flight of the black middle class from these areas.

An important area that get short shrift in Eberts's paper is employer discrimination. Employers clearly *perceive* lower skills, poor attitudes, and worse job performance among blacks, especially males. To the extent that these perceptions are correct *on average*, we may still have a problem of "statistical discrimination," in which these characteristics are attributed to *all* blacks by employers whose ability to screen accurately across different individuals is very limited. To the extent that employers exaggerate these differences, or cater to the prejudices of their customers and employees as well as their own, we may have "pure discrimination" as well. Either way, the results of recent audit studies by the Urban Institute and others suggest these employer perceptions are major additional barriers.[4]

If Eberts's list of causes (along with my additions) is now more complete, what do these causes imply for our national urban policy? Eberts's call for policies to encourage higher economic growth is certainly warranted, though these issues are largely beyond the scope of urban policy; and his call for regional governments and tax-base sharing is certainly appealing, although extremely controversial and difficult to implement politically.

I was pleased that Eberts argues against favorable tax treatments or subsidies for businesses in specific geographic areas, of which I would

---

[3] See Holzer et al. (1994) for evidence on transportation costs and other barriers limiting travel during job search and employment for young inner-city blacks.

[4] See Turner et al. (1991) for results of the Urban Institute audit studies of matched pairs of black and white job applicants that were sent out to employers in Washington, DC and Chicago. Job offers went to 29 percent of white applicants and 19 percent of blacks who were matched in terms of observable characteristics.

include inner cities. To be blunt, we have little evidence that *any* of these policies are cost-effective ways of generating employment for the disadvantaged. In particular, recent evidence suggests that urban enterprise zones are particularly costly ways to generate jobs for low-income zone residents.[5] Instead, policies that seek to improve quality of life for residents of very low-income urban neighborhoods (focusing on police protection, schools, etc.) seem to be preferable.

How, then, do we raise employment opportunities for residents of these areas, especially for those who do not seem to be able to gain any private-sector employment on their own in the current labor market? I would endorse the greater reliance on job creation for the less-skilled through wage subsidies and public service employment that Eberts advocates, but here the evidence has not been so encouraging as Eberts suggests in his final paragraph. The Targeted Jobs Tax Credit, designed specifically to subsidize employers who hire the disadvantaged, has generated few new jobs for these people, as an individual's eligibility for the credit seems to stigmatize him/her more than it opens doors. Perhaps we can make these credits more appealing by broadening the wage base on which they are paid.

In the end, some public-service employment will be necessary as well. More generally, we must recognize the failure of many work experience and public training programs for minority youth to generate significant post-program effects—which has consistently been found in government programs (such as the Job Training Partnership Act or JTPA), and many other demonstration projects. Work experience must be *stable* and in the *private sector* to have meaningful effects on future employment and earnings. We must also be able to provide more than just minimum-wage jobs to lure back to legitimate employment many of those who have recently found more lucrative opportunities in the illegal sector.[6]

Thus, in addition to modified versions of these job-creation efforts in the central cities, we need special efforts to link inner-city workers to existing jobs in growing suburban labor markets where they might gain such early private-sector experience. Here, I endorse much of Eberts's strategy to increase the "access" of inner-city residents to these suburban employment opportunities. "Mobility" strategies that combine transporta-

---

[5] Papke (1993) estimates that the cost of each new job created by state-level enterprise zones which actually goes to a zone resident can be as high as $30,000. A preferable alternative might be to provide wage subsidies to *any* employers (regardless of location) who hire residents of these zones (see Lehman 1993).

[6] Indeed, the dramatic rise in criminal activity among young black males seems to reflect the combination of declining earnings potential in regular employment along with growing profitability of criminal work, in part because of the rising demand for "crack" in the late 1980s. See Holzer (1994).

tion, job placement, and some counseling may be particularly cost-effective ways of doing this for those young workers who appear to be "employable," especially where suburban demand for less-skilled labor is strong (as it sometimes was in the pre-recessionary markets of the late 1980s).[7] If major suburban employers continue to resist the hiring of inner-city minorities who now have greater "access" to where they are located, heightened federal monitoring of their hiring behavior (as part of Equal Employment Opportunities activities) might be an appropriate complement to the mobility strategy. Furthermore, improving the access of inner-city minorities to housing markets in these areas is clearly an appropriate strategy for a national urban policy as well.[8]

Finally, we come to the issues of skills, education, and job training. Clearly, these issues will have the greatest affect on the *long-run* earnings prospects of inner-city minorities. Although there is once again little clear evidence of exactly what works in this context, a few more specific suggestions might be in order.

For one thing, we need to build on relatively successful early interventions such as "Head Start," providing more sustained basic-skill remediation in these schools as children age, and more workplace-relevant skills later on that employers must help schools to identify. We might also use the schools to provide support for "mentoring" programs for adolescent males (which Eberts advocates) and expanded links to community institutions that might provide them with useful social contacts. Finally, the potential role of post-school training programs for the disadvantaged, whether public (e.g. Job Corps) or private, needs to be reconsidered as well.

References

Holzer, Harry. 1994. "Black Employment Problems: New Evidence, Old Questions," *Journal of Policy Analysis and Management* (Fall).

Holzer, Harry, Keith Ihlanfeldt, and David Sjoquist. 1994. "Work, Search and Travel among Young Whites and Blacks," *Journal of Urban Economics*.

Hughes, Mark, and Julie Sternberg. 1992. *The New Metropolitan Reality* (Urban Institute).

Lehman, Jeff. 1993. "Updating Urban Policy." Mimeo, University of Michigan.

Moss, Philip, and Chris Tilly. 1993. "Soft Skills and Race: An Investigation of

---

[7] See Hughes and Sternberg (1992) for data on central-city vs. suburban employment growth and for a review of "mobility" strategies.

[8] See Rosenbaum and Popkin (1991) for an analysis of data from the Gautreaux Project, in which employment rose for black household heads who were relocated to the suburbs from the central city.

Black Men's Employment Problems." Mimeo, University of Massachusetts at Lowell.

Murnane, Richard, John Willett, and Frank Levy. 1993. "The Growing Importance of Cognitive Skills in Wage Determination." Mimeo, Harvard University.

O'Neill, June. 1990. "The Role of Human Control in Earnings Difference between White and Black Men," *Journal of Economic Literature* (October).

Papke, Leslie. 1993. "What Do We Know about Enterprise Zones?" National Bureau of Economic Research Working Paper, 1993.

Rivera–Batiz, Francisco. 1992. "Quantitative Literacy and the Likelihood of Employment among Young Adults in the U.S.," *Journal of Human Resources.*

Rosenbaum, James, and Susan Popkin. 1991. "Employment and Earnings of Low-Income Blacks Who Move to Middle-Class Suburbs," in C. Jencks and P. Peterson (eds.), *The Urban Underclass* (Washington, DC: The Brookings Institution).

Turner, Margery, et al. 1991. "Opportunities Denied, Opportunities Diminished: Discrimination in Hiring," (Urban Institute).

Assessing the Well-Being
of Urban Households and Residents

Robert D. Plotnick

An urban area is thriving if its residents enjoy a high, increasing, and fairly shared level of well-being. The performances of an urban area's economy, labor market, infrastructure, and public sector may reasonably be assessed by their direct and indirect contributions to the quality of its residents' lives. In this sense, the issues and outcomes considered in this article are in part products of the "inputs" discussed in several of the others. If this viewpoint is accepted, the many diverse issues that might be addressed in a national urban policy report should be framed to an important degree in terms of their relationship to and impact on residents' well-being.

"Well-being" or "quality of life" (I shall use the two terms interchangeably) is a broad construct that encompasses economic well-being but goes far beyond it. Public concern and policy debate about the problems of urban America properly address the level, growth, and distribution of economic well-being, but extend beyond these matters to others such as health status, environmental quality, physical security, and the ability to take part in the life of the community. Consequently, the national urban policy report must also look beyond matters of economic well-being to fully address the range of issues involved in improving the urban quality of life.

The Notion of Well-Being

We may view how we live our lives as a set of interrelated "functionings" that consist of activities we pursue and our physical and psychological conditions (Sen 1992; Dasgupta 1993). Functionings range from basic—such as being adequately nourished or sheltered—to more complex—such as having self-respect or emotional security, or taking part in the life of the community. Functionings fundamentally constitute a person's being and hence an evaluation of personal well-being must assess these functionings.[1]

Possessing income is not in itself a basic element of well-being. Rather, it is one important means to achieving well-being, since it is used to purchase goods and services needed to achieve many functionings. Important as it is, income falls well short of indicating the quality of life. Individuals trade off income against climate, environmental amenities, and social conditions such as the crime rate, which also affect the quality of life (Berger and Blomquist 1988). Other functionings important to the quality of life, and some of the means to achieving them, are not for sale in any well-defined market. Families cannot buy a happy home life; children cannot buy self-esteem; civil liberties are not for sale. Measuring income as comprehensively as possible and adjusting it for needs improves the measurement of economic well-being, but still fails to measure broadly conceived well-being.

What Aspects of Well-Being Deserve Attention in National Urban Policy Reports?

Future national urban policy reports should devote primary attention to those functionings of the urban population which are most open to policy intervention. This section proposes a set of such functionings and, working from this conceptual framework, suggests statistical indicators of these functionings. The indicators include standard ones describing economic status, labor-market conditions, and crime that several urban policy reports have considered, but range beyond them. Many are currently published or could be developed from special analyses of currently collected data such as the Current Population Survey. Others may call for expanded data collection efforts. Since different reports would likely develop different broad themes, they would correspondingly change the relative emphasis given to the various classes of indicators of well-being.[2]

The premise behind many urban policy initiatives is that social and economic conditions of urban areas and large cities in general, or of many specific urban areas and large cities, are worse than those elsewhere and deteriorating in either absolute or relative terms. The main function of indicators of well-being in discussions about urban policy is to provide systematic information about such conditions. Public policy makers, advo-

---

[1] In this formulation, well-being is neither pleasure, happiness, nor utility.

[2] Reports will also address, at least implicitly, the factors responsible for each indicator. Such analysis is beyond the scope of this paper.

cates, policy specialists, and other participants in the policy process rely on them to provide comparisons of conditions among and within metropolitan areas and cities, to track how they are changing in absolute terms and relative to each other, and to make the case for one policy approach over others (Kingdon 1984). Thus, a useful indicator ideally sheds light on the current level of an important aspect of well-being and on its recent trends.

Urban residents' *material well-being*—access to and control over economic resources—is the most obvious functioning to focus on because its level and trend are better measured than most others, and because it is probably most easily affected by public policy. Perhaps the best summary measure of this for an urban area, at least under current data constraints, is the median of a comprehensive measure of annual real income, adjusted for needs and measured over all persons.[3] A similar measure of consumption is the obvious alternative. The wide availability of income data and limited consumption data suitable for analysis of urban conditions suggest reliance on an income-based measure.

The poverty rate based on the same comprehensive income measure is an important complementary indicator of the extent to which urban residents fail to achieve a minimally decent level of economic well-being. Rates of extreme poverty (for example, the percentage of persons below half the poverty line), poverty gap data, and information on the persistence and spatial concentration of poverty usefully supplement standard poverty rate data.[4] Because this aspect of well-being evaluates minimally decent consumption levels, using an absolute poverty line is appropriate.

These summary indicators do not necessarily correlate highly with other measures of material well-being, and therefore need to be augmented with information about the extent of specific material hardships (Jencks and Torrey 1988; Mayer and Jencks 1989). Information on specific hardships could include, for example, the proportion of households

---

[3] At the individual level, a permanent income measure (or at a minimum an income measure covering several years) is clearly preferable to one using a one-year accounting period, and produces more accurate comparisons of economic well-being. However, given the extensive individual geographic mobility among urban areas and between urban and non-urban areas, it is not clear that an analogous long-term measure can be constructed when cities or metropolitan areas are the units of observation. For comparisons among urban areas and between urban and non-urban areas, a one-year accounting period may well be adequate and appropriate. The nuances of measuring income and economic well-being have been widely discussed and are not covered here in detail. See Ruggles (1990) for a thorough discussion in the context of measuring poverty.

[4] Reports should avoid the temptation to present poverty data derived from axiomatically based indices of poverty that have become popular in the technical literature (see Sen 1992 for a guide to this literature). They have stronger conceptual bases than the standard indicators, but lack the intuitive and widespread understanding of what the latter mean.

who cannot afford to buy food or report being hungry at some time during the year. It could include the proportion of persons who live in substandard housing, spend a disproportionately high share of their income on housing, suffer a spell of homelessness, lack telephone service, or experience other housing-related hardships. Similar data about accessibility of medical care and consumption of clothing and transportation would also help assess the level of economic well-being.[5]

The *ability to be economically self-supporting* (alternatively, not being economically dependent on others) is a second important constituent of well-being. Avoiding economic dependence on others (outside of family), moreover, may enhance more subjective aspects of well-being such as self-respect and the perception by self and others that one has a respected role in the community.

General indicators of this functioning include rates of employment and unemployment and median earnings and, as a predictor for youth of future outcomes, high school graduation rates. Of greater interest are more direct indicators of economic dependence such as pretransfer, prewelfare, and earnings-capacity poverty. Pretransfer poverty identifies persons who fall below the poverty line when only their income from markets and other private sources is counted. Prewelfare poverty identifies persons below the poverty line when all sources of income except public assistance are counted. prewelfare income includes social insurance benefits because they are based on an individual's (or spouse's) past earnings. They are generally perceived as earned and reliance on them to escape poverty is not considered evidence of economic dependence. The earnings-capacity poor include persons in families who would be unable to generate enough income to be over the poverty line even if all working-age adults work year-round full-time. Such families will be poor unless assisted financially by private or public assistance.[6]

Data on AFDC, food stamp, and other public assistance caseloads provide programmatically specific indicators of economic dependence. Data on the duration of spells of welfare use and prewelfare poverty would be valuable supplements to standard cross-section statistics.

Economic security—the capability of a family to endure an unanticipated temporary loss of income or large involuntary medical expenses

---

[5] One can think of many other indicators of physical and material well-being such as use of personal services, the availability of cultural and recreational amenities, or climate conditions. However, since urban policy seeks to do something about social conditions perceived or interpreted as social problems (Kingdon 1984), these sorts of indicators would seem to deserve little attention in national urban policy reports.

[6] In practice, measures of pretransfer and prewelfare poverty have counted only cash-income sources; conceptually they could include other forms of income. See Haveman and Buron (1993) for a discussion of earnings-capacity poverty and its trends.

without a substantial decline in its standard of living—captures another aspect of economic well-being. One indicator is the extent to which families have liquid assets equal to, say, three months of disposable income. A second is a measure of families' access to either formal or informal sources of credit (Mayer and Jencks 1989). Data on the proportion of families lacking health insurance and the mean and distribution of spells of non-coverage provide other important indicators of economic insecurity.

Higher income can buy better medical care, but not necessarily better health. *Health status,* therefore, is a fourth independent aspect of well-being deserving attention in national urban policy reports. Suitable indicators include the infant death rate, the percent of babies with low birth weight, overall life expectancy, and morbidity measures such as sick days and the incidence of specific diseases (e.g. HIV/AIDS) and chronic conditions, and the prevalence of drug and tobacco use and alcoholism. Data on environmental conditions linked to health status are also appropriate.

Physical security surely deserves careful attention in any assessment of the quality of urban life. Crime and victimization rates and related statistics on crime and the criminal justice system, especially those for violent crime, are the primary indicators. Since violence creates major health problems, violent crime rates might also be regarded as an indicator of health status. Data on residents' fear of being outside in their neighborhood or elsewhere in their urban area and their feelings of safety would provide more subjective indicators.

Having a respected role in the community and *being able to take part in the life of the community* are social functionings important to a person's quality of life. In this society success in attaining these functionings partly depends on being economically independent, and thus may be partly gauged by the same indicators. Labor-market participation, enrollment in school, and avoidance of juvenile crime are other indicators of attempting to take or prepare for responsible social roles. A measure of "economic inactivity," such as the percentage of adolescents and working-age adults neither participating in the labor force, in school, nor caring for a young child, would provide further information on this aspect of well-being.

Fear of crime inhibits participation in community life; hence indicators of physical security reflect the likelihood of success in this function. Data on the extent of residential segregation and on discrimination in housing, mortgage, and labor markets are critical indicators of limitations on minority residents' access to important community opportunities.[7]

Persons with incomes substantially below the average in their society are effectively excluded from participating actively in the social and

---

[7] Data on involvement with local civic organizations and other community organizations, volunteer activities, election turnout, and similar behavior capture other aspects of taking part in community life.

political life in their community and are accorded little community respect. Indicators of *relative* economic status, such as statistics on income inequality and relative poverty, help capture this dimension of these aspects of well-being. Data on basic literacy measure another personal attribute necessary to participate fully in this society.

The *quality of private family life* is a final functioning that national urban policy reports should address. It is probably more important to individuals' overall well-being than the social functionings just discussed. Statistical indicators of this aspect of well-being include the percentage of children living in single-parent families, the rate of nonmarital childbearing (both among all women and among adolescents), the divorce rate, rates of child abuse and neglect, and the level of spouse abuse and family violence. Some indicators of health status, such as rates of alcoholism and drug use, may also reflect the quality of family life.

A discussion of useful indicators of well-being among urban residents would be incomplete without mention of the "underclass." In terms of the analytic framework developed here, the most widely cited underclass measure (Ricketts and Sawhill 1988) is a hybrid measure of well-being. The components that examine male labor-force involvement, high school dropouts, and households dependent on welfare address the ability to be economically self-supporting and having a respected role in the community. The component that examines mother-only families with children helps gauge the quality of family life. All four are indirect predictors of absolute and relative poverty; none directly measures these aspects of well-being. The Ricketts–Sawhill measure cuts across several functionings but does not provide a well-rounded picture of any.[8]

The Level and Trend of Well-Being in Urban America: Selected Indicators

This section presents selected indicators of the aspects of well-being discussed in the previous section.[9] The tables show differences between metropolitan and non-metropolitan areas. More importantly, because disparities in well-being between central cities and their suburban rings are of wide interest, they portray differences between these two major parts of metropolitan areas. The tables also provide comparisons among major

---

[8] Other hybrid measures include the suicide rate, measures of happiness, and subjective measures of overall well-being, all of which are likely to be related to most of the constituents of well-being discussed here.

[9] Because of the limited scope of this article and limitations in available data, the tables do not provide information for all the indicators suggested earlier.

Table 1

Real Median Household Income in Metropolitan and Non-Metropolitan Areas, 1980–1992 (1992 dollars)

	1980	1985	1990	1992	% change 1980–1992
all metropolitan areas	32,463	33,345	34,160	32,694	0.7
areas > 1,000,000	34,122	35,260	36,311	35,036	2.7
in central city	26,055	27,798	28,695	26,872	3.1
outside central city	39,328	41,476	41,683	40,460	2.9
areas < 1,000,000	30,488	31,049	30,678	29,952	−1.8
in central city	27,240	27,529	26,729	26,179	−3.9
outside central city	33,735	33,697	33,701	32,289	−4.3
non-metropolitan areas	26,168	23,927	25,450	24,991	−4.5
all U.S.	30,191	30,796	32,142	30,786	2.0
metropolitan as % of non-metropolitan	124	139	134	131	
large central city as % of all U.S.	86	90	89	87	
other central city as % of all U.S.	90	89	83	85	

Sources: For 1980—U.S. Bureau of the Census, "Money income of households, families and persons in the United States: 1980," *Consumer Population Reports*, Series P–60 No. 132 (Washington, DC: USGPO, 1982), p. 10. For 1985—U.S. Bureau of the Census, "Money income of households, families and persons in the United States: 1985," *Consumer Population Reports*, Series P–60 No. 156 (Washington, DC: USGPO, 1987), p. 6. For 1990 and 1992 and for price index, U.S. Bureau of the Census, "Money income of households, families and persons in the United States: 1980," *Consumer Population Reports*, Series P–60 No. 184 (Washington, DC: USGPO, 1993), pp. 1, B–2.

metropolitan areas and central cities, and show how the differences have changed over time.[10]

Differences *within* urban areas and central cities among residents characterized in terms of race, ethnicity, economic status, residential neighborhood and other policy-relevant characteristics clearly would de-

---

[10] The tables are gleaned from a wide range of sources. The unit of observation varies depending on the available source. It includes the aggregate of all metropolitan areas (for comparisons with all non-metropolitan areas) or urban places, as well as specific Metropolitan Statistical Areas (MSAs), Primary MSAs (PMSAs), Central MSAs (CMSAs), and major cities.

serve extensive analysis in national urban policy reports. Attention to such differences is particularly apt when examining the 1980s and early 1990s, a period characterized by high and rising inequality along a number of dimensions of well-being both between and among demographic groups. The statistics presented here, then, are meant simply to illustrate the kinds of data that assess well-being and are only suggestive of what a more detailed analysis would show.

Material Well-Being

In recent years median household income in metropolitan areas has been about one third larger than in non-metropolitan areas (Table 1, row 10). The differential has fallen since 1985, but there is no apparent trend since 1980. However, the central cities of both large and other metropolitan areas have consistently had median incomes 10 to 15 percent *lower* than the rest of the country (rows 11, 12). The relative affluence of metropolitan areas is concentrated in their suburban rings.

For large metropolitan areas there is no clear trend in the differential; for the others, perhaps a slight downward trend. Real household income in the United States has barely grown since 1980. The modest growth that has occurred has mainly been in the larger metropolitan areas, including their central cities. Other metropolitan areas and non-metropolitan areas have faced declining real household incomes. Overall, then, larger metropolitan areas and their core cities have not experienced a decline in income relative to the rest of the country.

Table 2 displays a different summary measure of economic well-being—real per capita money income—for the ten largest cities based on 1990 population. The variation in both growth rate and level is striking. New York experienced a 31 percent increase between 1979 and 1989. Income in Philadelphia and San Diego grew substantially. Four cities had gains in the 10 percent range, while two had declines. In 1989 New York, Los Angeles, San Diego, and Dallas were about 13 percent above the mean, while San Antonio and Detroit were 25 and 35 percent below, respectively. These comparisons do not adjust for cost-of-living differences among cities and may therefore be misleading.[11]

The poverty data in Table 3 are consistent with those in Table 1 in showing less poverty in metropolitan areas and more poverty in central cities compared to other areas in all years. The same is true in 1992 for

---

[11] The correlation between reported per capita personal income and income deflated by a proprietary cost-of-living index is only 0.43. The index is reported only for smaller MSAs, but the results suggest considerable caution in interpreting intercity income differences as intercity differences in the standard of living. Sound, regularly measured cost-of-living indices for major urban areas are needed if future urban policy reports are to draw accurate comparisons among them.

Table 2

Real Per Capita Money Income in the Ten Largest Cities, 1979 and 1989, in 1992 Dollars (ranked by population in 1990)

	1979	1989	% change
New York	14,061	18,435	31.1
Los Angeles	16,274	18,330	12.6
Chicago	13,408	14,606	8.9
Houston	17,069	16,148	−5.4
Philadelphia	11,706	13,690	16.9
San Diego	15,502	18,571	19.8
Detroit	12,019	10,692	−11.0
Dallas	16,645	18,456	10.8
Phoenix	14,605	15,961	9.3
San Antonio	11,145	12,324	10.6
all U.S.	14,113	16,328	15.7

Source: U.S. Bureau of the Census, Statistical Abstract of the United States, 1993, 113th edition (Washington, DC: USGPO, 1993), Tables 734 and 744.

"extreme poverty," measured by the percent of persons with incomes less than half the official poverty line. Central cities' poverty has been 41 percent higher than for the entire United States in recent years and their extreme poverty has been 51 percent higher.

Unlike the income trend, poverty in metropolitan areas and central cities has steadily increased compared to other areas. The central city poverty rate, for example, was only 13 percent higher than the overall U.S. rate in 1970, compared to 32 percent in 1980 and 41 percent in 1992.

Table 4 contains poverty data for the same cities in Table 2. Variation in level and change is again considerable. Poverty declined in New York and Philadelphia by less than one percentage point from 1979 to 1989. It rose by between 1.0 and 4.2 percentage points in six cities. Houston and Detroit suffered enormous increases of 8.0 and 10.5 percentage points. By 1989 poverty rates in the ten largest cities ranged from 13.4 percent in San Diego to 32.4 percent in Detroit, with most between 18 and 23 percent. For children under six years of age the poverty rate was generally 50 to 60 percent higher than the rate for all persons.

Approximately 5 percent of the urban population has been persistently poor—defined as being poor at least 80 percent of the time. The probability that an urban resident who was poor in one year would exit

Table 3

Official Poverty Rate for Persons in Metropolitan and Non-Metropolitan Areas, 1970–1992

	1970	1975	1980	1985	1990	1992	income/pov line < 0.50 1992
metropolitan areas	10.2	10.8	11.9	12.7	12.7	13.9	5.7
in central city	14.2	15.0	17.2	19.0	19.0	20.5	8.9
outside central city	7.1	7.6	8.2	8.4	8.7	9.7	3.8
non-metropolitan areas	16.9	15.4	15.4	18.3	16.3	16.8	6.4
all U.S.	12.6	12.3	13.0	14.0	13.5	14.5	5.9
metropolitan as % of non-metropolitan	60	70	77	69	78	83	89
central city as % of all U.S.	113	122	132	136	141	141	151

Sources: For 1970–1980: U.S. Bureau of the Census, "Characteristics of the Population below the Poverty Level: 1980," Consumer Population Reports, Series P–60 No. 133 (Washington, DC: USGPO, 1982), pp. 11, 19. For 1985: U. S. Bureau of the Census, "Poverty in the United States: 1985," Consumer Population Reports, Series P–60 No. 158 (Washington, DC: USGPO, 1987), p. 6. For 1990: U.S. Bureau of the Census, "Poverty in the United States: 1990," Consumer Population Reports, Series P–60 No. 175 (Washington, DC: USGPO, 1991), p. 1. For 1992: U.S. Bureau of the Census, "Poverty in the United States: 1992," Consumer Population Reports, Series P–60 No. 185 (Washington, DC: USGPO, 1993), p. 1 and Table 17.

poverty in the next declined between the mid 1970s and early 1980s. In contrast, poverty did not become harder to escape for non-urban residents. (The figures are from Adams, Duncan, and Rodgers 1988).

In metropolitan areas the number of persons living in areas of concentrated poverty (defined as a census tract with an official poverty rate of 40 percent or more) was 8.43 million in 1990, a significant increase from the 5.36 million persons in 1980 and 3.57 million in 1970. Underclass data present a somewhat different picture. The number of persons living in underclass neighborhoods (census tracts meeting the Ricketts–Sawhill definition) jumped from 0.75 million in 1970 to 2.45 million in 1980, but then barely rose to 2.51 million in 1990. In 1980, 96 percent of concentrated poverty and 99 percent of persons in underclass areas were in metropolitan areas. In 1990, the metropolitan shares were 81 and 95

Table 4

Official Poverty Rate for Persons and Children under Age 6
in the Ten Largest Cities, 1979 and 1989
(ranked by population in 1990)

	1979	1989 (all persons)	1989 (children under 6)
New York	20.0	19.3	30.9
Los Angeles	16.4	18.9	27.7
Chicago	20.3	21.6	35.8
Houston	12.7	20.7	31.3
Philadelphia	20.6	20.3	31.9
San Diego	12.4	13.4	21.0
Detroit	21.9	32.4	52.4
Dallas	14.2	18.0	27.9
Phoenix	11.1	14.2	22.8
San Antonio	20.9	22.6	35.6
all U.S.	12.4	13.1	NA

Sources: For 1979: U.S. Bureau of the Census, *County and City Data Book, 1988* (Washington, DC: USGPO, 1988). For 1989: U.S. Bureau of the Census, *Statistical Abstract of the United States, 1993*, 113th edition (Washington, DC: USGPO, 1993), Table 742 and tabulations of the 1990 Census of Population and Housing, Summary Tape File 3C on CD-ROM.

percent (Mincy and Weiner 1993). Concentrated poverty and underclass areas remain overwhelmingly urban problems.

Ability To Be Economically Self-Supporting

The rate and trend in prewelfare and pretransfer poverty are among the most useful indicators of the difficulty persons experience in being self-supporting. Such data, as well as data on earnings capacity, are currently not available for metropolitan areas and cities.

Employment and unemployment data help indicate the ability to earn an adequate living. The employment-to-population ratio was essentially constant or slightly increased in large metropolitan areas between 1983 and 1992 (Table 5). The Detroit area had the largest increase. Some cities joined in the employment growth in their labor market, while others did not. Table 6 shows that New York, Chicago, and Detroit experienced increases in tandem with their wider metropolitan areas. Houston and

Table 5

Employment and Unemployment Conditions in Selected Large Metropolitan Areas, 1983 and 1992

	employment/population ratio		unemployment rate	
	1983	1992	1983	1992
New York PMSA	50.3	52.4	9.0	10.0
Los Angeles– Long Beach PMSA	58.2	59.3	9.7	9.6
Chicago PMSA	58.4	62.7	11.2	8.1
Washington DC MSA	67.7	69.9	5.6	5.9
San Francisco PMSA	64.0	64.9	7.8	7.4
Philadelphia PMSA	57.0	59.5	9.4	7.9
Boston PMSA	62.6	62.8	6.5	7.8
Detroit PMSA	53.5	59.8	15.3	8.9
Dallas–Fort Worth CMSA	70.1	69.8	4.9	6.6
Houston PMSA	63.6	66.4	10.1	8.0
all U.S.	58.3	61.4	9.5	7.4

Sources: U.S. Bureau of Labor Statistics, "Geographic Profile of Employment and Unemployment, 1983," *BLS Bulletin* 2216 (October 1984); "Geographic Profile of Employment and Unemployment, 1992," *BLS Bulletin* 2428 (July 1993).

Philadelphia did not and Dallas's ratio dropped, although its metropolitan area ratio held steady. Central-city unemployment rates consistently exceed those of their metropolitan area and move in the same direction. The data all imply that residents of central cities find it harder than other urban residents to be economically self-supporting. Improving the labor markets in central cities, especially those for low-skill workers, deserves high priority on the urban policy agenda (see the article by Randall Eberts for further discussion).

Economic Security

The proportion of persons not covered by a private, public, or military health insurance plan serves as the only indicator of economic (in)security. Non-elderly residents of metropolitan areas have slightly better protection against high health-care expenses than those in non-metropolitan areas, but both groups lost coverage during the 1980s. Among persons under age 65 living within metropolitan areas, lack of coverage

Table 6

Employment and Unemployment Conditions
in the Ten Largest Cities, 1983 and 1992
(ranked by population in 1990)

	employment/population ratio		unemployment rate	
	1983	1992	1983	1992
New York	48.7	50.2	9.4	10.8
Los Angeles	NA	59.3	NA	10.7
Chicago	50.1	56.7	16.8	11.0
Houston	63.2	62.5	12.0	10.0
Philadelphia	49.1	48.4	13.6	11.3
San Diego	NA	57.5	NA	8.0
Detroit	41.2	43.2	24.7	17.8
Dallas	69.0	65.3	6.0	8.9
Phoenix	NA	66.3	NA	8.6
San Antonio	NA	55.8	NA	8.0
all U.S.	58.3	61.4	9.5	7.4

Sources: U.S. Bureau of Labor Statistics, "Geographic Profile of Employment and Unemployment, 1983," *BLS Bulletin* 2216 (October 1984) and "Geographic Profile of Employment and Unemployment, 1992," *BLS Bulletin* 2428 (July 1993).

rose from 11.3 percent in 1980 to 15.1 percent in 1989. Over the same period lack of coverage for non-aged persons living outside metropolitan areas rose from 14.8 percent to 17.8.

Lack of coverage among the elderly is far less common and declining. Within metropolitan areas it fell from 5.3 to 4.5 percent between 1980 and 1989. Outside them it fell from 3.7 to 2.6 percent.[12]

Health Status

The infant mortality rate and related measures are widely regarded as key indicators of a population's health status and access to minimally adequate health care. Data on the percentage of infants with low birth weight and the infant mortality rate in Table 7 clearly show that metro-

---

[12] Data are from National Center for Health Statistics, *Health United States 1992 and Healthy People 2000 Review*, DHHS Pub. No. (PHS) 93–1232, 1993, Tables 135 and 136. Central city–ring comparisons were not provided.

Table 7

Low Birth Weight Infants and Infant Mortality Rates in Metropolitan, Urban, and Non-Metropolitan Areas, 1978 and Late 1980s

	% of infants with low birth weight (< 2,500 grams)		infant mortality rate per 1,000 live births	
	1978	1988	1978	1989
metropolitan counties	7.3	7.0	13.8	9.9
urban places	7.8	7.5	13.9	10.5
non-metropolitan counties	6.7	6.5	14.8	9.5
all U.S.	7.1	6.9	13.8	9.8

Sources: Columns 2, 3: For 1978: Computed from data in National Center for Health Statistics, *Vital Statistics of the United States, 1978*, vol. 1, *Natality*, DHHS Pub # (PHS) 90–1100 (Washington, DC: USGPO, 1982), Table 2–2. For 1988: computed from data in National Center for Health Statistics, *Vital Statistics of the United States, 1988*, vol. 1, *Natality*, Washington, DC: USGPO, 1990, Table 2–2. *Columns 4–5:* For 1978: National Center for Health Statistics, *Vital Statistics of the United States, 1978*, vol. 2, *Mortality Part A*, DHHS Pub # (PHS) 83–1101 (Washington, DC: USGPO, 1982), Table 7–2. For 1989: National Center for Health Statistics, *Vital Statistics of the United States, 1989*, vol. 2, *Mortality Part A* (Washington, DC: USGPO, 1990), Table 8.2.

politan counties, and especially urban places, fare worse than non-metropolitan counties. Table 8 suggests a reason for the difference—a higher percentage of mothers in urban places receive minimal prenatal care.

Since 1978, both indicators have improved. Improvement in the infant mortality rate was noticeably slower in urban places. While it was the same as the national average in 1978, by 1989 it was clearly above. The disaggregated data in Table 9 are consistent with this last observation. Infant mortality in every central city is always higher than in its metropolitan area, in some cases by 6 to 10 percentage points. In Washington, DC and Detroit the level is more than double the national average; in Chicago and Philadelphia it is 70 percent higher.

Other data support the conclusion that residents of urban areas and major cities have poorer health. Rates of vaccination against serious childhood diseases are lowest in central cities (Table 10). They have fallen markedly since 1970 for DPT and polio, but substantially increased for measles, mumps, and rubella since the mid 1980s. Use of all types of illegal drugs and the prevalence of AIDS is higher in large metropolitan

Table 8

Minimal Prenatal Care in Metropolitan, Urban, and Non-Metropolitan Areas, 1978 and 1988

| | % of births to mothers with two or fewer prenatal care visits | |
	1978	1988
metropolitan counties	3.0	3.4
urban places	4.2	4.7
non-metropolitan counties	3.0	3.0
all U.S.	3.0	3.3

Sources: For 1978: computed from data in National Center for Health Statistics, *Vital Statistics of the United States, 1978*, Vol. 1, *Natality*, DHHS Pub. (PHS) 90–1100 (Washington, DC: USGPO, 1982), Table 1–89. For 1988: computed from data in National Center for Health Statistics, *Vital Statistics of the United States, 1988*, vol. 1, *Natality* (Washington, DC: USGPO, 1990), Table 1–94.

Table 9

Infant Mortality Rate per 1,000 Live Births in Large Metropolitan Areas and Their Central Cities in the Late 1980s

New York Northern NJ Long Is. CMSA (New York City)	10.9	(13.1)
Los Angeles Riverside Orange County CMSA (Los Angeles)	8.9	(10.1)
Chicago Gary Kenosha CMSA (Chicago)	11.9	(17.0)
Washington DC Baltimore CMSA (Washington, DC)	11.5	(22.9)
San Francisco Oakland San Jose CMSA (San Francisco)	7.8	(9.9)
Philadelphia Wilmington Atlantic City CMSA (Philadelphia)	11.7	(17.6)
Boston Brockton Nashua NECMA (Boston)	7.7	(10.5)
Detroit Ann Arbor Flint CMSA (Detroit)	12.3	(21.1)
Dallas Fort Worth CMSA (Dallas)	8.8	(10.7)
Houston Galveston Brazoria CMSA (Houston)	9.6	(11.2)
all U.S.	10.0	

* These are the ten largest metropolitan areas in terms of population, defined as of 31 December 1992. CMSA data are for 1988; central city data are for 1989.

Source: U.S. Bureau of the Census, *Statistical Abstract of the United States, 1993*, 113th edition (Washington, DC: USGPO, 1993), Tables 91 and 92 and Committee on Ways and Means. *1993 Green Book: Overview of Entitlement Programs* (Washington, DC: USGPO, 1993), pp. 1162, 1163.

Table 10

Vaccination Rates for Children Ages 1–4, 1970, 1983, and 1991

	1970	1983	1991
Diphtheria–Tetanus–Pertussis			
metropolitan areas			
in central city	68.9	55.4	60.1
outside central city	80.7	69.4	68.7
non-metropolitan areas	77.1	69.4	68.2
all U.S.	76.1	65.7	65.8
Polio			
metropolitan areas			
in central city	61.0	47.7	47.3
outside central city	70.8	60.3	52.2
non-metropolitan areas	64.7	60.3	52.1
all U.S.	65.9	57.0	50.6
Measles–Mumps–Rubella*			
metropolitan areas			
in central city	NA	57.5	75.6
outside central city	NA	63.9	78.8
non-metropolitan areas	NA	65.4	77.9
all U.S.	NA	62.8	77.6

* For 1983, means of individual vaccination rates for the three diseases.

Source: National Center for Health Statistics, *Health United States 1992 and Healthy People 2000 Review*, DHHS Pub. No. (PHS) 93–1232 (1993), Table 51.

areas than small metropolitan or non-metropolitan areas (Tables 11 and 12).[13]

Current rates of drug use among high school seniors are roughly the same in large, small, and non-metropolitan areas. Usage has declined fastest in large metropolitan areas (Table 13). On this health indicator large metropolitan areas appear no worse off than the rest of the country.

Table 14 shows trends since 1980 in air quality in major metropolitan areas. Most areas experienced decreases in the number of days of unhealthful air quality and by 1991 rarely experienced such days. The New York and Los Angeles areas showed the most improvement. The Houston area suffered deterioration in its air quality. By 1991 only residents of the Los Angeles area faced large numbers of days with unhealthful levels of air pollution.

---

[13] Tables 9 and 12 also demonstrate the wide variation in health status among major cities and metropolitan areas.

Table 11

Estimated Prevalence of Drug Use by Residence, 1991
(in percentages)

	large metro area	small metro area	non-metro area
ever used			
marijuana	36.3	32.7	28.4
cocaine	13.5	11.1	8.6
inhalants	5.6	5.5	4.8
hallucinogens	8.9	7.9	6.9
PCP	4.1	3.4	3.1
heroin	1.5	1.1	1.3
use of any illicit drug	7.0	6.2	5.2
within past month			

Source: Kathleen Maguire, Anne Pastore, and Timothy Flanagan (eds.). *Sourcebook of Criminal Justice Statistics, 1992* (U.S. Department of Justice, Bureau of Justice Statistics, Washington, DC: USGPO, 1993), Tables 3.98, 3.99, 3.100, and 3.101.

Table 12

AIDS Cases per 100,000 Population
Reported October 1992 through September 1993

MSA, ranked by 1990 population of central city		metropolitan vs. non-metropolitan areas	
New York	155.3	*metropolitan areas*	
Los Angeles	61.1	*> 500,000*	50.9
Chicago	34.5	*< 500,000*	22.0
Houston	72.8		
Philadelphia	42.5	*non-metropolitan areas*	10.0
Detroit	28.7		
Dallas	64.4	*all U.S.*	37.5
San Francisco	279.8		
Washington, DC	58.7		
Boston	40.2		

Source: Centers for Disease Control and Prevention, "HIV/AIDS Surveillance Report," October 1993.

Table 13

Reported Marijuana, Cocaine, and Heroin Use among High School Seniors, 1983 and 1992 (in percentages)

ever used		large metro area	small metro area	non-metro area
1983	marijuana	62.3	58.8	50.5
	cocaine	22.6	16.0	11.6
	heroin	1.2	1.1	1.5
1992	marijuana	32.5	32.6	32.7
	cocaine	6.6	6.4	5.0
	heroin	0.9	1.4	1.2

Sources: For 1983: Edmund McGarrell and Timothy Flanagan (eds.), *Sourcebook of Criminal Justice Statistics, 1984* (U.S. Department of Justice, Bureau of Justice Statistics, Washington, DC: USGPO, 1985), Table 3.61. For 1992: Kathleen Maguire, Anne Pastore, and Timothy Flanagan (eds.), *Sourcebook of Criminal Justice Statistics, 1992* (U.S. Department of Justice, Bureau of Justice Statistics, Washington, DC: USGPO, 1993), Table 3.84.

Physical Security

The widely held belief that urban residents are less well off because they face higher risk of crime is well founded. The upper panel of Table 15 shows the victimization rate for all crimes, a reliable indicator of the objective risk of crime. About 12 percent of central-city residents and 9 percent of other metropolitan area residents were criminal victims in 1991. These rates were 72 and 28 percent higher than those experienced by non-metropolitan residents. Perhaps surprisingly, victimization rates for residents of the largest metropolitan areas are no higher than those for smaller ones. Victimization rates for all crimes have declined since 1980 in all areas, but there has been little improvement since 1986. The biggest declines have occurred in the suburban ring and in central cities of the larger metropolitan areas.

The lower panel of Table 15 focuses on violent crimes, which create greater insecurity. On this indicator, central cities also compare unfavorably. The risk of violent crime has recently been about 76 percent higher in central cities than in non-metropolitan areas. Rates outside central cities have been about equal to those in non-metropolitan areas since 1986. Residents of the largest central cities were actually slightly less likely to be victims of violent crime than those of other large cities in 1986 and

Table 14

Air Quality Trends in Major Urban Areas, 1980–1991

PMSA ranked by 1990 population of central city	*no. of days when pollutants standards index is greater than 100**			
	mean			absolute change
	1980–81	1985–86	1990–91	1980–81 to 1990–91
New York	110	18	13	−97
Los Angeles	224	204	160	−64
Chicago	3	5	6	+3
Houston	21	29	37	+16
Philadelphia	41	23	18	−23
Detroit	18	4	5	−13
Dallas	11	9	3	−8
San Francisco	2	5	1	−1
Washington, DC	31	13	11	−20
Boston	5	1	3	−2

* The index integrates information from many pollutants across an entire monitoring network into a single number representing the worst daily air quality experienced in the urban area. Values of the index exceeding 100 are deemed unhealthful.

Source: U.S. Council on Environmental Quality, *Environmental Quality* (Washington, DC: USGPO, 1993), Table 42. For Chicago and Detroit, values for 1980 are not reported; the table entry is the value for 1981.

1991. The reverse was true in earlier years. In discouraging contrast to trends in the upper panel, the chances of being victimized by violent crime have not declined since 1980 either in the central cities of all metropolitan areas or in non-metropolitan areas. Violent crime in suburbs and in the central cities of the largest metropolitan areas did decline substantially by 1986. It rebounded in later years but still remains below 1980 levels.

Table 16 complements data on actual experience with crime by reporting perceived danger from crime. The data are consistent with Table 15. Half of all urban residents feel a sense of danger from guns, compared to 32 and 29 percent for suburban and rural residents, respectively. Similarly, fear of being outside at night in one's neighborhood is strongly and positively correlated with city size. This fear has shown no trend during the past decade.

Table 15

Criminal Victimization Rates for Persons Age 12 and Over by Location of Residence (per 1,000 Persons)

	1980	1984	1986	1991	% change 1980–1991
all crimes					
all metropolitan areas					
central cities	143	128	116	119	−17
outside central cities	124	108	91	88	−29
metropolitan areas > 1,000,000					
central cities	154	123	97	115	−25
outside central cities	127	108	92	90	−29
non-metropolitan areas	82	76	79	69	−16
all U.S.	116	103	96	92	−21
violent crimes					
all metropolitan areas					
central cities	45	43	36	44	−2
outside central cities	33	30	24	26	−21
metropolitan areas > 1,000,000					
central cities	55	45	28	39	−29
outside central cities	33	30	23	27	−18
non-metropolitan areas	23	22	26	25	+8
all U.S.	33	31	28	31	−6

Sources: U.S. Department of Justice, Bureau of Justice Statistics. "Criminal Victimization in the United States," reports for 1980 (Table 19), 1984 (Table 20), 1986 (Table 17), and 1991 (Table 18). Note: The boundaries of metropolitan areas changed between the 1984 and 1986 reports. Hence, earlier and later rates are not exactly comparable.

Functioning in the Community

The level of relative poverty is an excellent summary indicator of the extent to which persons are excluded from mainstream community life, but such data are currently not available for metropolitan areas and cities. Income inequality also is a proxy for this functioning. Central cities exhibit considerably more inequality than their surrounding areas and than non-metropolitan areas (Table 17).

Table 16

Perceptions of Danger from Crime

A. Perceived danger from gun violence, 1993*		
residence	yes	no
urban area	50	50
suburban area	32	68
rural area	29	70

* Responses of a national sample to the question: "Do you feel any sense of danger from gun violence where you live and work, or not?" Excludes those with no opinion.

Source: Kathleen Maguire, Anne Pastore, and Timothy Flanagan (eds.), Sourcebook of Criminal Justice Statistics, 1992, U.S. Department of Justice, Bureau of Justice Statistics (Washington, DC: USGPO, 1993), Table 2.28.

B. Percentage of respondents reporting that they feel afraid to walk alone at night in their own neighborhood, 1982 and 1992			
1982		**1992**	
city > 1,000,000	57	large city	60
city 500,000 to 1,000,000	54	medium city	56
city 50,000 to 499,999	53	suburb	42
town 2,500 to 49,999	50	small town	36
town < 2,500 and rural areas	31	rural area	31

Sources: For 1992: Table 2.35 of above source. For 1982, Edmund McGarrell and Timothy Flanagan (eds.), Sourcebook of Criminal Justice Statistics, 1984. U.S. Department of Justice, Bureau of Justice Statistics (Washington, DC: USGPO), 1985.

Quality of Family Life

Living in a single-parent family has a range of negative consequences for children (McLanahan 1988). The percentage of children living with both parents declined in the largest cities between 1979 and 1989 and throughout the nation (Table 18). The decline was dramatically large for Detroit, and in all but one of the nine other largest cities, the decline was faster than the national average. By 1989 only about half the children of New York, Chicago, and Philadelphia were living with both parents, while in Detroit only one third were.

Table 17

Inequality of Household Income in Metropolitan and Non-Metropolitan Areas, 1992 (measured by Gini coefficient)

all metropolitan areas	0.430
areas > 1,000,000	NA
in central city	0.465
outside central city	0.403
areas < 1,000,000	NA
in central city	0.441
outside central city	0.403
non-metropolitan areas	0.407
all U.S.	0.430

Source: U.S. Bureau of the Census, "Money Income of Households, Families and Persons in the United States: 1980," *Consumer Population Reports*, Series P–60 No. 184 (Washington, DC: USGPO, 1993), p. 9.

Table 18

Percentage of Children Less than Age 18 Living with Two Parents in the Ten Largest Cities, 1979 and 1989 (ranked by population in 1990)

	1979	1989	% decine		1979	1989	% decine
New York	59.5	53.5	10	San Diego	71.3	67.7	5
Los Angeles	65.6	61.7	6	Detroit	48.1	32.7	32
Chicago	56.0	49.8	11	Dallas	65.2	59.7	8
Houston	70.3	60.7	14	Phoenix	75.2	67.6	10
Philadelphia	57.3	48.6	15	San Antonio	72.5	64.3	11
all U.S.	71.3	67.7	5				

Source: For 1979: U.S. Bureau of the Census, *1980 Census of Population: General Social and Economic Characteristics, Part 1, U.S. Summary* (1983), Table 246. For 1989: U.S. Bureau of the Census, *1990 Census of Population: Social and Economic Characteristics,* (individual state volumes), 1992, Table 1 and *General Population Characteristics, U.S.,* Table 37.

Table 19

Births to Teenage Women as a Percentage of All Births, Metropolitan, Urban, and Non-Metropolitan Areas, 1978 and 1988

	1978	1988
metropolitan counties	15.6	11.8
urban places > 50,000	NA	14.0
non-metropolitan counties	18.7	15.0
all U.S.	16.6	12.5

Sources: For 1978: computed from data in National Center for Health Statistics, Vital Statistics of the United States, 1978, Vol. 1, Natality, DHHS Pub # (PHS) 90–1100 (Washington, DC: USGPO, 1982), Table 1–58. For 1988: computed from data in National Center for Health Statistics, Vital Statistics of the United States, 1988, Vol. 1, Natality, Washington, DC: USGPO, 1990, Table 1–67.

Table 20

Births to Unmarried Women as a Percentage of All Births, Metropolitan, Urban, and Non-Metropolitan Areas, 1988

	births to all unmarried women as % of all births	births to unmarried teenagers as % of all teenage births
metropolitan counties	26.4	69.3
urban places > 50,000	35.0	75.1
non-metropolitan counties	23.0	56.3
all U.S.	25.7	65.9

Source: Computed from data in National Center for Health Statistics, Vital Statistics of the United States, 1988, vol. 1, Natality (Washington, DC: USGPO, 1990), Tables 1–67 and 1–76.

Births to teenagers, especially if the mother does not marry, generally lead to a number of adverse social and economic outcomes for both mother and child. (See Hayes 1987, and for a contrary view Geronimus and Korenman 1992). Table 19 shows that births to teenage women are actually a smaller percentage of total births in metropolitan counties and urban places than in non-metropolitan counties. In seven of the largest

Table 21

Births to Teenage Women in the Ten Largest Cities, 1991

	births to teens as % of all births	nonmarital teen births as % of all teen births
New York	10	83
Los Angeles	13	76
Chicago	19	89
Houston	16	52
Philadelphia	18	94
San Diego	11	69
Detroit	24	92
Dallas	18	66
Phoenix	16	79
San Antonio	17	40
all U.S.	13*	69

* Author's estimate.

Source: Child Trends, Inc., "Facts at a Glance," Washington, DC (January 1994), based on unpublished data from National Center for Health Statistics.

cities, however, the percentage of births to teenagers was well above the national average (Table 21). In New York and San Diego it was below.

In urban places larger than 50,000, 35 percent of all births and 75 percent of births to teenagers are out of wedlock (Table 20). These percentages are well above those for non-metropolitan counties. In Detroit and Philadelphia more than 90 percent of births to teenagers are nonmarital (Table 21, col. 2). The percentages in several other cities also far exceed the high national average of 69 percent. Houston and San Antonio have relatively low percentages of births that are nonmarital.

Systematic information on family dysfunctions that seriously degrade the quality of life, such as child maltreatment, domestic violence, and spouse/partner abuse, is not available at the city or metropolitan-area level.

How Well Off Are Urban Residents: A Summary Judgment

It almost going without saying that the indicators of well-being presented in this paper, although they are diverse and touch on many aspects, simply illustrate the kinds of data needed to assess well-being and are only suggestive of what a more complete analysis would show. Nonetheless, it would be remiss not to suggest a few straightforward conclusions about the levels and trends in well-being based on the indicators presented here. Metropolitan areas have higher median income, less poverty, and better health-care coverage than non-metropolitan areas, and so score better in terms of material well-being and economic security. Indicators of physical security show that metropolitan areas are far worse off than non-metropolitan areas. Measures of health status mostly show the same thing. Because crime reduces the ability to take part in community life, this aspect is lower in metropolitan areas. However, another indicator of this functioning—income inequality—shows parity between metropolitan and non-metropolitan areas. The very incomplete indicators of family life presented here suggest that this component of well-being is lower in metropolitan areas as well. The well-being of metropolitan-area residents in general therefore compares unfavorably to that of non-metropolitan residents, unless one weights material well-being strongly.

Within metropolitan areas it is clear that central cities have lower levels of well-being than their surrounding smaller cities and suburbs, and often substantially so. Most of the nation's largest cities are also worse off than average on most of the indicators presented here, but there is considerable variation among these cities on every indicator.

The generally low performance of central cities across a wide range of indicators suggests that no single policy intervention can hope to raise the average well-being of city dwellers to national levels. Rather, a comprehensive policy strategy embracing labor-market performance, income-support programs, health care, crime prevention, and supportive family services will be necessary. At the same time, the clear differences between cities and metropolitan areas on every indicator mean it would make little sense to apply a uniform mix of policies to all. Policies tailored to each city's or area's particular problems and strengths holds greater promise.

The findings and conclusions drawn from the tables presented here mask wide disparities in overall well-being and its constituent functionings among the residents of each urban area. Such differences among residents characterized in terms of race, ethnicity, sex, age, economic status, neighborhood, and other policy-relevant characteristics would require careful exploration in national urban policy reports and serious attention in the design and implementation of new urban policy initiatives.

Conclusion

Though much useful information for assessing the well-being of persons and households is available from currently available and routinely published statistics, these sources fall short in many respects. Some unavailable important indicators can be readily generated from special analyses of existing data sets. For example, rates of prewelfare and relative poverty can be computed at many geographic levels from census microdata. Other federal microdata files may also have enough cases to generate reliable estimates at the individual city and metropolitan level. For other classes of indicators, such as some of the specific aspects of material hardship, the quality of life in the community, and the quality of family life, expanded data collection will be needed.

In many cases, indicators of children's current well-being are also predictive of the likelihood of their becoming successful adults, and hence of future well-being. National urban policy reports may therefore particularly want to upgrade measures of child functioning and well-being, with a focus on aspects closely related to the successful transition to adulthood.

References

Adams, Terry, Greg Duncan, and Willard Rodgers. 1988. "The Persistence of Urban Poverty," in Fred Harris and Roger Wilkins (eds.), *Quiet Riots: Race and Poverty in the United States* (New York: Pantheon), pp. 78–99.

Berger, Mark, and Glen Blomquist. 1988. "Income, Opportunities and the Quality of Life of Urban Residents," in Michael McGeary and Laurence Lynn Jr. (eds.), *Urban Change and Poverty* (Washington, DC: National Academy Press), pp. 67–101.

Dasgupta, Partha. 1993. *An Inquiry into Well-Being and Destitution* (New York: Oxford University Press).

Geronimus, A., and S. Korenman. 1992. "The Socioeconomic Consequences of Teen Childbearing Reconsidered," *Quarterly Journal of Economics* 107 (4): 1187–1214.

Haveman, Robert, and Larry Buron. 1992. "Escaping Poverty through Work—The Problem of Low Earnings Capacity in the United States, 1973–1988," *Review of Income and Wealth* 39 (2): 141–157.

Hayes, Cheryl (ed.). 1987. *Risking the Future*, vol. 1 (Washington, DC: National Academy Press).

Jencks, Christopher, and Barbara Torrey. 1988. "Byond Income and Poverty: Trends in Social Welfare among Children and the Elderly since 1960," in John Palmer, Timothy Smeeding, and Barbara Torrey (eds.), *The Vulnerable* (Washington, DC: Urban Institute Press), pp. 229–73.

Kingdon, John. 1984. *Agendas, Alternatives and Public Policies* (New York: HarperCollins).

Mayer, Susan, and Christopher Jencks. 1989. "Poverty and the Distribution of Material Hardship," *Journal of Human Resources* 24 (1): 88–114.

McLanahan, Sara. 1988. "Family Structure and Dependency: Early Transitions to Female Household Headship," *Demography* 25 (1): 1–16.

Mincy, Ronald, and Susuan Weiner. 1993. "The Under Class in the 1980s: Changing Concept, Constant Reality," The Urban Institute, July.

Ricketts, Erol, and Isabel Sawhill. 1988. "Defining and Measuring the Underclass," *Journal of Policy Analysis and Management* 7 (2): 316–325.

Ruggles, Patricia. 1990. *Drawing the Line: Alternative Poverty Measures and Their Implications for Public Policy* (Washington, DC: Urban Institute Press).

Sen, Amartya K. 1992. *Inequality Reexamined* (Cambridge: Harvard University Press).

Commentary

Assessing Well-Being
in an Era of Uneven Tides

Sheldon Danziger

Robert Plotnick has done an excellent job of showing the many dimensions over which well-being can be measured—material well-being, economic self-sufficiency, economic security, health, physical safety, and the quality of family life. Then, using available published data, he illustrates how these concepts vary across space. He duly notes that the 1980s were "characterized by high and rising inequality along a number of dimensions of well-being both between and among demographic groups." Plotnick nonetheless overlooks the increased within-group differences and concludes that "metropolitan areas have higher median income, less poverty, and better health-care coverage than non-metropolitan areas." Yet, mindful of his caveat about inequality, the reader should notice that some of the highest-income metropolitan areas—New York, Chicago, Detroit, and Philadelphia—have above-average poverty rates (Table 4) and above-average infant mortality rates (Table 9), especially in their central cities.

The large and growing extent of within-group inequality is a serious problem for any national urban poverty report. By calling attention to a set of spatial categories, it leads Plotnick and the rest of us to derive conclusions based on *between-group* comparisons even though these differences are smaller than the *within-group* differences in every locale. Indeed in the paragraph following the conclusion I have just questioned, Plotnick cautions, "within metropolitan areas it is clear that central cities have lower levels of well-being than their surrounding smaller cities and suburbs." Because this is the case, we should *avoid* drawing conclusions and making policy decisions based on a metro/nonmetro or other dichotomy.

As Plotnick's tables show, the variation in economic circumstances among areas is so large that it is difficult to characterize a metropolitan experience. Consider income changes. Between 1979 and 1989, some central cities experienced rapid per capita income growth, while others experienced losses (compare Detroit to New York in Table 2). Moreover, these differences in growth rates across cities obscure a wide diversity of experiences within each area. Many college graduates did very well in the labor market of the 1980s, regardless of where they chose to live, while most high school graduates fared badly; female workers in any education group, regardless of locale, experienced more inflation-adjusted wage growth than similarly-educated males; central-city residents who live further from areas of suburban job growth fared worse than those who lived closer to those suburban areas.

In other words, a national urban poverty report tends to focus our attention on poor places, despite the fact that we have gone through an era characterized by a large number of economic winners and losers in every place. This growing inequality within places is a recent economic phenomenon. In the quarter century following World War II, economic growth was rapid and a "rising tide lifted all boats." If the economic fortunes of an area lagged, most residents of that area tended to fare badly; if a place prospered, most residents fared well. In fact, most geographic areas and most families fared very well over the period from the late 1940s to the early 1970s, when inflation-adjusted incomes roughly doubled. During this era, a focus on *between-group* differences was a reasonable one, as *within-group* differences were relatively constant.

However, the stability of within-group differences has broken down over the last two decades. Wage growth, especially for males, and family income growth was much slower in the 1980s than in post-World War II decades, and earnings and family-income inequalities increased. This was an era in which "uneven tides" lifted the most advantaged but buffeted the disadvantaged (see Danziger and Gottschalk 1993).

Figure 1 is based on an analysis of the computer tapes from the public use samples of the Censuses of 1980 and 1990. Each point on the figure represents one of the fifty largest metropolitan areas. The horizontal axis shows the percentage change in inflation-adjusted annual earnings for men between the ages of 25 and 54 who were in the civilian labor force. The vertical axis shows the percentage point increase in the low earnings rate—defined as the percentage of men earning less than the poverty line for a family of four if they work fulltime, full year at their current wage rate ($12,674 in 1989 and $7,564 in 1979) (see Acs and Danziger 1993; U.S. Bureau of the Census 1992).

If a rising tide had lifted all boats, those metropolitan areas which experienced earnings growth would have had reductions in their low earnings rates. In the most straightforward case, if every worker's wage grew at the same rate, then a downward-sloping line would pass through the origin (no change in the mean; no change in the low earnings rate) and the data points would be clustered in the northwest quadrant (areas with declining average wages would have rising rates of low earnings) and in the Southeast quadrant (areas with rising wages, declining low earnings rates).

This did not happen in the 1980s. The data in Figure 1 do conform to a downward-sloping line, but the line is shifted out toward the northeast quadrant. Mean male earnings grew in twenty-six of the fifty largest metropolitan areas, but the low earnings rate fell in only five of them. The line indicates that, on average, an area with no real wage growth had about a 4 percentage point increase in the percentage of men with low annual earnings and that the low earnings rate did not fall except in the few areas where earnings growth exceeded 10 percent.

Table 1 presents the data used to form Figure 1 for the ten largest metro areas. The low earnings rate increased in eight of these areas, even though real wages grew in seven of them. Wage growth in Boston, for example, was the most rapid, at 19.4 percent, yet the low earnings rate there fell by only one-half percentage point.

The data in the figure and table also emphasize how difficult it is to talk about growth in metro areas being more rapid than that in non-metro areas, as there were actual wage declines in about half of the largest fifty areas. This was a decade of uneven tides—slow growth in the mean and rising inequalities, with increased variation both between and within metropolitan areas. In addition, most of the largest areas contain inner-city neighborhoods of concentrated poverty in which living conditions are bleak, regardless of the overall economic conditions in the city or metropolitan area.

While Plotnick presents important indicators of well-being in a number of dimensions, I would nominate several others for consideration for a national urban poverty report. These would include an index of racial residential segregation, information on the quality of local institutions, such as schools and public services, high school graduation rates for young people, and the percentage of families spending a large proportion of their budget on housing expenses.

Data should also be disaggregated to document differences among and between racial and ethnic groups in the measures presented. For example, consider the central-city poverty rates in Plotnick's Table 5. Detroit and Chicago and Philadelphia appear among the poorest cities. Yet, the 1990 Census data on poverty rates for their entire metropolitan areas reveal that the white poverty rates in these three areas are among the lowest in the nation. Because they are among the most segregated metropolitan areas in the country, they have the greatest disparity between economic conditions in the central city, where most of their minority residents live, and the suburbs, where most whites reside. In sum, if we are to assess the well-being of urban residents, we need data that better reflect

Figure 1

Relationship between Changes in Mean Earnings and Low Earner Rate, 1980–1990

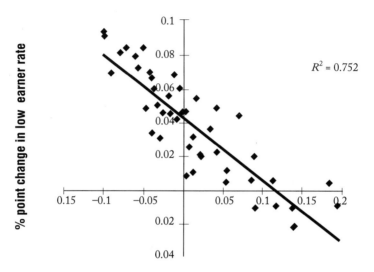

% change in mean male earnings

the growing differences not only between places, but within places for residents who differ in race, ethnicity, location, and economic position.

The slow and uneven growth of the economy requires a new urban policy focus that directly addresses the poverty and joblessness of those who have been left behind for the past two decades, even when the economy has expanded. Rather than focus on large development projects that pour concrete into depressed areas, we should promote a labor-intensive urban development strategy. We should subsidize private employers, wherever they are located, to hire the jobless, especially residents of inner-city areas with high concentrations of poverty. And we should offer minimum-wage public service jobs of last resort to those whom private employers do not hire. These jobs should be funded by the federal government, but the workers could be supervised by state or local governments or nonprofit organizations (see Danziger and Gottschalk 1995). These workers could be employed as playground monitors, day-care or nursing-home aides, or in the delivery of other services. Because of large reductions in federal aid to urban areas over the past fifteen years, and a shortage of local revenues, these are the very areas in which public services have deterio-

Table 1

Changes in Male Earnings, Largest Metropolitan Areas, 1979–1989[a]

metropolitan area	% increase in earnings	mean earnings 1989	% pt. change in low earner rate	% low earner rate 1989
Boston	19.4	37,946	−0.53	10.4
Chicago	0.2	35,385	4.75	14.0
Dallas	−1.2	32,299	6.94	18.8
Detroit	−1.8	36,300	4.64	13.5
Houston	−9.8	32,212	9.12	20.2
Los Angeles	4.2	33,906	5.01	19.0
New York	18.5	38,447	0.82	14.1
Philadelphia	11.8	35,559	−0.56	11.2
San Francisco	9.0	37,639	2.32	13.0
Washington, DC	5.3	38,907	0.79	10.5

[a] Sample includes men between the ages of 25 and 54 who were in the civilian labor force. The low earner rate is defined as the percentage who would earn less than the poverty line for a family of four persons if they worked full-time for a full year at their current wage rate.

Source: Computations by author from Public Use Data samples of the 1980 and 1990 Census of Population

rated. At a minimum, the jobs would directly reduce economic hardship for those employed; at a maximum, they might even improve the quality of life enough in pockets of concentrated poverty to induce increased private-sector investment.

References

Acs, Gregory, and Sheldon Danziger. 1993. "Educational Attainment, Industrial Structure and Male Earnings through the 1980s," *Journal of Human Resources* 28 (Summer): 618–48.

Danziger, Sheldon, and Peter Gottschalk (eds.) 1993. *Uneven Tides: Rising Inequality in America* (New York: Russell Sage Foundation).

_____. 1995. *America Unequal* (Cambridge, MA: Harvard University Press).

U.S. Bureau of the Census. 1992. *Workers with Low Earnings: 1964 to 1990.* Current Population Reports. Consumer Income. Series P–60, No. 178 (Washington, DC: USGPO).

The Public Sector:
A New Urban Strategy
for America's Large Cities

Anita A. Summers

Introduction

As population and employment within metropolitan areas have decentralized over the last several decades, the socioeconomic and political fabric of many of America's largest cities has thinned. In the absence of a coherent set of government policies, America's large cities, particularly those larger than a quarter of a million, will continue to unravel. Existing jurisdictional boundaries make fiscal crises virtually inevitable for the cities with the highest concentration of the poor, putting at risk enormous investments in private and public urban infrastructures. Though the Clinton administration has been energetic in the development of functional policies that are relevant to central cities—health care, welfare reform, the macro economy—it has not articulated a strategic plan for a set of geographically grounded policies. Some would regard this void as a policy statement in and of itself. A national urban policy report is the communication of choice for the articulation of such a strategy.

Urban agendas have arisen from time to time—mid 1960s, late 1970s, early 1980s—and the country has learned from the lack of success. We have learned that the density of high-need populations in cities gives rise to exponentially serious and costly problems, that management efficiencies in cities are associated with the segmentation of cities into strong subcity units, that many federal policies have exacerbated urban problems, and that there are significant legal and institutional constraints on the ability to attain the efficiencies of regionalization. The Wharton Real Estate Center at the University of Pennsylvania is engaged in a research project designed to address each of these, and to provide a new set of short- and long-term options.

Our view is that the most important statement a national urban policy report could make is to explicitly recognize that basic structural problems have to be attacked. Ameliorating the problem of homelessness in a city will not put the city on a more solid economic footing—the fundamental problems remain.

Underpinnings of an Urban Strategy

A serious national urban policy report by a new administration from a party long out of the White House should make clear that short- and long-term urban strategies are required. The basic economic principle—that when markets do not work perfectly, there is a case for government intervention to either help them work well or to supplement them—provides grounding for developing these strategies. We believe that, under the existing legal and legislative federalist framework, cities are being assigned an increasing share of the *nation's* poverty-related burdens, without being allocated increased resources to deal with those burdens. In general, cities cannot control these expenditures. Further, we believe that the political structure in many of the largest cities contributes to the relatively inefficient management of the limited local resources that are available. This is associated with a more controllable set of expenditures. Today's potentially explosive urban environment is the result.

We suggest these three intellectual underpinnings to a newly articulated urban strategy:

- Apart from explicit redistributional considerations, efficiency requires that those who benefit from federal, state, or local urban policies should pay for those benefits. Resources should be allocated to reflect the gains to, and the burdens borne by, each level of government. Cities should not and cannot bear the burdens of national policy decisions and mandates without the associated resources.
- Efficiency in government, as elsewhere, requires the use of incentives rather than microregulation to achieve desired results. Allocation criteria of state and federal governments to cities should reward those cities which implement institutional structures yielding efficiently delivered services and penalize those which do not. Allocation criteria of the federal govern-

ment to state governments should reward those states which
enable local governments to develop these structures.

- Redistributional policies, properly, are the functions of state
  and federal governments, not municipalities. Local governments are so severely constrained by their boundaries that efforts to redistribute may be counter-productive and certainly
  will be very costly. The main job of municipal government is
  the efficient delivery of important public services.

The translation of these tenets into structural changes in the large-
city urban economies of America involve both long- and short-term proposals. In the longer run, existing legal and fiscal frameworks can be
altered. A key aspect of a long-run strategy is that federal and state governments should implement policies that work to reduce the concentration
of people in poverty in the urban core. Clearly, this calls into question the
wisdom of a host of existing programs—such as most of the low-income
housing programs and empowerment zones—that encourage the urban
poor and immigrants to remain in or near areas already burdened by a high
density of poverty. In addition, it calls for new incentives to encourage the
regionalization of tax and service delivery systems. But, in the short run,
existing jurisdictional boundaries make fiscal crises inevitable for these
cities with the highest concentrations of the poor. A fiscal life line is
essential—an expenditure-neutral one that would involve reallocating the
sums currently going to cities, so that the ones bearing more national
burdens receive more, with others receiving less.

Empirical research into several areas is needed, of course, to
ground these strategies:

- measurements of the extent to which cities have uncontrollable expenditures because they are bearing the costs for
  national responsibilities;
- analysis of the factors accounting for differences in the relative
  efficiencies of city government—many of which are controllable;
- evaluation of the impact of the institutional constraints (fiscal,
  social, legal) on the plight of large central cities; and
- evaluation of the impact of existing policies on the concentration of poverty.

Several policy recommendations are emerging from the theoretical
underpinnings and the empirical research:

- the use of an intellectually-grounded "formula" for the use of
  federal and state governments that will provide the criteria for

allocating funds to cities for bearing national and regional burdens, and the incentives for encouraging efficient (and discouraging inefficient) municipal management;

- the development of incentives for encouraging state governments to enact legislation that will build regional tax and service delivery units;
- changes in federal policies that have inadvertently concentrated poverty populations within cities, and within particular neighborhoods of cities;
- the development of both local and state policies that will help private-property owners and government officials in the newer suburban "cities" from falling prey to the problems of their central cities.

The objective is to help our large cities become more livable—to enable them to deliver the social, cultural, political, and economic services they perform for the nation efficiently and with appropriate compensation.

Why Are We So Concerned about Large Cities?

It is tempting to some to argue that cities should compete like firms. If they are inviting places in which to live and work, they will flourish; if they are not, they will decline. The argument continues—if they are not attractive, this reflects the preferences of residents and employers for packages of taxes and public services, then so be it. The flaw in this chain of "perfect market" reasoning is that these markets are far from perfect. (1) Most of the big central cities of the nation take on responsibilities that extend far beyond their "markets," with enormous uncontrollable fiscal consequences. (2) Many of the factors behind the crises in large cities arose from past federal policies (housing, investment tax credits, transportation) that, inadvertently, helped to empty cities. (3) The absence of price and profit gauges to assess the efficiency with which municipal services are delivered inevitably complicates the process of good city management. (4) The size and extended power of municipal unions introduces a significant monopolistic element into the budgetary issues. (5) City governments are there not only to deliver services efficiently— they are also there to deliver them equitably, however their multiple, strong-voiced constituents define equity.

Public finance theory effectively addresses the first issue, the burden of delivering public services—apart from conscious redistributive allocations, those who benefit from the public services should pay. Bluntly stated, because suburban residents can live without the disamenities of poverty—partly because of affluence, partly because they enact various zoning and other regulations—they help concentrate poverty in the urban core, and they should compensate core residents.

The second issue, inadvertently harmful past federal policies, requires a thorough review of their effects on central cities—and an assessment of policies that would be consistent with the robust findings that policies attracting residents exert important positive influences on urban economic development. Federal housing policies merit particular attention.

There is no shortage of excellent techniques for coping with the problem of the absence of prices and profit gauges—the third issue. But there is a shortage of the political will to require their use, complicated by the role of municipal unions (the fourth issue) and the demands for "fairness" (the fifth issue). This lack of will, greatly exacerbated in cities by the large and increasing heterogeneity of the population, significantly impedes the ability to eliminate union-imposed inefficiencies—and it frequently paralyzes the ability of the municipal governing bodies to arrive at a consensus on what constitutes an equitable distribution of services.

The net effect of all these factors is a nation whose central cities are in acute distress, and whose central-city populations are in circumstances increasingly disparate from the remainder of their region and country.

The cost to the cities, their states, and the nation as a whole is substantial. Private and public investment is reduced in value; and concentrations of poverty add to the probability of crime, adolescent pregnancies, dropouts, drug cultures, and groups of homeless people. Moreover, the dynamics of America's urban areas provide no support for the notion that somehow cities will restore themselves to a former—or even better—state of economic well-being. Analyses of these metropolitan entities show clearly that there has been massive decentralization among and within them. There has been a considerable population and employment movement from the older densest urban areas in the Northeast and Midwest to new urban areas in the southern and western parts of the country, and, very important, movement from the central city to the suburbs.

Increasingly, as people enjoy higher incomes, they and their jobs move to the suburbs. Tables 1 and 2 show population and employment changes in the sixty largest metropolitan areas between 1970 and 1990. The disparate rates of growth between the cities (CC) and the rest of the metropolitan area (OCC) are obvious from the overwhelming number of minus signs in front of the CC percentages, and from comparison of the CC and OCC averages. Their preferences were fueled by federal policies (interstate highways, housing subsidies, tax policies), and technological advances (TV, cable, fax). Metropolitan areas are no longer characterized by one overwhelmingly large urban core—they still have one larger core, but they now have many large and growing suburban nodes. The urgency of these dynamics derives from the fact that this pattern is not reversible in the foreseeable future, and is in fact continuing. The net effect is the substantially changed income distribution in central cities and within metropolitan areas over the last two decades—the proportion of people with incomes below the poverty line living in central cities has been increasing even when the macroeconomy has relatively low unemployment rates.

In brief, America's large central cities are in trouble, and the trouble will not go away in the absence of a concrete ameliorative strategy.

Poverty and Resource Mismatch?

Poverty is an overwhelming fact of life in most of America's large cities. A successful urban strategy must address the realities of the growing relative concentration of poverty in cities, the role of federal policies in fostering that concentration, and the mismatch of resources from the federal and state governments to care for the poor and the social problems associated with the concentrations. What are these realities?

Poverty Concentration

The growing level and density of poverty in central cities lead to a fiscal burden that many central cities cannot continue to bear for the nation without proper recompense. Poverty clearly is a national problem. The size and allocation of the welfare safety net is determined primarily at the national level. Moreover, while poor local service delivery has stimulated the migration of the middle class to the suburbs, cities did not invite the poor to concentrate within their borders. A complex web of socioeconomic factors and the dynamic of historical demographics helped produce the current location patterns.

The levels of poverty in central cities, and the growing disparities between those levels and the levels in their suburbs, are a force to be reckoned with. There are several ways of measuring this disturbing characteristic. John D. Kasarda, in a recent Department of Housing and Urban Development study, uses census data to show for ten large central cities the proportion of census tracts in poverty (at least 20 percent of the households have incomes below that year's poverty income levels), and in extreme poverty (at least 40 percent of the households have incomes below that year's poverty income level) for 1970, 1980, and 1990. Nine out of ten had significant increases in both categories between 1970 and 1980 (Philadelphia's percentages went from 28.1 to 40.2 percent, for example). Detroit's data are staggering—the proportion of census tracts in poverty increased from 34.8 to 75.8 percent between 1970 and 1990; the proportion in extreme poverty increased from 5.5 to 41.3 percent over the same time period. Janice Fanning Madden, in her work on the Wharton Real Estate Center project, has generated poverty-level data (Table 3) for large cities that show:

Table 1

Population Changes for the Sixty Largest
U.S. Metropolitan Areas, 1970–1990 (percentage)

	1970–1990			1980–1990		
	CC	OCC	SMSA	CC	OCC	SMSA
1. Akron	−13.9	5.1	−3.8	−6.0	2.7	−0.4
2. Albany	−12.2	4.7	2.2	−0.6	5.1	4.3
3. Allentown	−5.3	9.7	7.0	1.3	9.4	8.1
4. Anaheim	88.9	31.4	36.1	21.5	25.1	24.7
5. Atlanta	−14.5	45.8	27.0	−7.3	43.4	32.8
6. Baltimore	−13.1	19.1	5.0	−6.5	16.2	8.0
7. Birmingham	−5.4	20.7	10.5	−6.5	7.0	2.5
8. Boston	−12.2	−2.6	−4.7	2.0	2.6	2.5
9. Buffalo	−22.7	0.0	−7.9	−8.3	−2.7	−4.3
10. Charlotte	30.3	2.0	14.2	25.9	16.1	21.0
11. Chicago	−10.6	13.5	4.5	−7.4	9.2	2.2
12. Cincinnati	−14.8	9.0	1.2	−5.6	7.1	3.7
13. Cleveland	−23.6	0.0	−8.0	−11.9	0.0	−3.5
14. Columbus	4.7	10.4	7.4	12.0	10.6	11.3
15. Dallas	7.1	35.0	25.1	11.4	42.1	32.8
16. Dayton	−16.5	3.3	−2.4	−10.5	5.6	1.7
17. Denver	−4.3	56.2	31.0	−5.0	22.6	14.2
18. Detroit	−20.4	−13.9	−15.8	−14.6	6.5	0.7
19. Ft. Lauderdale	9.8	80.0	64.2	−2.5	27.9	23.3
20. Gary	−13.3	7.1	1.5	−23.2	−0.6	−6.0
21. Grand Rapids	−7.9	22.9	11.6	4.0	18.9	14.4
22. Greensboro	7.9	16.0	14.4	17.9	8.8	10.5
23. Hartford	−13.7	5.3	1.1	2.5	6.7	5.9
24. Honolulu	12.4	30.6	21.2	0.0	18.5	9.7
25. Houston	29.4	70.9	45.3	2.2	42.2	20.2
26. Indianapolis	−5.9	27.5	5.1	4.4	11.3	7.1
27. Kansas City	−11.7	15.0	4.4	−2.9	15.2	9.1
28. Los Angeles	5.4	6.9	6.3	17.5	19.2	18.5
29. Louisville	−17.4	20.1	4.5	−9.8	3.5	−0.9
30. Memphis	3.6	27.1	9.5	−5.6	39.0	7.5

continued on following page

Table 1, continued

	1970–1990			1980–1990		
	CC	OCC	SMSA	CC	OCC	SMSA
31. Miami	3.5	37.1	28.2	3.4	23.4	19.1
32. Milwaukee	−11.3	10.8	0.0	−1.3	5.7	2.5
33. Minneapolis	−14.6	14.5	8.1	−0.7	18.8	15.4
34. Nashville	1.7	54.2	20.8	7.2	25.8	15.8
35. New Orleans	−6.1	39.2	13.5	−10.9	4.7	−2.6
36. New York	−10.4	1.0	−8.1	3.5	0.0	2.8
37. Newark	−13.9	−2.1	−4.3	−16.4	1.3	−1.6
38. Oklahoma City	10.0	30.0	19.5	10.3	12.6	11.5
39. Orlando	29.6	61.4	54.5	28.4	58.8	53.2
40. Philadelphia	−13.4	5.6	−2.1	−6.1	8.0	3.0
41. Phoenix	35.8	86.4	56.0	24.5	58.3	40.6
42. Pittsburgh	−18.5	−2.2	−5.7	−12.8	−6.1	−7.4
43. Portland	−4.1	40.7	23.1	19.4	11.3	13.7
44. Providence	−12.5	12.8	7.5	2.5	8.1	7.1
45. Richmond	−12.2	38.6	15.4	−7.4	30.0	17.0
46. Rochester	−18.4	9.7	1.0	−4.2	5.7	3.2
47. Sacramento	8.4	35.2	26.7	34.0	33.5	33.6
48. Salt Lake	−7.3	46.0	32.7	−1.9	21.4	17.4
49. San Antonio	20.1	22.3	20.7	19.1	28.0	21.5
50. San Diego	25.7	49.2	37.1	26.8	40.7	34.2
51. San Francisco	−5.1	7.4	4.5	6.6	15.2	13.4
52. San Jose	41.0	7.7	21.6	24.3	7.5	15.6
53. Seattle	−7.0	25.0	13.1	4.5	30.8	22.7
54. St Louis	−27.2	6.5	−2.2	−12.4	6.5	2.8
55. Syracuse	−13.8	7.7	1.0	−3.7	4.9	2.6
56. Tampa	−2.2	60.0	44.2	3.1	30.0	25.3
57. Toledo	−7.7	15.4	3.8	−6.1	−26.5	−17.4
58. Tulsa	8.8	50.0	25.2	1.8	14.2	7.7
59. Wash. DC	−15.6	12.6	5.2	−4.9	26.1	19.6
60. Youngstown	−17.4	5.0	−1.0	−17.1	−4.6	−7.3
mean	−1.9	21.9	12.0	1.7	15.6	11.1
median	−7.7	15.4	7.5	0.0	11.3	9.1

Source: U.S. Department of Commerce, *Census of Population and Housing,* 1970, 1980, 1990.

Table 2

Employment Changes for the Sixty Largest
U.S. Metropolitan Areas, 1970–1990 (percentage)

	1970–1990			1980–1990		
	CC	OCC	SMSA	CC	OCC	SMSA
1. Akron	−9.3	22.0	9.4	−1.0	11.7	7.4
2. Albany	−7.4	17.2	13.3	9.5	18.9	17.6
3. Allentown	−0.1	18.4	14.7	4.7	18.0	15.8
4. Anaheim	63.3	81.4	79.1	24.4	33.7	32.6
5. Atlanta	−16.4	87.4	45.8	0.2	59.3	48.6
6. Baltimore	−13.2	45.3	19.9	2.8	29.2	20.9
7. Birmingham	0.0	43.6	25.5	−3.9	18.7	11.3
8. Boston	−3.9	17.0	12.3	12.8	11.8	12.0
9. Buffalo	−23.6	13.9	1.3	−0.2	6.9	5.1
10. Charlotte	52.1	14.8	31.0	34.5	24.2	29.4
11. Chicago	−11.0	36.8	13.6	−2.3	16.2	9.2
12. Cincinnati	−8.9	27.6	15.4	−0.3	19.7	14.4
13. Cleveland	−25.4	16.3	1.8	−14.8	4.3	−0.6
14. Columbus	19.7	30.5	24.7	24.1	20.0	22.2
15. Dallas	24.3	64.3	49.3	10.0	49.0	36.8
16. Dayton	−25.0	17.7	5.2	−2.7	15.9	12.0
17. Denver	15.1	102.5	65.1	−4.6	29.4	19.2
18. Detroit	−29.7	26.5.	7.4	−15.0	18.9	11.3
19. Ft Lauderdale	29.1	110.6	90.7	0.9	44.6	37.3
20. Gary	−16.4	23.4	12.8	−24.3	6.7	0.5
21. Grand Rapids	0.0	53.6	34.6	9.3	31.2	25.3
22. Greensboro	20.9	30.2	28.3	32.2	17.9	20.6
23. Hartford	−16.3	26.3	16.9	−0.0	13.8	11.6
24. Honolulu	25.1	66.8	40.1	6.7	41.3	22.1
25. Houston	60.4	116.9	80.6	−4.7	45.3	16.8
26. Indianapolis	8.0	46.1	20.4	13.6	25.7	18.4
27. Kansas City	−1.4	40.2	22.9	0.5	22.9	15.4
28. Los Angeles	21.2	23.9	22.8	19.8	22.0	21.1
29. Louisville	−14.8	40.6	17.2	−4.0	14.6	8.9
30. Memphis	12.7	71.3	24.6	−0.7	71.1	19.3

continued on following page

Table 2, continued

	1970–1990			1980–1990		
	CC	OCC	SMSA	CC	OCC	SMSA
31. Miami	6.5	60.4	44.7	−4.9	28.6	21.4
32. Milwaukee	−5.0	26.8	10.8	−3.9	14.0	6.2
33. Minneapolis	−2.9	42.9	31.9	0.9	27.2	22.5
34. Nashville	19.5	82.3	41.2	15.5	40.9	26.9
35. New Orleans	4.7	73.2	34.4	−14.9	7.6	−2.4
36. New York	−8.6	14.7	−3.6	11.6	7.4	10.6
37. Newark	−19.8	12.4	7.2	−4.1	11.1	9.3
38. Oklahoma City	26.0	52.8	38.3	9.2	15.3	12.3
39. Orlando	48.5	105.7	92.8	48.1	79.7	74.2
40. Philadelphia	−18.2	22.4	5.9	4.3	21.3	16.0
41. Phoenix	59.5	124.7	83.2	31.0	77.0	51.6
42. Pittsburgh	−11.4	13.2	7.8	−9.7	0.2	−1.6
43. Portland	11.2	96.6	59.9	25.9	20.1	21.8
44. Providence	−11.6	31.1	21.9	5.2	17.0	15.2
45. Richmond	−4.4	63.5	32.7	−3.4	41.6	26.9
46. Rochester	−16.9	27.6	13.6	0.9	15.4	12.1
47. Sacramento	20.0	67.9	52.2	42.8	45.8	45.1
48. Salt Lake	5.1	70.2	52.1	−0.1	30.2	24.4
49. San Antonio	37.6	76.1	46.1	27.4	43.7	31.8
50. San Diego	57.2	96.6	75.7	46.4	55.9	51.4
51. San Francisco	7.6	31.7	25.7	12.9	21.7	19.8
52. San Jose	90.1	42.9	61.6	32.4	13.1	22.1
53. Seattle	10.4	63.9	42.1	13.6	42.3	33.3
54. St. Louis	−25.3	24.1	11.5	−6.7	16.2	12.3
55. Syracuse	−10.5	24.8	13.2	−0.2	19.7	14.6
56. Tampa	9.2	91.9	68.4	14.6	52.3	45.3
57. Toledo	−6.3	29.8	11.1	−0.2	−14.3	−8.1
58. Tulsa	33.3	79.5	50.2	−0.8	21.8	9.0
59. Washington, DC	−11.0	44.3	28.7	2.0	41.3	33.7
60. Youngstown	−21.5	17.2	2.9	−23.3	2.7	−2.2
mean	6.7	49.0	31.8	6.4	26.3	20.0
median	−0.1	42.9	25.5	0.5	21.3	17.6

Source: U.S. Department of Commerce, *Census of Population and Housing,* 1970, 1980, 1990.

- increases in center-city poverty levels for the majority of cities between 1979 and 1989 (e.g. from 16.4 to 18.3 percent for Los Angeles);
- decreases for some (e.g. from 18.6 to 14.5 percent for Washington, DC);
- 1989 levels ranging from 12.7 percent (San Francisco) to 30.6 percent (New Orleans) among the largest sixteen cities;
- *and* increases in the ratio of city to suburb poverty levels in eleven of the sixteen largest metropolitan areas, even where the absolute levels declined in the cities. (Boston's center-city levels declined from 20.2 to 15.4 percent, but its city-to-suburb poverty level ratio increased from 2.97 to 3.21).

Madden's analysis (1994) of intermetropolitan variations in household income distribution—using Gini coefficients for the metropolitan areas—shows clearly that demographic structure has a significant and substantial effect on inequality within the areas. Greater proportions of households headed by women strongly increase inequality—and in central cities there are much greater proportions of households headed by women. Beyond that, as the Gini coefficients for 1979 and 1989 in Table 3 indicate, the inequalities for all metropolitan areas for which data are available have increased significantly over the decade.

These poverty data are, in and of themselves, evidence of the concentration of significant responsibilities in center cities. What do we know about the fiscal magnitudes associated with those responsibilities?

Resource Mismatch

Estimating the fiscal burdens borne by the nation's cities for the public expenditures that grow out of poverty is a complicated problem beset by a number of conceptual and data challenges. Janet Rothenberg Pack, in her work on the Wharton Real Estate Center project, has taken on this effort (Pack 1994).

Pack first sorts out which of the many expenditures cities make are attributable to the size of the population living in poverty. Three categories seem most clearly so—means-tested public welfare programs, health, and hospitals. Other public functions are clearly associated with poverty, though not to the same extent—education, police, corrections, judicial and legal administration, fire, recreation, and housing and community development. Tables 4 and 5 document strikingly the substantially heavier fiscal burden large local governments cover in delivering services to the poor.

In Table 4, the proportion of total general expenditures spent on functions attributable to poverty are shown for different-sized municipalities. The seven cities in the one-million-or-more group are dominated by the figures for New York City, and are also quite heterogenous with respect to other characteristics. The averages, therefore, are not very meaningful. In cities of 500,000 to one million persons, 13.3 percent is spent on direct poverty functions, compared to 4 to 5 percent for cities. On the whole, the direction is the same for the other poverty-associated expenditures but less strikingly so. On a per capita basis (Table 5), the differences between the large and smaller cities are much more pronounced. Total per capita expenditures are nearly $1,500 for cities of 500,000 to one million, less than $1,200 for cities between 300,000 and 500,000, and about $1,000 for smaller cities. The comparable poverty expenditures per capita show even greater differences—$200 and less than $100.

The issue, of course, is not just whether the expenditures are higher in the larger cities with higher concentrations of poverty, but the role their own tax base plays in covering these costs. The lower part of Table 4 speaks to that question. Intergovernmental revenues cover a larger proportion of total expenditures for larger cities—*but* intergovernmental revenues as a proportion of direct poverty expenditures are inversely related to size. Bigger localities have a smaller proportion of their poverty costs covered by federal and state governments.

Pack concludes that there are a number of important implications for an urban strategy that emerge from her work:

- There is a strong equity argument for assistance to large cities. They cover, relatively, the highest proportion of direct poverty expenditures from their own tax base.
- Federal assistance should be directed to both state and local governments, with the proportions going to each related to the state–local fiscal structure. Variations in this structure account for the very great variation in the proportion of direct poverty costs borne by local governments even when they have the same poverty rates.
- Either state and federal aid should be higher for cities that are coterminous with counties than those with more regionalized fiscal jurisdictions, or states should be encouraged to make legislative changes to move to regionalization.

A well-functioning urban strategy must incorporate the realities of the concentration of poverty in the large central cities of the United States. The concentration is growing, and with it the growing fiscal burdens for these cities. In the short run, fiscal life lines are essential if we are not to lose the public goods cities provide for the nation. In the long run, assistance will be required, but efforts to deconcentrate the poor and regionalize the urban tax bases will produce permanent structural improvement.

Table 3

**Poverty Rates for All Persons in the Sixteen Largest
Metropolitan Areas (1969, 1979, 1989)
and Gini Coefficients of Household Income (1979, 1989)**

	1969	1979		1989	
	rates	rates	Gini	rates	Gini
Atlanta		12.2		10.0	
city	20.5	27.5		25.9	
suburbs		8.3		7.2	
ratio		3.31	0.374	3.60	0.411
Baltimore		11.9		10.1	
city	18.4	22.9		21.4	
suburbs		5.6		4.7	
ratio		4.09	0.383	4.55	0.404
Boston		9.4		8.3	
city	16.2	20.2		15.4	
suburbs		6.8		4.8	
ratio		2.97	0.374	3.21	0.421
Buffalo		10.3		12.2	
city	15.4	20.7		25.6	
suburbs		6.1		5.4	
ratio		3.34	0.356	4.74	0.416
Chicago		11.3		12.4	
city	14.5	20.3		21.2	
suburbs		4.7		4.3	
ratio		4.32	0.386	4.93	0.420
Detroit		10.2		12.9	
city	14.9	21.9		30.2	
suburbs		5.7		6.2	
ratio		3.84	0.382	4.87	0.420
Houston		10.1		15.1	
city	14.2	12.7		20.6	
suburbs		7.1		9.4	
ratio		1.79	0.377	2.19	0.435
Los Angeles		13.4		15.1	
city	13.3	16.4		18.3	
suburbs		11.2		12.1	
ratio		1.46	0.352	1.51	0.443

continued on following page

Table 3, continued

	1969	1979		1989	
	rates	rates	Gini	rates	Gini
Memphis		20.0		18.3	
city	20.8	21.8		23.0	
suburbs		15.4		9.7	
ratio		1.42	0.425	2.37	NA
New Orleans		17.6		21.2	
city	27.0	26.4		30.6	
suburbs		9.9		14.5	
ratio		2.67	0.412	2.11	0.478
New York City		16.8		17.5	
city	14.8	20.0		19.2	
suburbs		5.6		6.5	
ratio		3.57	0.439	2.95	NA
Philadelphia		12.0		10.4	
city	15.4	20.6		20.9	
suburbs		7.1		4.8	
ratio		2.90	0.394	4.35	NA
Pittsburgh		8.7		12.2	
city	15.6	16.5		21.6	
suburbs		6.9		10.0	
ratio		2.39	0.354	2.16	0.438
San Francisco		10.3		9.0	
city	14.1	21.8		12.7	
suburbs		7.6		6.0	
ratio		2.87	0.373	2.12	0.417
Saint Louis		9.8		10.8	
city	20.2	18.5		22.3	
suburbs		13.7		7.0	
ratio		1.35	0.384	3.19	NA
Washington, DC		8.2		6.4	
city	16.9	18.6		14.3	
suburbs		5.5		4.4	
ratio		3.38	0.267	3.25	NA

Source: Janice F. Madden, "Changes in the Distribution of Income and Earnings Within U.S. Cities and Suburbs." Draft Working Paper, Wharton Real Estate Center, University of Pennsylvania, 1994.

Table 4

Poverty and Other City Expenditures by City Size: 1989–1990 (Expenditures in Millions)

	all	1,000,000 or more*	500,000 to 99,999	300,000 to 499,999	200,000 to 299,999	100,000 to 199,999	75,000 to 99,999	less than 75,000
				municipalities having a 1988 population of:				
total general expenditure	153,684	43,679	18,344	12,387	6,664	14,933	7,227	50,450
public welfare	7,890	6,078	1,013	176	78	218	51	276
% of total expenditure	5.1	13.9	5.5	1.4	1.2	1.5	0.7	0.5
hospital	6,581	2,838	901	272	96	365	200	1,909
% of total expenditure	4.3	6.5	4.9	2.2	1.4	2.4	2.8	3.8
health	2,560	1,015	522	250	119	1	76	71
% of total expenditure	1.7	2.3	2.8	2.0	1.8	1.2	1.0	0.8
total poverty expenditures	17,031	9,931	2,436	698	293	759	322	2,592
% of total expenditure	11.1	22.7	13.3	5.6	4.4	5.1	4.5	5.1
housing & community development	7,661	2,919	908	576	413	675	335	1,835
% of total expenditure	5.0	6.7	4.9	4.7	6.2	4.5	4.6	3.6
education	17,368	7,071	2,059	931	899	2,237	1,111	3,060
% of total expenditure	11.3	16.2	11.2	7.5	13.5	15.0	15.4	6.1

police	7,266	929	1,796	762	1,472	2,078	3,880	18,183
% of total expenditure	14.4	12.9	12.0	11.4	11.9	11.3	8.9	11.8
correction	89	10	57	42	136	662	1,286	2,282
% of total expenditure	0.2	0.1	0.4	0.6	1.1	3.6	2.9	1.5
judicial and legal	507	61	146	77	177	429	744	2,141
% of total expenditure	1.0	0.8	1.0	1.2	1.4	2.3	1.7	1.4
general revenue from own source	39,363	5,528	10,607	4,828	9,506	133,129	30,034	112,995
intergovernmental revenue:								
from federal government	1,782	247	552	386	795	2,091	1,692	7,545
from state government	10,433	1,476	2,987	1,283	1,809	3,316	12,939	34,243
total from federal and state government	12,215	1,723	3,539	1,669	2,604	5,407	14,631	41,788
% of total expenditure**	24.2	23.8	23.7	25.0	21.0	29.5	33.5	27.2
% of poverty expenditure***	471.3	535.1	466.3	569.6	373.1	222.0	147.3	245.4

* Seven cities are included in this group and the figures are dominated by those from New York City. The remaining six cities are quite heterogeneous in that three are joint city/county governments and three have separate county governments with major expenditure responsibilities

** IGR/TGE

*** IGR/Poverty

Source: U.S. Department of Commerce, Bureau of the Census, City Government Finances, 1989–90, Table 2.

Table 5

Poverty and Other City Expenditures per Capita by City Size: 1989–1990 (Dollars)

		municipalities having a 1988 population of:						
	all	1,000,000 or more*	500,000 to 99,999	300,000 to 499,999	200,000 to 299,999	100,000 to 199,999	75,000 to 99,999	less than 75,000
total general expenditure	1,004.47	2,282.77	1,497.63	1,189.02	1,096.39	1,006.15	1,000.13	607.44
public welfare	51.57	317.67	82.67	16.88	12.78	14.67	7.08	3.33
hospitals	43.01	148.32	73.57	26.09	15.82	24.61	27.73	22.98
health	111.31	519.03	198.85	66.95	48.15	51.12	44.64	31.22
total poverty expenditures	111.31	519.03	198.85	66.94	48.15	51.12	44.64	31.22
% of total expenditure	11.1	22.7	13.3	5.6	4.4	5.1	4.5	5.1
housing and community development	50.07	152.55	74.15	55.27	67.91	45.5	46.29	22.11
education	113.52	369.53	168.10	89.39	147.92	150.69	153.75	36.86
police	118.84	202.78	169.68	141.34	125.37	120.98	128.50	87.48
correction	14.91	67.23	54.05	13.05	6.90	3.84	1.40	1.07
judicial and legal	13.99	38.87	34.98	16.95	12.62	9.80	8.41	6.13
general revenue from own source	738.52	1,569.65	1,071.80	912.50	794.42	714.63	764.63	764.97

* See note 1, Table 4.

Source: U.S. Department of Commerce, Bureau of the Census, *City Government and Finances,* 1989–90, Table 2.

Immigration and Resource Mismatch?

Immigration may provide the clearest illustration of the disparity between those who benefit from and those who pay for the consequences of a national policy. Immigration policy is unambiguously nationally designed. Numerous studies show that immigrants provide a net benefit to the nation. They are so productive over the long run that they more than make up for the high costs they generate upon arriving. For several reasons, however, this is not the case for cities that have experienced the biggest influx of immigrants. First, most of the tax revenues immigrants pay goes to federal and state governments while the bulk of the services they use is provided by counties and cities. Second, the costs associated with new immigrants may exceed the costs associated with older cohorts of immigrants, because of differences between the cohorts in the rate at which their wages catch up to those of natives.

In 1990, 59 percent of all immigrants who entered the United States within the previous ten years lived in nine cities; 43 percent lived in three cities—Los Angeles, New York, and Miami. Los Angeles alone is home to nearly one-quarter of all recent immigrants. Kermit Daniel, in his work on the Wharton Real Estate Center's urban project, is researching the question of the net cost to cities of immigrants (Daniel 1994). Each city involves separate data analysis, and the work is in progress, but preliminary evidence suggests that the net costs they bear are substantial.

Estimating these net costs is a complex problem. On the revenue side, their tax contributions to each level of government need to be calculated. Estimates must be made not only for recent legal immigrants and those granted lawful status under amnesty agreements, but also for the large number of undocumented immigrants and their citizen children. In Los Angeles, for example, the total immigrant population is estimated at 25 percent of the total population—recent legal immigrants are 6.9 percent, amnesty-granted immigrants 7.8, undocumented immigrants 7.6, and their citizen children 2.7. Cost estimates must be developed for the extra expenditure involved in delivering services to immigrants beyond those for the rest of the population. (At the local level, these costs are heavily education and health-care related.) Finally, estimates should be made of the indirect costs imposed on the wages and employment of native workers, if indeed that is the case. Potentially, this gives rise to significant cost to city governments.

The most detailed data available—for Los Angeles County—support the finding that, while the bulk of services immigrants use is supplied at the local level, the bulk of tax revenues they generate goes to the federal and state governments. The U.S. Government Accounting Office (U.S. General Accounting Office) made a particularly detailed set of estimates for Los Angeles County. Tables 6 and 7 show their calculations of the propor-

Table 6

Percent of Revenues Generated by All Immigrants in L.A. County Going to Each Level of Government, 1991–92

government level	%
federal	60.0
state	28.6
county	3.2
other local	8.2

Source: U.S. Government Accounting Office (1992).

tion of revenues going to each government level, and the proportion of Los Angeles County expenditures accounted for by immigrants (excluding schooling, a major expenditure). Although the four categories of immigrants constitute 25 percent of the total population, only 3.2 percent of the revenues they generate go to the county, and 8.2 percent to other local governments. On the other hand, the state of California received 28.6 percent of the revenues they generated, and the federal government 60 percent. Although immigrants constitute 25 percent of the total, they account for 31 percent of the Los Angeles County expenditures. (If education costs were included, that number would be even higher.)

There is a second major pressure on the cities that are major gateways for immigrants. New immigrants and their children require more expenditures at first than later—when they and their children get jobs and earn more. Essentially, the nation invests in the new immigrants and their children, and receives the return later. But the recent large increase in the number of immigrants means that the return from the earlier cohorts of immigrants cannot finance the new cohorts. More than half of the foreign-born populations in five cities—Atlanta, Dallas, Houston, Los Angeles, and Washington, DC—arrived in the 1980s; about one-fifth in Atlanta, Los Angeles, and Washington arrived after 1985. The children of these immigrants born in the United States are not, of course, immigrants, but many of the costs are associated with them.

Beyond the issue of surging immigration costs not offset by past returns is the issue of the rate at which immigrants' wages catch up to those of natives—the rate of assimilation. There is evidence that the immigrant pool is becoming less skilled over time (La Londe and Topel 1991)—and therefore are contributing less taxes and using more resources than in the past.

Table 7

Immigrant Share of L.A. County Costs* and Population, 1991/92

	share of costs (%)	% of population
recent legal	11.5	6.9
amnesty	6.3	7.8
undocumented	10.1	7.6
citizen children	3.0	2.7
immigration total	30.9	25.0

* Excluding education
Source: U.S. Government Accounting Office (1992).

The U.S. GAO study calculated the costs of and the tax revenues generated for Los Angeles County. Their estimate of the *net* financial costs to the country in 1990–91 was $808 million, or about $350 per immigrant—contrasted with $126 per capita for the nonimmigrant population. Daniel estimates that if schooling costs are included, the net financial costs rise to $1,936 million, or about $870 per immigrant—equal to about 17 percent of total city and county expenditures, and 26 percent of total operating expenditures. The GAO study estimates that immigrants generated $538 per capita for the state of California, and $1,130 per capita for the federal government—a net financial gain for the United States as a whole. This implies, if the California experience can be generalized, that in principle the county and local governments could be compensated for the costs of providing services to immigrants out of tax revenues generated by the immigrants themselves for higher levels of government.

What is clear from the work thus far is that the net costs of our *national* immigration policy to *local* governments is high, and far from fully reimbursed. The basic tenets of public finance dictate that it is the nation's responsibility to do so.

City Government Efficiency: Resource Misuse?

There are strong reasons for thinking that some cities deliver public services much more efficiently and at a higher quality than others. To the naked eye, the quality of public services looks much better in Minneapolis than in New York. That might be entirely due to the relative ethnic and racial homogeneity of the Minneapolis area, and/or to the relatively low rates of poverty. If these were the only factors accounting for the differences in public services, then there would be a strong case for helping New York more to support the needy population concentration that history and state and government policies produced. But it might also be true that Minneapolis's relatively high quality of public services flowed from good internal management policies and a strong centralized form of municipal government. Robert P. Inman (Inman et al. 1994), in his work on the Wharton Real Estate project, is analyzing this issue. He and two others—Stephen Craig of the University of Texas at Houston and Thomas Luce of the University of Minnesota—are studying in depth the government functioning of three cities: Houston, Minneapolis, and Philadelphia. Houston is a useful case because it took a severe economic shock that had nothing to do with its internal management, so one can study how it coped. Philadelphia experienced significant changes in the politics of public finance during the 1970s and 1980s. And Minneapolis–St. Paul is a "good" government model that has a relatively homogeneous population and a regional tax base.

Which institutions accompany relatively strong public service delivery? The evidence suggests strong, more centralized forms of municipal government and tax-base sharing, which fully reflect who benefits from the service, contribute to more efficient public service delivery. Unlike concentrations of immigrants and poverty, these factors are choices local and state governments can make. The consequences of the increased empowerment of individual constituencies and sharply delineated geographical parts of municipalities may be counterproductive to local government's efforts to improve its economy. When elected officials from constituencies and neighborhoods vote on allocating a city's resources, they typically do so to maximize the welfare of their political base rather than to achieve what is best for the city as a whole. Inefficient expenditures are the result. The political will power to resist higher-than-market public employeee demands for wages and benefits must come from within city political systems. Rewards from higher levels of government are a way to encourage this.

A national urban strategy based on rewarding cities that provide frameworks and incentives for efficiency (and penalize cities that fail to do so) will need to keep close track of these developments in each city. Intergovernmental grants are the tools for such an incentive system.

Legislative and Legal Context of an Urban Strategy

There are federal policies—particularly housing policies—that, inadvertently perhaps, have contributed to the economic and fiscal decline of American cities. And there are aspects of our legal system that have been discouraging to the regionalization of their responsibilities. Both of these institutional factors have played a significant role in bringing about the large city scenes we now see—and changes in both will have to be part of a long-term strategy for improving the viability of America's cities. What have been their roles, and what options are there for change?

Federal Housing Policies and the Concentration of Poverty

There are a large number of federal policies that have the worthy objectives of helping the low-income population, improving the nation's transportation network, facilitating home ownership for veterans, and encouraging capital investment—but which, inadvertently, have contributed to the distress of the nation's largest cities. It is important to underscore the fact that these policies were designed to contribute to the well-being of various groups—but their potential impact on cities was ignored. The concentration of low-income housing in cities warrants particular attention. It was destructive to cities and to housing development residents. The expanded transportation network helped to empty cities; the criteria for Veterans Administration mortgages encouraged the move to suburbs; and the requirement, for many years, that lower investment tax rates be applicable only to new investments meant that investments in places other than old cities were subsidized. Some of these policies might well be important to carry out, even if they have negative effects on cities—but a country that wants to preserve the public good characteristics that cities have will accompany them by offsetting policies that are beneficial to cities.

Michael H. Schill and Susan M. Wachter, in their work on the Wharton Real Estate Center's urban project, argue that "Throughout the twentieth century, federal housing policy has exhibited a locational bias that has promoted the growth of large concentrations of poor people in the inner city" (Schill and Wachter 1994).

The federal government and cities incur substantial direct costs in providing housing assistance to low-income families. At the federal level, the grants have been substantial, although their form has changed. Funding for supply-oriented programs such as public housing has been reduced dramatically over the past decade. In place of these production subsidies, however, HUD has increasingly funded demand-oriented assistance such as Section 8 housing certificates and vouchers. In many instances, local governments have responded to federal production subsidy cutbacks by instituting a wide variety of housing programs that focus on facilitating the construction of low- and moderate-income housing. As a proportion of the total amount spent by cities on housing programs, local funds are dwarfed by federal subsidies.

Schill and Wachter have examined how the public housing program and the homeowner mortgage assistance programs contributed to the poverty concentration in central cities. Several important points emerge from their analysis:

- In 1935, following the passage of Congressional legislation authorizing the federal government to build publicly-owned housing, a federal court struck the legislation down, saying that providing low-income housing was not within the scope of the government's eminent domain powers.
- The result was that the Housing Act of 1937 stated that public housing would be owned and operated by local public housing authorities, effectively placing the decision of where to locate public housing in the hands of local authorities. This permitted many communities, particularly suburban ones, to avoid participating in the supply of low-income housing.
- To economize on the high cost of urban land, where the public housing was being placed, high-density construction was employed—adding another dimension to low-income housing concentration.
- Subsequent legislation added requirements that public housing be filled with extremely low-income residents.
- Inefficient management and undermaintenance resulted in physical deterioration and further ghettoization.
- Public housing authorities were subjected to increasingly strict requirements before they could screen out potentially troublesome tenants.

Schill and Wachter document the negative spillover effects of concentrations of public housing units through econometric analysis of Philadelphia data from 1950 to 1990. They conclude, decisively, that federal housing programs have promoted the concentration of low-income households in central cities—and with that concentration has come a complex set of social ills. In theory, housing certificates and vouchers need not create the concentrations of low-income residents, but they find that restrictions on the portability of those subsidies have made it difficult to move to suburban jurisdictions. They conclude that low-income housing placed a direct drain on city resources of 4.5 to 4.8 percent of their budgets during the 1980s—but the biggest drain on these resources came from the more indirect effects of concentrated poverty.

American housing policy over the last half century has been counterproductive to the health of American cities. We can ill afford such policies if we want to continue to have cities be the important birthplaces of the arts and the "melting pots" for the nation.

The Constitutional and Legal Context of Regionalization

Understanding the constitutional and legal environment in which cities and urban policy currently operate is necessary for determining the shape of a long-run urban agenda. Georgette Poindexter and Kenneth Shropshire, in their research on the Wharton Real Estate Center's urban project, report that our legal system historically has favored strong municipal government (Poindexter and Shropshire 1994). This is important because it has tended to strengthen the hand of suburban governments, particularly with respect to annexation by a central city. Few suburbanites now desire to append themselves to the urban core, and the law provides them strong defenses against having to do so. They are reviewing and assessing the legal potential for the redistribution of the economic burdens carried by large central cities.

This analysis is directly relevant to the likelihood of regionalization of fiscal responsibilities. For decades many have advocated this policy, but few have opted for it in the voting booth. On the whole, suburban residents do not visibly see the benefit to them of transferring some of their tax revenues to the central city. That cities are the caretakers of the area's poor, the providers of the infrastructure, the location of major cultural and sports activities, and the processors of many of the world's refugees does not visibly translate into the fiscal responsibilities of suburban residents. Transportation networks and environmental issues are transparently regional issues, which is why regional fiscal and organizational arrangements for them form readily. Without state constitutional changes, regionalization will not occur. Barring annexation, the Constitution and common law effectively require that regionalization of burden-sharing be approved by state or federal legislators or be imposed by state courts.

In the absence of voluntary agreements, numerous parties have petitioned their state courts to impose burden-sharing across regions or the entire state for both education and housing services for the poor. The Mount Laurel decisions in New Jersey regarding low-income housing are perhaps the most prominent example of court-ordered sharing of burdens. This set of decisions illustrates both the power and weaknesses of the courts. The New Jersey Supreme Court issued a clear ruling mandating that some type of burden-sharing result. The actual process by which the burden-sharing occurred was determined by the state legislature. The court established that communities in New Jersey have a constitutional obligation to provide low-income housing based on the needs of the region, not just on the needs of the individual community. A community cannot prevent the building of low-income housing through its zoning laws if it is not meeting its regional "fair share."

The successive Mount Laurel decisions are particularly interesting. In Mount Laurel I, the power of developing municipalities to erect barriers to lower-income residents was limited; in Mount Laurel II, the court articulated the constitutional duty of each community to provide a regional "fair share" of low-income housing; and in Mount Laurel III, and later cases, the court cedes power to the legislature to implement a regional planning agenda for the state. The legislative response was to establish regional contribution agreements. Municipalities can either "pay or play" for their fair share of the region's low-income housing—they can buy out a portion of their obligation by paying another municipality to build up to 50 percent of the paying municipality's fair share of low-income housing.

This "pay or play" implementation mechanism has resulted in almost no dispersion of the poor from New Jersey's central cities. Poindexter and Shropshire conclude that essentially a legal framework has been developed to establish a constitutionally permissible method of regional sharing of public responsibilities—but implementation has barely occurred. This suggests that state and federal governments will have to provide incentives for those outside the city to consider regionalization seriously. It is a policy advocated by urban experts for decades—but few jurisdictions have opted for it at the ballot box. Nevertheless, regionalism remains a vital part of a long-term urban agenda.

Short- and Long-Term Urban Strategies

For federal, state, and local governments and their constituents, there is a need for a short- and a long-term strategy. Short-term strategies involve a fiscal life line, a framework for long-term solution, and accepts the existing fiscal, political, and legal institutions as given. Long-term strategies generate some changes in these framework institutions which, in many cases, helped form the environment in which the costly socioeconomic phenomena associated with dense poverty concentrations arose. Fiscal constraints are severe at all levels of government, and fiscal restraint is a requirement for political acceptability and for sharpening the real choices. These recommended strategies are intended to be expenditure-neutral.

Short-Term Strategy

The imperatives of America's cities today dictate immediate action. If the large social risks in cities are to be mitigated, and if the huge private and public infrastructure investments in cities are not to be written off rapidly, then some actions must and can be taken now. Until long-term solutions can be implemented, a fiscal life line is needed. In the short term, new allocation formulas for the flow of funds to cities from the state and federal governments need to be instituted with two major elements:

- criteria that alter the standard per capita allocation to reflect the extra social, economic, and fiscal costs of the dense concentrations of the poor and immigrants, both of which arose from history and from past state and federal policies;
- criteria that allocate more resources to cities with efficiency-driven organizational structures—open to privatization, appropriate use of user fees, and evidence of political will power to maintain market wages and benefits for public employees.

An "urban audit report" is required to track the extra costs of the nationally-dictated urban burdens, and to "score" the efforts at efficiency. The national urban policy report should present those "scores." But, most importantly, these audits should drive the allocation of federal and state funding among cities. More dollars should flow to cities with larger shares of these burdens, and more dollars should flow to cities that are actively pursuing efficiency initiatives such as privatization, user fees, rigorous budgeting procedures, productivity incentives in the wage structure, and market-set wages and benefits. Less dollars should flow to cities with smaller burdens, and to those that are less efficient.

Long-Term Strategy

In the longer term, policies that reduce the concentration of the poor now living in central cities are needed. And regionalization is an important part of any long-run urban strategy. An econometric exploration (Summers and Brooks 1994) of the economic relationships between cities and their suburbs in the sixty largest metropolitan areas in the United States shows that there is indeed a complementarity in the employment and population pattern of suburbs and their central cities. Central-city employment growth results in suburban employment growth. A long-term strategy should include these elements:

- A macro policy that emphasizes high levels of employment is a necessary condition for reducing the numbers of people in the poverty group. But it is not a sufficient condition.
- The poverty population in central cities should be deconcentrated, as they are in Western European cities. To do this requires:

  — federal and state legislation to facilitate the formation of regional tax and service institutions,
  — a supportive judiciary to help bring this about,
  — some interim subsidization to encourage legislatures to see gain from regionalization, and

    —   changes in federal policies that inadvertently concentrate poverty within cities, or within neighborhoods in cities.

- The formulas for allocating resources to central cities described under the short-term agenda should be continued and refined.

Long-term changes will require state "report audits" as well as urban ones. States that implement legislation encouraging regionalization of tax and service delivery systems get higher grades—and relatively more federal funds.

Summary

It is the nation's responsibility to address the imperative need in America's large central cities. Urban America requires a separate agenda. Health-care reform, welfare reform, and a strong macroeconomy will all contribute to helping our cities—but they will not improve significantly without a strategic plan directed at cities, as the unifying entity.

The work of our research team on the development of an urban agenda yields some recommendations on the direction that needs to be taken. Sheer density, the concentrations of poverty of immigrants, heterogeneity, and existing legislative and legal structures underlie much of their difficulties. In the short term, we need to compensate cities for the extra burdens of the poor and the immigrants, and reward them for developing efficient services delivery structures. In the long term, we need to create incentives and mechanisms for deconcentrating the high-need groups, and change the legal and legislative framework to encourage regionalization and eliminate policies that contributed to poverty concentration.

This is an agenda for federal, state, big-city, and suburban governments and their stakeholders—and it could be a planning document for the governments and constituents of the newly emerging cities in metropolitan areas.

It is easy to assume that every new public agenda is a call for additional dollars. That is not the case here. *We are proposing an expenditure-neutral agenda.* The intergovernmental grants now going into city budgets should be reallocated, so that the cities bearing more national burdens receive *more*—and the others receive *less*. Similarly, the cities with more efficient structures should get *more*—and the others *less*. Many cities are now receiving large amounts of federal, state, local, and foundation funding to increase the autonomy of individual communities within cities—a path we believe operates against improving the city as a whole. We think, consistent with an expenditure-neutral approach, that these dollars would be better directed toward strengthening collaboration across neighborhoods to improve the city as a whole. Beyond this, only a firm expenditure-neutral approach will sharpen the real choices that have to be made—enforcing the tradeoffs between efficient and less efficient use of resources. Expenditure neutrality is harsh in the face of deteriorating urban environments, but the approach will enable city officials to make the necessary but politically difficult tradeoffs between efficient and inefficient resource usage.

In the long term, policies that encourage deconcentration of the high-need groups are vital, while maintaining the short-run policies that give municipalities incentives to become more efficient over time. Experience with what works may lead to increased allocation of revenues to cities in the long run. But additional revenues should only be provided if they are clearly helping to make the central city more livable, because only more livable cities will survive in competition with the new suburban cities.

We think there needs to be clear recognition that the responsibility for the fate of many large cities rests simultaneously with federal and state governments and with the cities themselves. Federal and state officials must acknowledge that cities are suffering under the strain of carrying a disproportionate amount of the nation's poverty-related responsibilities. And cities must restructure themselves so that they can become more appealing places in which to live and work.

References

Daniel, Kermit. 1994. "Bearing the Nation's Burdens: Immigration," Draft Working Paper, Wharton Real Estate Center, University of Pennsylvania, March.

Inman, Robert P., Steven G. Craig, and Thomas F. Luce. 1994. "The Fiscal Future for American Cities," Draft Working Paper, Wharton Real Estate Center, University of Pennsylvania, March.

La Londe, Robert, and Robert Topel. 1991. "Immigrants in the American Labor Market: Quality, Assimilation, and Distributional Effects." *American Economic Review* 81 (2).

Madden, Janice F. 1994. "Changes in the Distribution of Income and Earnings within U.S. Cities and Suburbs," Draft Working Paper, Wharton Real Estate Center, University of Pennsylvania, February.

Pack, Janet R. 1994. "Poverty and Urban Public Expenditures," Draft Working Paper, Wharton Real Estate Center, University of Pennsylvania, February.

Poindexter, Georgette, and Kenneth Shropshire. 1994. "The Constitutional and Legal Context of Regionalism," Draft Working Paper, Wharton Real Estate Center, University of Pennsylvania, February.

Schill, Michael H., and Susan M. Wachter. 1994. "The Spatial Bias of Federal

Housing Programs," Draft Working Paper, Wharton Real Estate Center, University of Pennsylvania, February.

Summers, Anita A., and Nancy Brooks. 1994. "The Interdependence of City and Suburban Employment Growth," Draft Working Paper, Wharton Real Estate Center, University of Pennsylvania, March.

U.S. General Accounting Office. 1992. *Impact of Undocumented Persons and Other Immigrants on Costs, Revenues and Services in Los Angeles County* (Washington, DC: GAO).

U.S. Department of Commerce. 1970, 1980, 1990. *Census of Population and Housing* (Washington, DC).

Acknowledgments

This paper, though written by me, draws directly on the work—in the form of preliminary drafts—of my colleagues at the Wharton Real Estate Center. We are in the midst of a several-year research project on the development of an urban agenda for America's large cities. Any errors of fact, omission or interpretation are, of course, my responsibility. The participants, and their subject areas, are:

Codirectors

Joseph Gyourko	Associate Professor of Finance and Real Estate (public and private urban investments)
Anita A. Summers	Emeritus Professor of Public Policy and Management, and Real Estate (city–suburban economic development links)

Participants

Steven G. Craig	Associate Professor of Economics, University of Houston (fiscal performance in Houston)
Robert P. Inman	Professor of Finance, Economics, Public Policy and Real Estate (political economy of urban fiscal performance)
Thomas F. Luce	Assistant Professor, H. H. Humphrey Institute of Public Affairs, University of Minnesota (fiscal performance in Minneapolis)
Janice F. Madden	Professor of Regional Science (measurement of urban poverty change)
Janet Rothenberg Pack	Professor of Public Policy and Management, City Planning, Real Estate (measurement of costs of poverty to cities)

Georgette Poindexter   Assistant Professor of Legal Studies and Real Estate (legal context of regionalization)

Michael Schill   Professor of Law and Real Estate (federal housing policies and the urban concentration of poverty)

Kenneth L. Shropshire   Associate Professor of Legal Studies and Real Estate (legal context of regionalization)

Susan M. Wachter   Associate Professor of Finance and Real Estate (federal housing policies and the urban concentration of poverty)

Commentary
The Public Sector

Helen F. Ladd

Anita Summers and her colleagues at the University of Pennsylvania are currently engaged in an important endeavor, namely, improving our understanding of the nature of the fiscal problems facing large American cities and developing policy proposals to alleviate them. The decision of the researchers to focus on large American cities, rather than on urban areas more generally, appropriately reflects the observation that jurisdictional boundaries matter for fiscal considerations and that within many of our large urban areas the large central city is typically far more fiscally stressed than suburban communities.

However, one must be careful to bear in mind that the fiscal institutions within which cities operate vary greatly from one city to another. For example, some cities have responsibility not just for standard municipal services such as street cleaning and public safety, but also for others such as education or social services that in other urban areas are provided by overlying counties or school districts. In addition, cities differ in their authority to levy taxes. Some cities, such as Boston, have access only to the property tax, while others, such as New York City, have access to income and sales taxes as well as to the property tax. As a result, some cities can easily capture tax revenue from commuters or shoppers while others cannot. This variation in fiscal responsibility and taxing authority greatly complicates both the analysis of city fiscal situations and the design of federal policy initiatives to assist fiscally overburdened cities.

Basic Themes and Policy Recommendations

The paper has two main themes that lead to three policy recommendations. The first theme is that, through no fault of their own, many large cities house disproportionate concentrations of groups (e.g. the poor and immigrants) who impose large fiscal burdens on the city. The second theme is that many large-city governments provide public services inefficiently. While the presence of high-demand groups and the fiscal burdens they impose are largely outside the control of local officials, the burdens associated with inefficient production are more controllable by city officials.

From these themes flow three recommendations for federal policy. The first two are short term in that they start from the existing concentration of poor people within cities and the existing set of intergovernmental fiscal arrangements. First, federal aid should be given to large cities specifically to compensate them for their fiscally burdensome populations. Aid should be formula-driven and targeted. Summers advocates an expenditure-neutral approach in which existing federal aid is redistributed from the undeserving cities to the most deserving cities. Second, federal aid should be used as an incentive to promote efficiency in the provision of urban public services. Not well spelled out, this proposal makes brief reference to the possibility of giving more aid to those cities which are open to privatization, make use of user fees, have centralized local governments, and have the political will to resist union pressures. The main longer-term policy recommendation involves decentralizing the poverty population. Possible mechanisms include incentives to facilitate the formation of regional tax and service institutions and changes in federal policies that inadvertently concentrate poverty within cities.

In my view, the fiscal problems associated with concentrations of population groups represent an important issue leading to a legitimate and compelling role for federal policy. Hence, they clearly deserve attention in an urban policy report. However, I am more skeptical about the inefficiency theme, especially as it is currently developed by Summers. In particular, I question the desirability of the type of federal role that Summers envisions to promote local government efficiency.

Concentration of Population Groups

Summers presents clear evidence of the concentration of the poor, and the rising concentration over time, in many cities. Noteworthy are the cities of Atlanta, Buffalo, Detroit, and New Orleans, where in 1989 more than 25 percent of the population was poor. Not mentioned, but relevant in terms of the political dimension, are the racial patterns of poverty in the various cities. In Atlanta, for example, the poverty rate was 35 percent for blacks, 31 for Hispanics, and only 10 for whites. Similar patterns emerge in Buffalo (38 percent for blacks, 52 for Hispanics, and 18 for whites) and in New Orleans (42.2 percent for blacks, 26.1 for Hispanics, and 11.8 for whites). In several cities, including Cincinnati, Cleveland, Miami, Milwaukee, Minneapolis, and New Orleans, more than two black residents out of five lived in poverty in 1989.

This concentration of poor households in cities primarily reflects past policies of other governments and governmental agencies. For example, Summers briefly alludes to the role of favorable federal taxation of home mortgages, VA lending policies, investment tax credits, and transportation policies that facilitated the movement of middle- and upper-income households to the suburbs, thereby increasing the concentration in the cities of the poor who stayed behind. Most fully developed in her paper is the role of public housing policy, which often channeled low-income households into high-rise buildings in the central city. Related, but not fully developed, is the role of local zoning powers that made it possible for suburbs to keep out all forms of low-income housing, not just public housing. Also alluded to, but deserving of more attention, are state policies on annexation that, for example, have made it easy for many southern and southwestern cities to expand their boundaries in order to keep many people in the city. One factor not mentioned at all emerges from the way the United States typically provides low-income housing. Most such housing is provided through a trickle-down process in which new housing is built for middle- and upper-income households, while low-income households move into the lower-priced old housing, most of which is located in the cities. Thus, the concentration of the poor in large cities largely reflects forces outside the control of city officials.

Summers argues, correctly in my view, that the concentration of poor people has significant adverse implications for the fiscal situation of cities. She provides three types of evidence. First are the direct spillover costs associated with public housing, which she reports average 4.5 to 4.8 percent of the local budget. Although I find this range plausible, I would like more information on how it was derived. Second, immigrants who tend to be concentrated in a few large cities impose a net cost on local governments because of the mismatch between the government level providing services and the ones receiving tax revenues. As elaborated by Summers, immigrants in Los Angeles pay disproportionate shares of their taxes to the state and federal government, while at the same time a disproportionate share of the services they receive is provided by local governments.

Third, she argues (based on Tables 4 and 5) that compared to smaller communities big cities spend more on poverty-related expenditure programs without full compensation in the form of intergovernmental aid. Unfortunately, the particular tables she presents are of limited usefulness since they do not account for the differing functional responsibilities of city governments. The limitations of this type of analysis are most clearly illustrated by the category of cities with populations greater than one million. As Summers notes, part of the problem is that this category is dominated by New York City, which is clearly unique not only in terms of its size but also in terms of the exceptionally broad range of its service responsibilities. These include paying half of the state and local share of Aid to Families with Dependent Children (AFDC) and Medicaid, providing social services typically provided elsewhere by county governments, and providing elementary and secondary education as well as a variety of other redistributive programs. Despite the fact that it represents only one of seven cities in this category, New York's population represents 38 percent of the population and its governmental spending accounts for a striking 68 percent of the governmental spending by all cities in this category.

Because New York City differs so much from other cities with populations over 1 million, it clearly should be examined separately. However, taking New York City out still leaves a heterogeneous set of six cities in this category. Of the six, three have separate overlying county governments that bear the bulk of the burden of providing social services. Consequently, the average share of spending on poverty programs in the six remaining cities is only 6.1 percent of total general expenditure, less than the average in the category of slightly smaller cities.

A more accurate sense of the poverty burden on city spending emerges from an analysis of the spending for cities grouped not by size but by their city–county status and their poverty rate. Janet Pack, the author of the background paper to which Summers refers, has done such an analysis with interesting and important findings (see Pack 1994: Table 7). She reports, for example, that within the set of separate cites (those without overlying counties), cities with high poverty rates spend about twice as much on poverty related functions (net of intergovernmental aid for those functions) per nonpoor person than do cities with low poverty rates. Similarly, within the group of city–counties, net spending on poverty-related functions in cities with mid-range poverty rates (about 20 percent) exceeds that in cities with low poverty rates by about 25 percent.[1]

In sum, I fully agree with the basic thrust of Summers's argument: characteristics of many large cities, such as high concentrations of poverty, which are outside the direct control of city officials can impose large fiscal burdens on cities and that a national urban policy report should monitor those trends and impacts. Moreover, I support the policy recommendation that federal aid be used to offset some of those burdens by directing aid to cities facing the greatest burdens, and, as a longer-run strategy, that the federal government should promote the deconcentration of poverty.

---

[1] Pack's sample size is too small to report similar results for joint city-county governments with high poverty rates.

The logical next task, but one beyond the scope of the work summarized by Summers, is to measure more precisely the fiscal effects of poverty and other city characteristics outside the control of city officials. Using multiple regression analysis, Pack (1994) finds that a 1 percentage point difference in the poverty rate leads to a 2 percent difference in total spending per capita. In our book on large cities, John Yinger and I also used multiple regression analysis to isolate the average effects of poverty and other characteristics such as population density on city spending in major central cities (Ladd and Yinger 1991). Our results indicated that a 1 percentage point difference in a city's poverty rate would on average lead to a 5.5 percent difference in the costs of providing an average level of police services and a 4.2 percent difference in the costs of providing fire services (ibid.: 84–86). Cities such as Newark, New York, and New Orleans with very high poverty rates face extremely high costs of providing public safety.

Several other issues arise in implementing the type of aid program recommended by Summers. City characteristics such as the poverty rate affect not only a city's expenditure need, but also its revenue-raising capacity. Hence, ultimately what is relevant is the balance between a city's per capita expenditure need, defined as how much the city would have to spend to provide an average level of public services, given its particular characteristics, and its capacity to raise revenue. Moreover, the huge variation across metropolitan areas in the fiscal responsibilities of cities complicates the design of a federal aid program. Ladd and Yinger (1991) argue that a federal aid program should direct aid to those cities with the largest gaps between their expenditure need and revenue-raising capacity, where such measures have been standardized for differing fiscal arrangements across cities or states. For example, according to the Ladd–Yinger proposal, federal aid should compensate a city like New York for the adverse fiscal effects of its social and economic characteristics (based on average impacts across all cities) but not for the fact that the city pays a portion of welfare and Medicaid spending. Otherwise the federal aid program would have the undesirable consequence of providing a disincentive for states to be generous to their large cities.

Governmental Inefficiency

Summers's second theme of governmental inefficiency is less well developed than her main theme; in my view, it has less clear implications for federal policy. The concept of inefficient provision is complex, and it is not obvious how the federal government would promote it even if promoting efficiency were deemed an appropriate role for the federal government.

Inefficiency has a variety of meanings in this context. First, it might mean inefficient production of a service such as street cleaning or protection from crime. For example, street cleaning would be inefficiently provided if a city used more workers than necessary to clean a mile of street, a situation that could plausibly occur in the public sector because of the lack of discipline from market competition. However, determining whether a city is cleaning its streets inefficiently is not a straightforward task. The simple approach of comparing the number of street cleaners per mile of city street with the comparable number in (presumably better managed) suburban districts is likely to generate misleading conclusions. How many workers are needed to achieve a given standard of cleanliness depends on how dirty the street is and the obstacles to cleaning it. In particular, a city street with a lot of trash and parked cars may take more workers and time to clean than a suburban street with less trash and more offstreet parking. A similar logic applies to police services. Because of their density of development and the presence of a large daytime population in the form of commuters, shoppers, and tourists, and demographic characteristics associated with high crime, large cities typically require more police officers per resident than small cities to achieve a similar level of protection. Thus, the challenge is to distinguish between the additional inputs justified by the characteristics of the city and those representing inefficiency and waste.

A second aspect of inefficiency or mismanagement could occur to the extent that city officials bargain ineffectively with city workers and consequently accept wage and fringe-benefit packages that are out of line with those offered by the private sector. Strongly entrenched municipal unions could lead to wages and fringe-benefit packages that exceed those in the private sector.

A third form refers to the mix and level of services. Summers suggests, for example, that the fact that many elected officials are elected by precinct rather than by city-wide districts may generate excessive spending as each official promotes the interests of his/her district rather than the interests of the city as a whole. However, in the context of heterogeneous cities, the meaning of the city's interests as a whole deserves close attention.

Inefficiency in one or more of these forms probably is common in many large cities, as it is likely to be in any large organization. The key question is whether the federal government could or should use its powers to promote local strategies that might increase efficiency. Summers mentions three types of local strategies: increased use of user charges, privatization, and more centralized forms of local government . Each of these (and particularly the last) raises complex issues that are beyond the scope of my comments. As an example of the problem, consider the call for privatization of public services. Privatization by itself need not increase efficiency. In general, its ability to do so depends on whether a sufficient number of firms are available to compete to generate the cost reducing benefits of market competition and whether the services can be sufficiently well defined so that the gains from privatization are not offset by the additional costs of monitoring service quality. Moreover, in the presence of large externalities, full privatization with no accompanying public subsidies would not produce efficient outcomes. Whether privatization increases efficiency will thus vary from service to service and from city to city. In light of these considerations, it is hard for me to imagine a federal policy or program designed to promote efficient provision of local public services within the existing structure of city governments.

An alternative and potentially more appropriate role for the federal government might be to promote structural changes within metropolitan areas. As emphasized by Summers and developed in some detail by others (e.g. Rusk 1993; Downs 1994), the current fragmentation of local governments leads to both inefficiencies and inequities in the provision of local services and to undesirable land-use patterns. Hence, more regionalization at the metropolitan level would be desirable. Although metropolitan governments are not politically feasible in most areas, other less ambitious approaches might be worth pursuing. One possibility is to create a federal incentive for regional institutions and regional decision-making. As elaborated by Anthony Downs (1994: 175–79), the federal government might consider consolidating into a single metropolitan grant all the grants it currently gives to separate state, local, and regional agencies operating in that area. To receive the federal funds, a regional agency would have to be set up to determine how to allocate the funds within the region, or alternatively a state agency would allocate the funds in line with federally specified principles. The goal would be to encourage regional planning, with appropriate attention to the needs and capacities of recipients throughout the metropolitan area.

This approach is fully consistent with Summers's call for federal and state legislation to facilitate the formation of regional tax and service institutions. Whether this approach or other federal incentives to promote regional decision-making at the metropolitan level are worth pursuing deserves further discussion and research.

References

Downs, Anthony. 1994. *New Visions for Metropolitan America* (Washington, DC: Brookings Institution).

Ladd, Helen F., and John Yinger. 1991. *America's Ailing Cities: Fiscal Health and the Design of Urban Policy*, updated edition (Baltimore: John Hopkins University Press).

Pack, Janet. 1994. "Poverty and Urban Public Expenditures." Draft, June. University of Pennsylvania.

Rusk, David. 1993. *Cities without Suburbs* (Washington, DC: Woodrow Wilson Center Press).

Urban Places and Spaces: Getting Serious about National Policy and Urban Physical Systems

Royce Hanson

The physical development of cities is a product of private invest-ment, public facilities, and regulations. With few exceptions (e.g. Wash-ington, DC, Oak Ridge, Tennessee) the facilities and regulations that influence and shape cities are those of state and local governments. Federal policy has had, however, a substantial marginal effect on the physical development of cities; in some instances federal policies have profoundly influenced the character of specific cities. For example, it is hard to imag-ine San Antonio without its River Walk, built with federal funds during the Great Depression. The suburbanization of America was spurred (if not spawned) by federal policies that facilitated mortgage financing of new homes and subsidized private automobile transportation.

Federal policy has not always done what its authors intended or expected it to do. In some cases it has fallen short, due to failures in design, financing, or execution. In other cases, it has had unintended or at least unexpected physical consequences for cities. This article is concerned with how national policy should address concerns related to urban physical sys-tems and their impact on other important functions cities perform in the national economy. It provides a historical interpretation of federal policies affecting the urban physical system, suggests a rationale for federal activity, and offers ideas for guiding policy in an era of limited national resources.

I.

Federal policies affecting urban physical systems fall into two broad categories: those explicitly designed to affect the form or process of urban development and facilities; and those designed to deal with specific "national" problems such as interstate transportation, environmental quality, or even national defense, but because of their physical incidence and scale have a profound effect on the way in which cities develop and function. The latter may be considered to provide a set of implied urban policies, even though their authors may not have envisioned them in that way.

Federal involvement in urban development following World War II had taken several forms. FHA home financing, urban renewal, and federal assistance for urban and regional planning greatly influenced the pattern and character of post-war urban development and redevelopment. The Department of Housing and Urban Development (HUD), which was created as a cabinet agency in 1965 was envisioned by its advocates as the federal agency that would provide a focus for explicit federal policies affecting cities and offer inspired leadership to make America's cities exemplars of humane prosperity, helping to transform them as the Department of Agriculture had helped rural America. The UD in HUD was in the eyes of its inventors the mission that would distinguish the new Department of Housing and Urban Development from its predecessor, the Housing and Home Finance Agency.

By the mid 1960s, programs in urban open space and mass transportation had been added to HUD's jurisdiction, although they were later transferred to other cabinet departments where they were presumed to have greater functional affinity (but lower bureaucratic priority). In addition, the interstate highway system was beginning to have a massive impact on the urban landscape. The euphoria for federal intervention in the urban physical system reached its apogee in the 1966 Housing and Urban Redevelopment Act, with the Model Cities program to address the needs of inner city redevelopment and Section 701g, which promoted regional planning through councils of governments.

Although enthusiasm for categorical federal involvement dimmed with the advent of the Nixon administration, federal aid continued to flow in increasing amounts until the middle of the Carter administration. Concern about forecasts of rapid urban growth produced the New Communities Development and National Urban Growth Policy Act of 1970. The authors of this ambitious legislation envisioned as many as one hundred planned new towns to absorb the expected urban population explosion of the next generation. The baby bust, underfunding, the lack of commitment of the administration and frequent changes in leadership, and rampant inflation in the ensuing decade (among other conceptual and practical defects) consigned the new communities portion of the program to an interesting but unsuccessful experiment (U.S. Department of Housing and Urban Development 1984). The urban policy mandate of the 1970 act has been, for the most part, an empty exercise. The biennial reports have been late, vague, self-serving, and fortunately obscure. There is no evidence that they have had any discernable effect on federal policy, much less on actual urban development.

The Nixon administration moved away from direct federal substantive concern with cities, replacing as many categorical grants as possible with block grants and revenue sharing. Although immensely popular with local officials, revenue sharing eventually was cashiered by the Reagan administration. The Community Development Block Grant became the principal HUD program that addressed urban physical conditions. This program has, without question, done much good, particularly in funding neighborhood projects and supporting community organizations. On occasion, however, it has degenerated into an exercise in distributive politics for the interest groups participating in the process of budgeting the federal funds.

The Carter administration's principal urban initiative, the Urban Development Action Grant (UDAG), provided an infusion of federal cash to leverage joint public/private projects in business and commercial districts. The objectives of the program were to attract private investment to locations it would otherwise avoid for business or bureaucratic reasons, speed up the development process, reduce its cost, and provide jobs for inner-city workers. While the wisdom and economic viability of some of the central city development it fostered can be questioned, the UDAG program demonstrated that a relatively small amount of federal financial participation can leverage substantial local public and private investment in cities and that it is possible to focus such investments in specific locations. UDAG, however, also expired during the Bush administration's continuation of the divestiture of urban programs, which was part of an explicit strategy of disowning federal responsibility for the physical condition of cities.

The greatest effects of federal policy on the urban physical environment have come not from HUD programs but other national policies that support infrastructure, regulate the environment, and stimulate real estate investment. The federal highway program has been one of the most powerful forces shaping the physical form and affecting the functionality of American cities. It has accommodated the metropolitan dispersion of population and economic activity. The improved mobility it offered fostered new concepts in retailing, such as the shopping mall. It facilitated the decentralization of employment and the general reorganization of metropolitan land use, making it feasible for people to live long distances from work. Federal assistance for rapid rail transit has made it possible to intensify development in the vicinity of some transit stations and has encouraged the selective reintroduction of mixed residential and business uses. At other locations vast parking areas and intermodal transfer facilities have had to be provided to serve commuters. But in spite of their sometimes spectacular effects on specific sites in the region, federal mass transit programs have had only a marginal effect on the overall patterns of metropolitan growth and development.

Federal river and harbor projects built by the Corps of Engineers and other federal agencies, such as the Tennessee Valley Authority, have also affected development patterns. Federally financed levees and other flood control projects have opened former flood plains to intensive urbanization. In some cases, they have also produced worse downstream floods, causing the depreciation of values and the deterioration of housing and commercial districts in the endangered zones. Waterways and harbor projects have undoubtedly produced a redistribution of economic activity among the new port cities created by the expanded system of water transportation.

In the last generation, environmental policies designed to reduce water and air pollution and to clean up or dispose of land pollution and solid waste have begun to impact on the patterns and densities of urban development. In its various permutations, the Clean Water Act has generally allowed cities and suburbs to continue to accommodate urban growth, albeit at an increased cost for wastewater collection and treatment. The protection of estuaries and wetlands from development has been a product of both specific federal regulations and general environmental concern stimulated by the act. New regulations dealing with nonpoint sources of pollution could begin to bite harder at the design of new development, requiring greater on-site management of storm water. They will also impose greater costs on cities to retrofit areas that were developed under less rigorous regulatory regimes to collect and treat storm runoff.

The Clean Air Act has continuously threatened to generate radical changes in land use patterns, but thus far has not delivered on the threats as emissions technologies have lagged behind political ambitions for cleaner air. The Superfund program for cleaning up hazardous waste sites has produced a list of urban areas subject to its strictures. Neighborhoods honored as Superfund sites tend to suffer property devaluation. The procedural sluggishness of the Superfund process tends to place the sites and the communities in their vicinity in environmental purgatory for extended periods of time, which produces difficulty in addressing their other physical and social needs until the cleanup has been completed.

By far the most pervasive effect of national environmental policies has been the support they have provided for the no-growth and slow-growth movements in cities and suburbs. The requirement of environmental impact statements for major federally funded projects has been a potent tool in challenging the location, density, and operational characteristics of many infrastructure projects, usually resulting in delays and increases in cost. The process, however, has occasionally led to improvements in design and selection of less environmentally damaging or costly alternatives.

At a minimum, federal environmental policies have led to much greater sophistication in urban and regional planning. Almost all major cities, and some states, now commonly consider the effects of proposed developments on the environment. Local governments have begun to resist absorbing the costs of the environmental externalities caused by development and are not only regulating against it, but often assessing impact fees to cover their costs. The effect of such rules has been mixed, sometimes only increasing private prices, but in many cases it has produced better development and reduced public costs.

Federal fiscal and monetary policies have had an enormous effect on urban development patterns. Combined with lower interest rates during the post-war generation, the interest deduction on home mortgages put the suburbs within reach of the middle class and much of the working class. Depreciation schedules for commercial real estate investments have varied over the last forty years, but when they have been generous, they have stimulated investment—often overinvestment—in apartment and office buildings. There is a strong relationship between the ending of accelerated depreciation for office construction in the 1986 Tax Reform Act and the collapse of the building boom. Similarly, deregulation of the savings and loan industry resulted in a mass migration of capital into speculative real estate ventures. This bubble of overinvestment produced a glut of office and apartment construction that changed the skyline of a number of cities, and left a legacy of vacant space and declining property values when it burst.

Finally, federal fiscal policy affects urban development through the tax exemption provided for municipal bonds. This allows municipal and school-system obligations to be issued at lower rates of interest, stretching their purchasing power for public infrastructure and land acquisitions. It has also allowed various forms of creative financing for urban development projects, such as industrial development bonds, to be used as subsidies for private development.

Only a small fraction of the federal policies that have influenced the physical form and character of cities was explicitly designed to do so. Policies that were designed primarily for other objectives, such as increasing intercity and interstate mobility and commerce, stimulating home ownership, or cleaning up the environment, have had a greater impact on the physical form and condition of the city than those deliberately designed to do so. Ironically, the most potent federal tools in shaping cities have been beyond the jurisdiction of the cabinet department with an explicit urban mission. In HUD itself, urban development policy has been driven toward the margin by jurisdictional and fiscal attrition. HUD's most substantial program remains public housing, and it is a deeply flawed instrument with which to lead urban development policy.

Table 1

Share of Metropolitan Employment in Six Major Urban Areas, 1976–1986

	1976	1986
Atlanta	18.1	11.9
Dallas	10.5	7.6
Houston	27.6	17.4
Phoenix	11.5	8.2
San Diego	17.6	12.6
San Francisco	16.8	13.9

Source: Wharton Real Estate Center, Urban Decentralization Project, 1989

II.

To the extent that there has been an explicit federal policy directed toward the physical environment of cities, it has been designed to revitalize the monocentric industrial city. It has been premised on the economic centrality of the central business district and the radial transportation patterns that supported it. The city, for the most part, was seen as the center of a metropolitan settlement and a hinterland that was progressively less densely settled. Accordingly, the agenda for urban policy was set primarily by central city mayors and congressional delegations.

At the same time, however, other, more powerful federal policies worked against the central cities in concert with pervasive demographic and economic trends that favored urban decentralization. After the 1970 congressional redistricting, the suburbs gained political ascendancy in national terms, although the constituency of the Democratic party remained heavily skewed toward older central cities. By the time of the Carter administration, in spite of strong efforts by the president and his HUD secretaries to maintain and even strengthen the emphasis on the central city, general support for that approach had already dissipated in Congress. The Reagan and Bush administrations, with a largely suburban constituency, essentially disavowed having an urban policy that was place-conscious, and disassembled as much of the prior system as possible.

It is time to reassess the role of federal policy in the urban physical system. Much has changed in urban America. Urban space has continued to be transformed. The restructuring of the national economy in the last two decades has led to an ever greater dispersion of urban housing and employment. It is now rare for a central business district (CBD) to contain

Table 2

Employment in the Dallas-Fort Worth Metropolitan Region
Percent by Geographic Sector, 1983 and 1987

	1983	1987
Dallas CBD	8.87	7.54
Fort Worth CBD	2.83	2.09
City of Dallas	47.20	44.13
City of Fort Worth	13.09	12.07
Dallas County	71.69	69.90
Tarrant County	25.14	25.31
four suburban counties	3.17	4.79

Source: Waddell and Shukla, "Employment Dynamics, Spatial Restructuring, and the Business Cycle," *Geographical Analysis* 25:47 (1993).

more than a sixth of an important urban region's employment or income generation. Table 1 shows the decline in economic significance of six central business districts as a proportion of total metropolitan employment. Table 2 contains data on the distribution of employment in one of these areas, Dallas-Fort Worth, for the four-year period from 1983 to 1987. It shows that even in such a short time span, the CBDs and one of the central cities experienced significant declines in employment compared to the suburban areas.

As a consequence of the rapid dispersion of employment, "polycentric" is no longer an adequate description of the extent of dispersion of economic activity in many urban regions. Figure 1 illustrates this phenomenon, again using the Dallas–Fort Worth region where the CBDs have become but two of several major employment centers. There, the 84 largest employment sites—one percent of the total number of such sites—contain only a third of the total metropolitan employment. An additional third is distributed in the 356 sites, but the remaining third is strewn across the metropolitan landscape in 7,990 smaller sites (Waddell and Shukla 1993).

Another important change that has taken place is that a number of the largest cities in the nation in 1970 have been displaced by other cities that were in a second tier of population twenty years ago. Many of the cities that long dominated American impressions of what was once urban have seen their economies shift from being strong centers of manufacturing employment to become major and more diversified service centers. At the same time, many of them, such as Cleveland, Philadelphia, and De-

Figure 1

Distribution of Employment in the
Dallas–Fort Worth Metropolitan Region

Source: Waddell and Shukla (1993).

troit, have lost large portions of their populations in absolute terms as well as a proportion of the metropolitan population.

The economic trends that have changed both the functions and the forms of major cities have also produced a new system or hierarchy of cities that is international in scope. Some cities have become nerve centers of the new international economy built around the transactions of multinational corporations and the international specialization of labor. The development of rapid international transportation and instantaneous communication has facilitated the separation of manufacturing and routine services from headquarters and research centers. Many cities are undergoing a process of simultaneous diversification of their economies and increased spatial specialization of their economic and social functions. A new hierarchy of cities has emerged, with a few functioning as command and control centers in the international economy and the remaining cities performing subordinate and specialized functions (Noyelle and Stanback 1983; Hanson 1983).

III.

The implications of this transformation of the urban system and its consequences for the use of urban space demand a fundamental revision—reinvention, to use a word currently in vogue—of federal urban policy. The first step is to come to terms with just what the national interest is in the physical networks, facilities, capital stock, and spaces of urban regions. Not all of the physical system of every city is of national concern. In our federal system, a definition of national interest requires more than the mere presence of a problem somewhere in the nation. It requires a nationally shared interest in it and a judgment that intervention by the national government is an appropriate use of its power and resources.

In this light, I argue that there is a national interest in four aspects of the urban physical system:

1. The elements of national infrastructure that support the urban base for U.S participation in an advanced international economy.

2. The facilities and environment that attract and sustain the institutional capacity needed to provide world leadership in value added through knowledge in products and services produced in American cities.

3. The regional planning and governance capacity to guide the development of a physical environment that allows American cities to compete successfully as the locations of the leading sectors of the world economy.

4. Investments in physical systems and regulatory policies that support domestic social policies.

For the foreseeable future, federal resources will be scarce. We cannot provide an indiscriminate array of fiscal transfers for a wide set of undeniable needs for local public works. Federal infrastructure investments should be deployed where a substantial return should be expected in the form of private investments and increased gross domestic product. This strategy suggests that the level and character of investment in a specific region should be greatly influenced by the function that it provides in the system of cities. Thus, the national government should give its highest priority to investments in facilities that help create an integrated and efficient national urban system that can advance national competitiveness.

The development of an advanced computing/telecommunications network connecting the system of cities and their principal public and private institutions is essential if the United States is to remain the world's economic leader. The actual federal investment in the information superhighway and its on-ramps will be minuscule compared with the amount of private investment needed to make the basic system a reality. The federal government should be involved, however, both through investments and regulations, to ensure that the system achieves its promise for the commonwealth by providing functioning access to every household and workplace. Leveraged investments by the federal government can help cities seize the comparative advantage that their informatization will give them in global economic competition. Federal leverage and leadership can also be critical in helping cities adapt to the new urban forms that will function more effectively in an information age.

There clearly is a national interest in the continuing development and maintenance of a high-quality intercity transportation system and in building international transportation centers. This suggests a high national value in the expansion of international airports and other regional transportation terminals that serve international trade and commerce. Resource constraints suggest that federal investments in port facilities, unlike the ubiquitous telecommunications system, must be strategically targeted to those urban areas with the highest potential for developing into strong international centers. Much of the transportation system will continue to require federal financial participation, coordination, and guidance, although most of it will be produced through state and local governments, with extensive private sector participation.

From a national policy perspective, it makes sense to increase the relative contribution of the federal government to building and maintaining these large-scale facilities that are part of an efficient national system and reduce the federal role in intracity transportation operations and maintenance. This national system of infrastructure is necessary for an advanced economy to function and it cannot be provided or effectively coordinated by either state and local government or the private sector. One way to offset the withdrawal of direct financial assistance to construction of urban infrastructure that has only tangential national significance would be instead to provide funding for the costs of local compliance with the substantive and procedural federal mandates that must followed in producing or operating local public facilities.

In addition to the communications and transportation facilities that are essential to a functioning national urban system, American cities need to be attractive places for the leading industries of a knowledge-based economy to locate and grow. One important component of this new economy's infrastructure is the facilities and amenities that sustain the research and development capacity in urban areas. The universities, medical centers, research institutes, and corporate research centers are the basic industries of the information age, much as steel and energy were basic to the industrial and automotive ages. As the Silicon Valley, Route 128 in the Boston area, the North Carolina Research Triangle, and the Telecom Corridor in Dallas demonstrate, these activities tend to be geographically clustered in high-amenity urban settings. The "mother ship" universities and high technology firms, their suppliers, and progeny also occupy vast amounts of urban space. Similarly, there is an increasing concentration of medical facilities in regional centers, such as Houston and Cleveland. Health is the basic industry of cities such as Rochester, Minnesota, and is now by far the largest single employer in a number of major urban regions. Health and research and development industries have a number of unique needs for infrastructure and amenities, as well as a wide range of high-quality urban services.

The federal interest in the urban environment of these leading industries has several elements. First of all, many of these organizations are footloose and highly conscious of the effect of environmental quality, educational opportunities, and the propinquity similar institutions have on their ability to attract and retain key staff, who are even more footloose than their employers. Another is in the strategic location and support of federal research centers and laboratories so that they (some with changed missions) can interact efficiently with universities and other research institutions. A third interest is in adequately funding basic research as well as providing the legal framework that facilitates diffusion of innovation.

The national government's interest in enhancement of national competitiveness must encompass an understanding that competitiveness involves not only a well-trained and resilient labor force, a stable economy, and a competent government, but attractive urban locations for the most sought after and footloose industries in the world. The federal interest in urban form and functionality is in assisting cities to become attractive and hospitable locations for the creation of new enterprises and the attraction of the most knowledge-intensive components of all industries. This suggests a value in reconfiguring federal support for urban planning and development to reorient it from its current disjointed focus on specific functions, such as surface transportation and air quality, to encouraging the building of greater capacity at the state and regional levels for comprehensive and strategic planning and management of urban development.

Building regional planning and governance capacity will involve more than the traditional federal approaches of grants in aid to regional planning agencies or regulations that require a minimum level of cooperative planning for eligibility for federal grants for sewage treatment plants and transportation facilities. These measures, while far more extensive than they would ever have been without the federal carrots and sticks, continue to fall well short of the need for effective management of urban development. To return to the argument that federal investments are entitled to a return, one such return on federal investment in nation-serving infrastructure should be the development of effective regional systems for the governance of development. The stakes are too high and the costs too great for the federal government to invest enormous sums in national infrastructure elements (e.g. international airports, research and development institutes, or highway and port facilities) not to demand that the states receiving these benefits organize their regional governance systems in ways that enable them to function effectively and capitalize on the investment. This does not require a common federal formula, but rather a flexible and individualized approach to providing federal infrastructure funding in a consolidated form to a state or region *if it can demonstrate that it has the planning and governance capacity to meet federal performance standards and has a strategy for improving the quality of its urban environment to promote, attract, and retain investment in the growth sectors of the economy.*

Environmental quality is now addressed through a battery of separate federal policies. Some of them, such as the Clean Water Act, involve the provision of new infrastructure such as wastewater treatment plants and improvements to sewer systems. The Safe Drinking Water Act imposes high standards (and costs) on municipal water systems. The Clean Air Act potentially has far-reaching implications for the physical form of cities as they try to meet mandated air quality standards. Technological improvements in control of emissions may reduce air pollution over the long run and thereby reduce pressure on development and transportation policies to reduce transportation-related pollution. It appears unlikely, however, that technology alone can adequately address the air-quality problems of most large urban areas. To the extent that it cannot and the attainment standards are not relaxed by Congress, cities will need to undertake development policies that internalize the costs of pollution. This will require a combination of fuel and parking taxes, road tolls and high-occupancy vehicle lanes, stricter emissions standards, and other measures to induce greater fuel efficiency and fewer trips. This, in turn, will increase the demand for new patterns of land use that allow shorter trips and greater use of the most efficient transportation modes, including walking, bicycling, pooling, paratransit, and buses. Such measures will also encourage the growth of telecommuting by the growing cadre of information workers. It is unlikely, however, that such measures will result in reductions of emissions sufficient to meet the federal standards for many cities.

The daunting task of urban planning in the next generation is to at last find means of reconciling the conflicting trends of information and other technologies that support even greater dispersion, spatial specialization, and lower densities than were spawned by the ubiquitous automobile, and environmental interests that tend to favor more compact forms of development, greater propinquity between home and work, and higher densities. This will entail fostering a considerable amount of experimentation in development patterns. Some experiments are likely to fail in an environmental sense even if they are market successes. And some environmental successes may be market failures. Whether successes or failures, they will entail a considerable enrichment of publicly and privately produced urban amenities and other collective goods imposing high costs on local governments. This underscores the need for improvements in the planning and governance capacities of urban regions, not to mention their fiscal capacities. It also reinforces the idea that the costs of complying with federal mandates regarding the physical systems of urban areas should be funded by the federal government.

In many tragic respects, federal policy affecting urban physical systems has been at odds with federal domestic social policy. For over a generation, national policy has discouraged racial segregation and discrimination, and has sought various means of alleviating poverty, which is concentrated in inner-city neighborhoods. At the same time, federal policy has maintained a deteriorating stock of public housing in much of which social pathologies have festered.

This administration appears to be reaching a turning point in federal public housing policy. It has begun to settle a number of lawsuits focused on the concentration of minorities in large scale projects and appears open to strategies designed to disperse the housing of poor families throughout metropolitan areas. This shift in policy would recognize research findings that the ghettoization of public housing has contributed to the spatial mismatch of low-income workers and jobs in major metropolitan area (Kain 1992; Ihlenfeldt and Sjoquist 1989). Limited experiments, such as the Gautreaux project in Chicago, suggest that relocation of poor households to better neighborhoods is in itself an important instrument in improving living standards and encouraging public housing recipients to succeed in the labor force (Popkin et al. 1993). Other research suggests that residential location in a non-poor neighborhood has a greater effect than any other factor on the likelihood of economic advancement for poor households (Jargowsky 1991, 1994).

High concentrations of public housing contributes to the spiral of urban decline in the neighborhoods within which it has been located. Scattered site housing does not appear to have such an effect. While desegregation of the broad housing market is beginning to be seen in the substantial relocation of the black middle class to the suburbs, the limited availability of housing vouchers has limited suburban access for poorer households. One consequence of improved housing opportunity for the better-off and economic confinement for the poor has been the intensification of their plight by creating neighborhoods in which there is little social support and even less economic opportunity (Wilson 1987).

An overhaul of federal housing policy should include strategies for the replacement of large-scale, largely segregated projects with widely dispersed, small-scale public housing developments and the broad, preferred use of vouchers throughout a metropolitan area. Eligibility for federal housing assistance should require state and local policies designed to avoid concentrations of poor families and the existence of development regulations that are inclusive of low- and moderate-income housing units. The experience of New Jersey, which has tried to overcome exclusive zoning practices, is not encouraging. Resistance to changing land use practices is strong and local governments have been inventive in avoiding compliance. While it would be foolish to contend that social behavior and economic success are determined by the physical environment of one's neighborhood, experience suggests that it materially contributes to improvement. Thus, to the extent that poverty and its related social problems operate as a drag on the national welfare, and to the extent that changing the physical environment affects the extent and persistence of those problems, the national government has an interest in so structuring its policies and programs that affect the physical environment to promote its social objectives. The national interest in equality of opportunity can also be supported by efforts to improve the physical quality of urban neighborhoods through programs designed to revitalize, maintain, and improve property values through more effective management of infrastructure and facilities. Potentially, one of the most potent federal policies affecting the vitality of neighborhoods is the Community Reinvestment Act and the Mortgage Disclosure Act, which require banks to reinvest in the communities from which they draw their deposits. If rigorously enforced, these policies can help staunch the outflow of capital from neighborhoods where structures are still sound and where middle-class families are willing to invest and improve their properties.

Policies that promote private investment in homes and businesses in older urban neighborhoods hold more promise for revitalization and reversal of decay than do programs such as Empowerment and Enterprise Zones. The former simply provide loans for projects that have bankable merit. They create net value for both the private investors and for the city. The latter offer inducements—usually in the form of federal and local tax expenditures—that tend merely to shift investments from one part of the city's geography to another, generating small net benefits, if any.

While the measures discussed above are not sufficient by themselves to prevent urban decline, improving private property values and maintaining the quality of the infrastructure system and public spaces and places serving a neighborhood are necessary elements for its stability. For the local government, maintenance of its physical stock is a central budget issue because it affects the property tax base. And local fiscal capacity to address issues such as neighborhood maintenance of infrastructure and public space is tied inexorably to the costs involved in participating in mandated and discretionary infrastructure programs that serve national as well as local interests. Thus, while the national government does not have a direct role in the fate of specific neighborhoods in most cities, its policies have a profound indirect effect on them.

IV.

The approach to federal urban policy respecting urban physical systems that I have advanced here is different from past policies in three fundamental ways. First, it proceeds from a different vision of the city as part of a national urban system, in which individual cities have distinct functions that require tailored strategies of physical and economic development. Second, it takes a selective approach to direct federal involvement in the physical city that is limited to areas of clear national interest and projects or programs that advance national economic objectives. Third, it argues that when federal resources are *invested* in urban development, there should be a return to the national interest.

It is not likely that federal policy will be the dominant influence on how cities develop. Federal policy could, however, be critical to how well they function as an urban system that defines the spatial economy of the country. It also can exert considerable leverage on the character of urban space through the infrastructure system it assists in building, the approach it takes to housing assistance to the poor, and the regulations it imposes on local governments, banks, and other private-sector activities such as home mortgages, taxes, and interest rates. One can only imagine the effect on housing segregation if mortgage interest deductions were available only for homes in jurisdictions that pursued inclusive zoning and housing policies.

Resources at the federal and local levels will be limited for the foreseeable future. There is diversity in the functions performed by different cities as well as within them. There are great differences in the ability to estimate the return on a federal investment in an international airport or an interstate highway system and in preserving the quality of an in-town neighborhood. Given these uncertainties in this vast and diverse nation, my argument is that we still must do the best we can. Cities are important. They are where an advanced economy happens. Their physical form and systems affect the vitality of the economy. They can be made more attractive as places for advanced economic activity by purposeful public action. The federal government should define, to the best of its ability, the infrastructure and other physical systems that are most important to the achievement of national objectives. It should then marshal its resources and powers in ways that give it the greatest return on its investment.

References

Hanson, Royce (ed.) 1983. *Rethinking National Urban Policy: Urban Policy in an Advanced Economy* (Washington, DC: National Academy Press).

Ihlenfeldt, Keith, and David L. Sjoquist. 1989. "Job Accessibility and Racial Differences in Youth Employment Rates," *American Economic Review* 80: 267–76.

Jargowsky, Paul A. 1991. *Ghetto Poverty: The Neighborhood Distribution Framework* (Cambridge: Harvard University, Ph.D. dissertation).

_____. 1994. "Ghetto Poverty among Blacks in the 1980s," *Journal of Policy Analysis and Management* 13: 288–310.

Kain, John F. 1992. "The Spatial Mismatch Hypothesis: Three Decades Later," *Housing Policy Debate* 3: 371–460 (Washington, DC: Fannie Mae Office of Housing Policy Research).

Noyelle, Thierry L., and Thomas M. Stanback, Jr. 1983. *Economic Transformation of American Cities* (Totowa: Allanheld and Rowman).

Popkin, Susan J., James E. Rosenbaum, and Patricia M. Meaden. 1993. "Labor Market Experiences of Low-Income Black Women in Middle-Class Suburbs: Evidence from a Survey of Gautreaux Program Participants," *Journal of Policy Analysis and Management* 12: 556–573.

U.S. Department of Housing and Urban Development, Office of Policy Development and Research. 1984. *An Evaluation of the Federal New Communities Program* (Washington, DC).

Waddell, Paul, and Vibhooti Shukla. 1993. "Employment Dynamics, Spatial Restructuring and the Business Cycle," *Geographical Analysis* 25: 35–52.

Wilson, William J. 1987. *The Truly Disadvantaged: The Inner City, The Underclass, and Public Policy* (Chicago: University of Chicago Press).

Commentary

Urban Places and Spaces

Charles J. Orlebeke

Royce Hanson has chronicled a history of frustration in the nation's attempts since the 1960s to fashion a coherent urban policy aimed at developing the physical systems of cities and metropolitan regions. On the one hand, "explicit" urban programs—mainly consisting of the program array administered over the years by the Department of Housing and Urban Development—have with rare exceptions had scattered and marginal impacts on urban systems, doing some good here and there, to be sure, but also some real harm as with highrise public housing in big cities. On the other hand, non-urban federal policies that address "national problems"—examples cited are interstate transportation, environmental problems, and national defense—have had much larger urban impacts although they were put forward without cities in mind and therefore with little understanding of their consequences.

For the future, "getting serious," according to Hanson, should involve selective investment-driven federal policies that recognize both the limits of federal resources and the opportunities for leveraging investments that bring national benefits. The general principles he would apply in guiding such investment decisions make good sense. The difficulty, I believe, lies in profound structural and political obstacles to federal *implementation* of a coherent set of policies aimed at particular cities and regions.

History is certainly not encouraging. As Hanson notes, the Department of Housing and Urban Development, launched with much rhetorical fanfare in 1965, fell far short of its promise. But I would add to Hanson's historical account that HUD's weakness as an effective lever of federal development policy was quite quickly recognized in the early

1970s. President Richard Nixon proposed as part of a complete revamping of federal domestic agencies a Department of Community Development, a kind of super-HUD that would include highways and transit from the Department of Transportation, rural development from Agriculture, and economic development from Commerce (Domestic Council 1971). The proposal landed with a thud in a hostile Congress and soon sank from view. President Jimmy Carter, however, revived the idea of sweeping executive reorganization. A special Office of Management and Budget task force worked for eighteen months and came up with a plan with some similarities to Nixon's; it also included a "super HUD" called the Department of Development Assistance, although the proposal left out the transportation components. The OMB plan was to be a highlight of Carter's 1980 State of the Union message, but did not survive the political scrutiny of the White House staff (Stanfield 1979).

The reason these two proposals—and their political fate—is interesting is that they would have positioned the federal government to (in Hanson's terms) "get serious about national policy and urban physical systems." A super-HUD could have put in the same powerful agency both the planning capacity and the budgetary leverage to contain metropolitan sprawl, channel investment into central cities, and pursue social goals of racial and economic integration. It could also have facilitated the sort of targeted/high-payoff investments in infrastructure and institutions advocated by Hanson.

Alas, it was not to be. Although a super-HUD made sense to urban policy specialists (and government reorganization advocates), it had little appeal to hardly anyone else. The cabinet departments that would have been obliterated did not like it; the Congressional committees that would have lost control over cherished programs did not like it; even the urban lobby that might have benefited saw too much risk in upsetting their existing programmatic and political networks.

Another relevant bit of history is the urban policy report of President Carter's Commission for a National Agenda for the Eighties, a prestigious body created by Carter to set an agenda for a hoped-for second term. In an embarrassing rejection of Carter's first-term urban policy initiatives, the commission advised against spending (and wasting) large sums of federal money on place-oriented strategies because powerful market forces and population shifts are too overwhelming to be affected much by deliberate federal action. Rather, the federal government should focus its efforts and resources on education, job training, and relocation of people to places where the economy is growing. In the classic "people versus place" urban policy debate, it was people who mattered (President's Commission 1980).

Carter repudiated his commission's analysis and recommendations, but they helped provide the underpinning for the non-urban (many would say anti-urban) urban policy of Ronald Reagan and George Bush, who stressed general economic growth as the centerpiece of domestic policy. A mobile population would seek economic opportunity wherever they could find it—"vote with their feet," as Reagan put it. As for federal investments in physical systems, these should flow (in reduced amounts) to state governments, which would be primarily responsible for any place-oriented strategies that might be devised.

President Bill Clinton's domestic policy is also notably non-place-oriented. His main initiatives, health care reform and welfare reform, are aimed squarely at the people side of the policy equation. For cities, Clinton has promised 100,000 police to fight crime—an unusual federal incursion into a basic municipal service. The only physical development initiative of any size is Empowerment Zones, but they will be tried in only six cities. I agree with Hanson that the zones may "tend to merely shift benefits from one part of the city's geography to another, generating small net benefits, if any."

In presenting his own rationale for national development policy, Hanson seeks to put the "national" back firmly into national urban policy. The federal treasury can no longer stand the cost of broad-based urban assistance programs; therefore, the federal government must be selective, investing only in high-pay-off facilities and institutions that will clearly advance the national economy and strengthen the U.S. position in a highly competitive world economy. These selective investments will be guided by an understanding of individual cities and regions that have "distinct functions" in a "national urban system." The places that offer the highest potential for leveraging the national investment will benefit the most. However, Hanson does not favor merely handing the money over; he would also require "the development of effective regional systems for the governance of development."

Hanson's emphasis on limited resources and investment selectivity raises the image of big winners and, necessarily, big losers in the competition for the federal nod of approval. But his subsequent excellent discussions of environmental and housing policies have a much broader focus. He advocates, for example, that the federal government pay the cost of state and local compliance with federal environmental mandates, and that federal housing policy should include replacing large-scale public housing with scattered-site housing and vouchers. Both of these good ideas, however, would be big-ticket federal budget items, and it is not clear how they mesh with the more hard-nosed investment banker tone that prevails elsewhere in the paper.

In general, Hanson presents a thoughtful and persuasive case for reinvigorating the urban policy debate as it relates to urban physical systems. I would like to have seen him engage more directly the implementation challenges that are implied in his proposals. Who would make these complex and fateful investment decisions, and on what basis? Drawing up the criteria for national or international significance as opposed to merely local benefit is a nightmarish task, and whatever the outcome, almost any self-respecting urban lobbyist could make a compelling (or at least plausible) case for *his* city's pet project. Hanson acknowledges the difficulties and uncertainties, but argues "we must still do the best we can."

A more fundamental problem is that the entire arrangement of the federal executive structure and Congressional political imperatives is stacked against a rational, intentional, location-specific investment strategy. Hanson mentions somewhat vaguely "a value in reconfiguring federal support for urban planning and development to reorient it from its current disjointed focus of specific functions." Although we do not get a peek at what he may have in mind here, one can only hope that its unveiling would draw more favorable attention than previous attempts to put the federal urban policy house in order.

References

Domestic Council, Executive Office of the President. 1971. *The President's Proposals for Executive Reorganization* (Washington, DC), pp. 20-23.

President's Commission for a National Agenda for the Eighties. 1980. *Urban America in the Eighties* (Washington, DC).

Stanfield, Rochelle L. 1979. "The Best Laid Reorganization Plans Sometimes Go Astray," *National Journal* (20 January), pp. 84-91.

Repairing the Community Fabric: The Role of Neighborhoods, Institutions, and Families in a National Urban Policy

Phillip L. Clay

Introduction

In past generations, residents in urban neighborhoods worked hard to realize the American dream of a secure job with benefits, a decent home, education for their children, security in old age, and personal safety. Indeed, efforts to achieve these goals have constituted the agenda for federal domestic policy since the Great Depression.

The progress in achieving social and economic progress has been steady. While members of minority groups have made far less progress than the white majority, even this population has made impressive gains when compared generation to generation.

Throughout, progress could be measured at the neighborhood level and at the level of the individual and family. Both measurements are traditional domains of concern. While labels changed (e.g. community, neighborhood, "target area," etc.), "place" has enjoyed a central role in both social science analysis and in public policy.

Institutions are also important. Strangely, however, their role is not always separately identified. Institutions are organizations, customs, trans-actions, and systems of belief created to embody, rationalize, and manage society's functions. These range from schools to housing markets. The family and the church are institutions. The criminal code, marriage, and Community Development Corporations (CDCs) are also institutions (Boskof 1962: 217–56).

Institutions are considered here because we now recognize that strong institutions are not only byproducts of community building, they are the basic elements of community. They are important levers when we aim to rebuild or re-create broken communities. Providing welfare or housing assistance to a family does not make the family better unless the resources facilitate transactions that the family uses to empower itself. We provide help toward empowerment for a family, for example, when they are able to buy more necessities or move into housing in a neighborhood network that offers family support, services, and access to jobs. When the family benefits in this way, institutions are validated and strengthened to serve the next client better. The neighborhood will not be better off and there is no institutional validation (D. Warren 1981: 133–79).

Where there is institutional strength in a city or neighborhood, a national urban policy should support it and use it as a means by which individuals, families, and areas leverage the help they might get from the federal government. Both the local hero and the federal angel are necessary (Schorr 1988: 291–93). Where such strength is absent, a goal of urban policy should be to support its development. As the urban crisis deepens and as we recognize the connection between various levels of government and individual players, this is increasingly the challenge presented when we discuss a national urban policy.

This paper explores the connection of neighborhood, family, and institutions in a national urban policy. The three are also part of a seamless local policy context that is critical to building and maintaining good communities (R. Warren 1970: 14–23). They incorporate people, markets, organizations, and behaviors that are beneficiaries of a national urban policy. Local contexts are aggregated to become the nation's urban challenge. Each city is special. Despite efforts to view cities with a wide angle, local views at the street level will define how well we do.

For federal policy to make families, institutions, and neighborhoods stronger, it has to advance the ability of each to help each other—for empowered individuals and families to take leadership in organizations and for strong organizations to take initiatives in their communities. Strong communities and community-centered organizations can then better help families who need it—both in terms of specific services and in terms of models for behavior and networks of support. The federal government brings resources that enable local players to perform their roles effectively. This is a type of leveraging that is a missing link in urban policy. The recommendations at the end of this article have as their goal the more effective use of resources and policy process to leverage local activity.

Unlike the housing construction and labor markets, where national parameters such as interest rates and change in gross national product are very important and the impacts identified quickly, the behavior of families, institutions, and the dynamics of neighborhoods are not influenced directly by federal policy. In addition, the impacts are often not immediate. The temptation may be to ignore them and to plan on advancing urban communities via economic development initiatives and with a "safety net."

Our main point here is that the reverse is true. There is no credible evidence of significant "trickle down" to the urban poor nor is there evidence that the "safety net" works as well as it needs to in order to protect the vulnerable (Jencks 1992: 70–91).

As we consider urban policy now, we are at a crisis point. It is not the case that the progress or the possibility of progress has disappeared. Evidence of both still exists. What is perhaps clearer now more than ever is that we have evidence of progress as well as indicators that show serious reversals in the fortunes of central-city residents and neighborhoods. For example, housing quality is better now than it has ever been in American history, yet we have a serious problem of homelessness (Rossi and Wright 1989: 132–42). Progress in expanding educational opportunities continues even though in central cities the gains are far short of what we now expect to be the academic and preparatory outcomes of young people. The gap between achievement and educational requirements grows larger, in part because the latter is changing faster than the former (Karsarda 1989: 29–36).

There is a sense that in recent years there has been a basic shift—a discontinuity with the history of the last several generations and that the vitality of urban neighborhoods, institutions, and social structure have been stressed, if not broken. We have in this generation, for the first time in our history, significant loss of middle-class status—actual and perceived—on the part of those who had it. Two bellwether indicators—the rate of home ownership among young families and real incomes—both declined during the 1970s and/or 1980s. For those below it, middle-class status seemed increasingly beyond reach (Joint Center for Housing Studies 1993: 1–15).

Despite a generation more attuned to participation, empowerment, and community control, increasingly evidence points to a growing number of urban neighborhoods that seem unable to frame or reframe the social contract, set and enforce community standards, or maintain the basic institutional infrastructure. In short, they lack a strong social fabric.

Policies in the recent past to address homelessness, youth, and other issues have run up against local institutional capacity deficits. This has prompted a host of foundation efforts to address the issues.

Whether drugs, teen pregnancy, child abuse, or some other problem, too little of the informal institutional power that used to be so powerful in neighborhoods now seems available in large sections of our cities. Agencies, housing authorities, schools, and jails are overwhelmed; urban residents who can afford private safety nets or migration away from such places are moving. Those who cannot move become the core of a community where people often live out quite desperate lives (Suttles 1968: 441–60; Keyes 1992: 135–62; Dunlap 1992: 181–7).

As the spiral of social problems tightens, the areas become more blighted. This puts every resident, business, and institution in the area and nearby "at risk." Our cities increasingly have a tornado-like character. Some core areas are racked with terrible social dislocation and upheaval. A short distance from the center of the storm, there is only the dark sky—and perhaps rain. All of this is in the shadow of new tall towers, convention centers, and restored elegance. Everyone in the area sees the cloud and hears the awful sounds of destruction, but the tornado itself touches down only in "at-risk" areas. The neighbors suffer the dark clouds and live in fear that the funnel will be broader and closer next time.

This is no simple phenomenon. The evidence clearly documents that we are creating an increasingly concentrated population that seems outside our economic, social, and political markets and institutions. There is a negative connotation associated with the label "underclass," which is often used to describe this group. There are young adult men and women who have never worked and who have no conception of what a regular job is. They are loosely attached to sometimes dysfunctional families. They are outside of wholesome family and institutional networks and caught up in gangs and street life, which are substitutes for effective and affective affiliation.

The young people in these communities in crisis have not been presented with a set of values, venues, and opportunities to conform to the American mainstream or the more traditional working-class urban versions that worked for previous generations of low-income people. They are not parties to a social contract (e.g. marriage, neighboring, citizen) nor have they taken responsibility for themselves or others.

This group is very different from the "hard-core unemployed" of the last generation. Many young people in the last generation were absorbed into the world of work and the social contract in their "community." Those who reached their late teens or early twenties and who seemed adrift would be, for the most part, pulled back on track by a combination of marriage, flight from the rural south (to the prospect of better opportunities in the north), a stable factory job, military service, or simple maturity. Poorly nurtured and ill-educated urban youth now appear too often as desperate parents who are often unable to nurture their own young.

This assessment is not meant to blame these victims. We neither provided them with an education for today's jobs nor managed the economy in ways that might benefit them even indirectly.

In describing this problem, it is also important to note that this most desperate group is a minority of inner-city residents. A comparable, if not larger, number of their brethren is doing better than ever before. These more prosperous young people are moving in ever larger numbers to the suburbs or to areas away from crisis communities. Even their poor peers who move out seem to do better in a different environment. The latter point underscores the power of place for transmission of opportunity

(Rosenbaum 1993: 223–46). The flight is part of the problem in that the low-income area is worse off for their leaving (W. Wilson 1987: 16–25). Those who leave are part of the solution in that they are often going to an area where their children will have more opportunities, face fewer risks, and enjoy a more supportive environment.

The possibility now is that the migrations and shifts described above will cause the loss of a whole generation of young people, break the fragile coalition for social policy initiatives (as resentment and class competition heat up), and stimulate an even wider spiral of urban decline. This fundamental sea change threatens to create trouble in neighboring urban domains—some lacking social control and filled with despair, and others deeply resentful and actively opposed to programs, etc. In limbo are still other neighborhoods trying hard to conserve their status against external forces they feel are pulling them into an abyss.

National Urban Policy and Local Dynamics

This article explores how to factor in the local dynamics of institutions, neighborhoods, and families in a national urban policy. This challenge prompts four questions:

- What are the changes in cities and in the nation's political economy that influence outcomes for institutions, families, and neighborhoods now and in the future, compared to the past?
- Cities are composed of many different groups whose relationship with each other is important and whose joint action is required for social change. What are the differences among these groups that matter with respect to framing and implementing urban policy? What are the dimensions on which their institutions and neighborhoods vary?
- A social fabric is critical to effective communities. What are the operational elements of the social fabric? What is the role of federal initiatives in improving the quality and strength of a community's fabric (or in repairing the fabric that has become frayed?) In such a difficult area of micro-planning, how do we factor in local empowerment of the community and at the same time achieve a coherent national policy?
- What is the legacy of the federal policy affecting neighborhoods, institutions, and families? Is that legacy now an asset or a constraint on action the feds might want to take under a new initiative?

The Changing Local Context

The first question focuses on changes in cities and their political economy. Historically, cities have been engines of opportunity. Immigrants arrived from distant locations to take jobs generated by an expanding industrial sector. Industry (usually at the insistence of, and in struggle with, labor) improved workers' pay and benefits. New technologies created additional opportunities. Growth swelled the public sector, which would then provide public and social services.

It appears now that the city as an economic engine has stalled (Logan and Molotch 1987: 52–7). Growth in manufacturing capacity of U.S. firms is now more likely to be in an emerging nation than in a depressed metropolitan region in the United States. Job growth is more selective in terms of location (suburban and outside the northeast and midwest), likely prospective workers (highly educated, part-time, or temporary), and quality ("better" as measured by pay and benefits) (Karsarda 1988: 148–98).

Public education in inner-city communities does not produce young people who can fit current employment requirements for better jobs. The years of underinvestment in education and training as well as in child development have made the labor force in many inner cities mismatched with changing demands in labor. While cities have expanded opportunities in some areas (health, financial services, etc.), the best jobs go to the suburbanites. The constant growth of well-paid factory jobs with security and excellent benefits are no more. Inner-city residents, including those who played by old rules and completed high school, find themselves more often in poorly compensated and unsteady service jobs.

Just as the city's economic engine has changed, so has the role of its markets. Housing investment has ceased to be an important sector for investment and with that went some of the incentives for maintenance and upgrading so critical in housing and economic development, where private funds are always the *sine qua non* (Logan and Molotch 1987: 277–80). Large areas of the cities are abandoned or disinvested, the result being a weakened market for almost any kind of development.

Cities also face a changing political relationship to their states. The large and medium-sized cities in a state no longer form a majority of a state's population (and legislative contingent). Suburbanites form the majority in most industrial states. The fiscal fallout of this shift is significant both in terms of the resources the local community is allowed to generate on its own and those redistributed to it by the state. States are often reluctant to let cities tax activities that might affect suburban people or businesses. More of the state aid is spread around rather than concentrated in inner cities. Often a state's policy to "help" urban communities is to mandate the provision of services without providing resources to defray the costs. (The feds have done this as well.)

The complexity of the challenge presented by this new context is daunting. Local resources and strengths are variable and increasingly difficult to muster. In a political system that finds it important to simplify and gloss over features not easily handled in the legislative and other processes, the complexity is all the more problematic in developing a national urban policy. Where counterforces are so prevalent and powerful, leveraging becomes critical, since no national urban initiative can be as powerful as the forces arrayed against it.

The Changing Demographics and Community Mosaic

There are two important aspects of the changing demographics of cities. First, cities face a changing demographic composition. This is a matter that goes well beyond the issue of their shrinking population, which by itself is not a major problem. Cities are faced with continuing out migration of the middle class, a growth of their low-income population, and an aging of their middle-class and working-class population. These trends create the possibility for generational conflict between those who have children and need public services, and those (with limited resources) who have no such need. It creates a sharper distinction between the city core (where the generational conflict is heating up) and the suburban ring, which is differentiating into subareas where residents have more fiscal flexibility in terms of what services they are willing to support.

The second aspect of demographic change has to do with the changing mix of groups with a stake in the city's future. Some of these groups are new. Some have been around for awhile. Yates may have overstated the point when he suggested that the city is ungovernable (Yates 1982: 6–7). It is clear, however, that the complex array of forces in cities does make governance and radical policy shifts difficult (Kirlin and Marshall 1988: 348–52). Figure 1 outlines some of the main demographic subgroups we find in cities today. The figure also presents some summary information about the group, the special features to their claim on cities, and the issues their needs stimulate.

Several things are clear from Figure 1. The first is the sharp conflict between the interest of some of the groups. For example, there is the juxtaposition of needs of a growing number of low-income families and an elderly homeowner group. The former needs costly support and the latter is increasingly inclined not to support such needs with local tax dollars. The homeowner group is powerful, politically active, and often financially pressed. Elderly owners are more likely to be white, while low-income families are increasingly minority.

The urban working and middle classes offer cities a Faustian bar-

Figure 1

Selected List of Demographic Groups
with a Neighborhood Stake

group	context	issues for planning and policy
low-income families	There are growing concentrations of such families. They have multiple needs. Individuals and families lack institutions that can address complex needs. Each family needs multiple supports. Behavior is often self-destructive.	Multiple services need to be available and should be articulated so that a given family or individual receives the full range of services for personal empowerment.
working-class families	Problems are more specific but assistance is required nevertheless. While they sometimes have some resources, they need incentives to use them. Leveraging is possible.	Potential for making limited resources have maximum impact. Important challenges exist in neighborhood conservation, public safety, and public education. Policies aimed at prevention are important. Failure to improve confidence will cause "flight" among those who are better off.
middle-class families	This group has faced declining real incomes and growing concerns about crimes, taxes and other urban problems. Education is a special concern to those with children. The suburbs are often within financial reach. During the 1980s, "gentrification" stimulated some evidence of a new commitment to city neighborhoods on the part of this population. This commitment will be tested as children reach school age.	Important to show progress in neighborhood "stabilization," public safety and education. They have the capacity to be investors but are often drawn away. Can be critical in institutional leadership which enhances their stake. in the community
elderly	While many have limited resources and choices, a growing fraction of property owners will be elderly. Important players in neighborhood conservation. Complex services needs to deal with physical and social needs that change over time. Needs and interests sometimes conflict with those of families.	Important to support elderly owners in conserving property and personal independence through a web of services that are sensitive to needs and changes in needs over time. Sources of cross-generation leadership and volunteer service. It is important to avoid the frequent cross-generational conflicts over community standards, services, etc.

continued on following page

gain. They want lower taxes, better education, and improved infrastructure. Instead of general social services, they prefer neighborhood conservation and enhanced public safety. While some of what the working and middle classes want would benefit all—improved education and violence reduction, for example—better-off households increasingly resist higher taxes to pay for social services.

Figure 1, continued

group	context	issues for planning and policy
youth	Complex and dependent group. Goal is to support education and human development. While most do not have serious problems, all have needs. "At-risk" youths are growing as a share of population. Services for complex needs and family support are often missing. Are often isolated from services. Services are sometimes mismatched or insensitive to their needs.	Neighborhoods need support in developing comprehensive assistance to the young.
commuter and non-residents	Want a safe, attractive city that meets their needs. Resist taxes and fees. Priorities are mismatched with those of residents. Despite problems, they are critical to job and tax base.	National urban policy must not allow cities to use scarce development dollars to serve this population as was sometimes the case with UDAG, for example. Serving this group should be viewed as part of the regional and state agenda and incentives and regulations should reflect this.
investors	Are critical for strength of housing, labor, and commercial markets. Have had less interest in cities lately and investment that has been made has been in a few locations away from low-income communities and rarely to their employment benefit.	Policy needs to support strategic local investment, maintenance, and expansion of areas of existing strength, and support for risk-taking by those who have a stake in the community.
homeless	Numbers continue to be large and growing and families as a share of the homeless population is up as well. Little hope of self-help. Cost of temporary solutions is high and public acceptance is waning.	Policy has to include permanent solutions in community settings as part of overall effort to help low-income people deal with changing housing markets. Public must not perceive that homeless are assisted to the exclusion of help for others who have need.
"community leaders"	Face a daunting task when they support piecemeal efforts that produce few results. Task made difficult when efforts focus on getting resources and making do. Little incentive to make strategic and long-term commitment. Receives mixed message regarding partnerships and collaboration. Leadership roles not clear.	Organizational suppot should be available to groups that are empowered by public policy. Commitment of resources should come at the end of organizational assessment and strategic planning. Avoid micro-management.

The working and middle class say, implicitly, that if they do not get what they want, they will leave. Many have already moved. If they are not in a position to move, past experience suggests they will disinvest and withdraw from civic and institutional life. Most mayors might prefer to have it both ways—promise to support the middle class while also helping the poor and their subconstituencies (e.g. the homeless, youth, etc.).

Another way of looking at the groups referred to in Figure 1 is to focus on the organizations and institutions through which various interests are mediated. We could outline comparable Faustian bargains involving, separately, the business community, residential investors, commuters, the upper class, etc. All of them demand to be attended to in ways that conflict with the poor, or demand a proportionately larger share of the limited resources, or both. They each make critical contributions that they threaten to withhold if their interests are not made more of a priority. The groups and institutions listed below are some of the groups that convey the messages of groups in Figure 1.

- social services agencies
- small business organizations
- civic and homeowners associations
- advocacy groups (each group in Figure 1 has one or more)
- nonprofit development organizations
- "good government" groups, commissions
- political parties
- civil rights groups
- professional associations
- local government
- foundations and charities
- major employers and corporations

The dynamics of the relations among interests, groups, and institutions are important because embedded within each is a certain calculus that determines what behaviors (i.e. cooperative, collaborative, defensive, or competitive) each will have in urban policy.

If national urban policy is effective, it will not be simply because major policy or programs caused or created progress but because the national initiatives stimulated a positive chain of behaviors in a set of local actors. The challenge is to stimulate activities on the part of individuals and institutions listed above that complement its own.

The various areas in which we develop local policy and for which there are national analogs give us a complex simultaneous equation at the local level. Each community will have a different set of equations and from its vantage point, the feds can do little to solve them directly. At its best (and beyond transfers), federal policy can stimulate and support local actors.

Figure 2 outlines the sharp and increasing sources of conflict built into urban communities. While these differences are presented here mainly to outline differences within and among racial and ethnic groups, they apply to other conflicts as well. Some of the past urban policy failures relate not to the fact that the federal government took inappropriate initiatives but that policies (or their implementation) were not sensitive to intra- and intergroup behavior. In other cases, policies that were applied were mismatched with the local demographic mosaic.

The rows in Figure 2 outline dimensions of group differences worth exploring in policy framing. The differences go to the heart of the calculus of groups in the urban mosaic and are important for understanding how various groups view the public policy process (Espiritu and Light 1991, pp. 37–49). Figure 2 helps us understand, for example, the different perspectives various minority groups have on an issue and the sources of conflict between the view of community people and policy makers.

These viewpoints are typically blurred or left unacknowledged at the national level but are often quite important at the local level. Figure 2 helps us to notice the various definitions of class and to expect an interaction between class and race (or ethnicity.) We can imagine the importance of the attitudes about victimization and oppression in framing incentives in training programs, for example. Understanding groups will also remind us that some groups view "the community" as a place to rebuild and commit to, while others view it simply as a way station en route to someplace else. This makes the debate about "people vs. place" concrete. These different perspectives will force academic debates to accept that within communities and between various people, there are conflicting visions that have to reconciled locally if any national resources are to stand a chance for being effective in local communities.

While no one labors under the illusion that federal policy will quickly solve urban problems by incorporating these considerations, we have an obligation to make sure the policies do no harm to constructive local mechanisms. The feds should signal local authorities to factor these into their requests for federal assistance and plans for implementation.

The Social Fabric

Our third question addresses social fabric, that intangible set of features which holds communities together and makes them operate as a kind of extended primary group. Community fabric is the means by which communities define and enforce their standards, implement the social contract, create and support formal and informal institutions, mobilize internal resources, and organize to obtain resources from outside. It is also the means by which communities support leadership.

Social fabric is a powerful set of internalized rules and traditions; it is more powerful than legislation and more durable than political structures (Goetze 1977: 77–90). Fabric can be strong or weak, tightly woven or loose. Fabric determines how the police operate at the street level, how teachers' expectations are set, and how politicians treat an area. The credibility and depth of leadership and the ability to deliver (e.g. votes, clients, etc.) are all framed by an underlying and invisible fabric. It is the glue of society—the stuff that binds elements of nations and neighborhoods. (There are, of course, other binders—regulations, contracts and mission in institutions; love, blood, and marriage in families.)

The two operative elements of strong social fabric are empowered individuals and strong institutions. Individuals initiate and carry out actions

Figure 2

Issues in Defining Inter- and Intragroup Differences

issue	description	significance for the implementation of urban policy
history	Each group brings to participation in the city a different set of historical benchmarks and traditions.	Different perspectives influence how policy and program elements will affect them and how they respond to challenges and possible incentives. In the Latino community, e.g., some came as immigrants from middle-class backgrounds and some as peasants; some are legal, other are not. Puerto Ricans are U.S. citizens. Some intend to settle in the United States while others may be waiting for the opportunity to return "home." Some want to build communities as ethnic beachheads; others may see the place they live as a mere way station to some other place when economic fortunes improve. Such variations may influence the extent to which residents will respond to "people" vs. "place" policies.
class	Class identification and striving vary in ways not totally related to income. Middle-class striving and modeling shape groups that look similar based on SES indicators. This includes attitude toward assimilation.	Ethnographers have noted that in the black community, within the "working class," there are at least two different value systems. One system is "very middle class" in striving while the other accepts and passes on to its children the values of the "street." Local institution-building depends on the degree to which the former makes an active commitment to community development and the latter can be engaged without being turned off.
power	In various settings groups differ in power and access to those who have power.	One's attitude toward accepting elements in an urban strategy depends on whether one sees the ability to get a share of the benefits in the local power arena. Implementation of urban initiatives must assess whether all affected groups are comparably empowered; resistance or non-participation may reflect confidence in gaining or using power.
		continued on following page

on a community agenda that grows out of shared values. They call others to act and model civic, parental, and social responsibility. They carry out the traditions and administer the rewards and sanctions. While leaders are critical, just as critical is a core group of followers who are not deterred from active and positive community citizenship. When these followers are active, they attract others, create groups, and stand as visible models.

Institutions incorporate the formal element and serve as the medium through which people work and by which the community is serviced. The service can be concrete, for example when a community center or school offers day care. The institution works as an important part of the fabric when it sets rules, provides alternatives to street life, educates the whole child, incorporates parents into the life of a school, and helps them

Figure 2, continued

issue	description	significance for the implementation of urban policy
blame for victim status and willingness to take personal responsibility	Groups and individuals vary in how they attribute blame for their victimization. Some blame specific "others" or the "system" and expect external change as the first step in reducing disadvantage. Others internalize and blame themselves, and/or are willing to take responsibility for changing their plight.	The group that internalizes is infinitely easier to work with and policy that empowers them by giving resources to them or to organizations that serve them will more likely have positive impacts. For the groups that externalize, it is difficult to stimulate institutional actions that moves individual who are less willing to take some initiative, especially when doing so exacts costs (e.g. giving up habits, accepting training, limitations on freedom, etc.). The group will push the institution and test the commitment and credibility of those involved. They may push for control but back off from being held accountable, which is a show of true commitment.
race or ethnic politics	Some place high value on such politics to deliver various benefits, including resources and jobs they assume would otherwise not be available. Others place less or no emphasis on such strategies. (The assumption in both cases is that resources are distributed on criteria other than need or merit.)	The distinction is best represented by the contrast between the black politician or leader (i.e. head of an institution) who is a "race man" and builds a political career around delivery of resources and power to blacks. (From this perspective, good urban policies are those which help blacks in relation to whites.) Coalitions are to be suffered if need be. The other type of politician serves "all the people" and believes that the fortunes of blacks are tied to those of the whole city. He/she places a high value on coalitions and on policies that build bridges. A good policy is one that helps all eligible people.
value placed on economic initiative and self-suffi-ciency	Some place high value on and are willing to endure sacrifice to obtain ownership or a stake in business. They will pursue economic development irrespective of whether a program exists and may not use a program if they feel it poses a problem of independence. Others place less value on self-reliance. Some see politics (rather than enter-prise) as the "game" to play for economic advantage.	Those who place high value on economic initiative and enterprise might sacrifice housing, service, education, and youth programs for help in business. Entrepreneurs who prosper and then leave the community stimulate resentment at the irony: a successful outcome for individuals reinforces isolation and deprivation for the community. In its guidelines, a national urban policy should address communities on the matter of balance between helping people and helping areas.

to parent and to become advocates for families and children. Models of parental support can also be communicated and enforced through churches. Schools pick up on parent and community expectations and continue the model through elementary and secondary schools.

Community values can be further inculcated in sports leagues and other activities that young people pursue. As success is experienced, values and behaviors become traditions and are infused into the culture. The values, including active responsibility for personal and community outcomes, are reinforced in the job market, in other institutions, and in the education of the next generation. Outside funding—from foundations to the feds—support and reinforce, or the in the worse case undermine, community initiatives.

In another example, combining the individual and institutional, one can have, as in law enforcement for example, one neighborhood in which law enforcement (on issues of public order, street and domestic behavior) is strict in enforcing certain community standards and has the formal and informal support of residents, and another community where there is no clear standard other than the one the police decide on their own. What the police do is determined externally with perhaps little connection to the interests of the local community (J. Wilson 1971: 277–90). In the former case, gangs might be pursued aggressively while in the other neighborhood, the gang is left alone and is free to prey on residents.

Community fabric is not rare nor is it always absent in low-income areas. The problem is that when it is absent, it places the community in crisis. Residents are not able to manage their own environment to protect themselves from predators or to effectively use services and development resources that assume a social infrastructure strong enough to overpower the forces of blight and fear. Calling a community meeting, for example, can be complicated by the fear of assembly after dark or by subtle intimidation from drug operatives. Simple initiatives become considerable risks.

Communities that have strong and tightly woven fabric are able to weather many of the difficulties they experience. These communities will be in a better position to handle racial transitions, take advantage of economic opportunities, organize to address local problems, provide constructive options for informal youth development, and support its leadership and institutions. They will also be able to request and use outside help.

No national program that simply gives dollars will help unless improving the fabric is part of the package. Just spending more money on social services or housing units will not empower people. While the federal role is discussed below, suffice it to say here that the federal government can require communities to explain how the implementation of federal initiatives will improve the social infrastructure. The feds can mandate a more strategic accounting of how its resources are used in local areas.

The Policy Legacy

The fourth question turns to the legacy of past federal policy and asks whether this legacy is an asset or a constraint. There is lots of evidence of a legacy. Welfare policy systematically discourages intact families; urban renewal and public works projects divided or disestablished neighborhoods with highways and other projects. Programs that force the creation of special boundaries set up artificial neighborhoods and undermine rather than build social fabric.

The fragmentation of social services into different agencies in an area prevents the servicing of all the needs of a family. One agency might offer job training, but day care is not available or is available only under rules that make participation in the training impossible. Beyond the fragmentation, there is no agency empowered to configure programs so that individuals are served comprehensively. The goal would be for people to move from powerlessness to empowerment.

Not all of the legacy has been bad, however. Fair housing has been added to the agenda in ways that would not have been possible without federal encouragement or mandate. Experiences such as the Gautreaux demonstration in suburban Chicago show the benefits of deconcentration for the poor. Community development organizations (e.g. CDCs, resident management, mutual housing associations) have been supported. They are stronger than ever and are leading an important non-profit community-based development sector that provides a venue for community leadership as well as development capacity. Requirements for citizen input have expanded urban democracy and individual empowerment.

A host of demonstrations in public policy—Neighborhood Housing Services, Headstart, neighborhood health centers and various education initiatives—have provided models of program development and community participation that strengthens neighborhoods and their institutions.

HUD is the lead urban policy agency. While its capacity and credibility are important, the roles played by Health and Human Services, Department of Labor, Commerce, and other cabinet departments are also important. The success of local coordination requires a reversal of the pattern of limited coordination within Washington agencies (Frieden and Kaplan 1975: 235–49; Hetzel 1993: 2–13).

HUD brings a considerable burden from the costs (and sometimes failures) of past policies. The facts, the perceptions, and the costs of these problems constrain our ability to develop new initiatives. The costs—expiring, use, Section 8 contract termination, and disposition of foreclosed properties—total several billions of dollars. The legacy reflected in these burdens calls for considerable new resources all by themselves before we factor in the cost of new initiatives. This tale of woe about the legacy of HUD is not intended to be discouraging. A new urban policy will need to build on positive aspects of the legacy, create or enhance mechanisms to use the new resources, and leverage non-federal and non-fiscal resources.

Toward a National Urban Policy

A national urban policy with respect to neighborhoods, institutions, and families should have the goal of strengthening neighborhoods, empowering people, and supporting community-based organizations. Some of the resources and program initiatives have to come from the federal government, some can come from state and local government, and many are non fiscal (i.e. regulations, land, development mechanisms, etc.). Additional support and opportunities for leverage will come from the private and charitable sectors if they see a national urban policy as a sound vessel in which they can have some confidence.

To achieve the goals outlined above, an effective national urban policy would be characterized by several features. Federal policy should:

- Provide significant new federal financial assistance for housing, community development, and related programs;
- Offer targeted discretionary assistance aimed at documenting "best practice" in local communities and in institutions;
- Support partnerships and collaborations that leverage resources from the federal government and engage charitable, corporate, and private resources in urban communities;
- Mandate and encourage a supportive role for state and local governments to develop policies, change regulations, and support planning in areas of federal action;
- Provide flexibility in priority setting and in the framing of local initiatives using federal resources;
- Require a statement outlining the likely impact of proposed projects on neighborhood development defined broadly, including specifically subareas that lack institutional strength and that have a high concentration of persistent poverty;
- Support a research agenda to document outcomes and the lessons from various initiatives and demonstrations;
- Coordinate federal departments to reduce the competition, overlap, and conflicting requirements of various federal programs and to maximize leveraging of those resources; and
- Empower community-based organizations, resident organizations, and other parties to be effective partners.

While this list may seem daunting, it does represent a set of features that we have learned the hard way are important if national urban policies are to be effective when they are implemented in local settings. Many of the items do not cost much but do require more coordination, planning, and partnership than has been typical. These process shifts are as important to community improvement as increased financial resources. The process shifts allow for greater effectiveness and provide more leverage because they directly alter behavior, incentives, and relationships at the local level.

Past experience also requires us to be careful about the legislative process. Politically crafted acts of Congress sometimes become blueprints for policy paralysis (Bardach 1977: 65–148). National urban policy has to avoid the difficulty that is often encountered where the messages given at various policy milestones—the authorizing legislation, appropriations process, rule-making, program selection, and implementation—are incompatible with each other. Based on past lessons, several criteria for the policy development process seem likely to assure effective implementation.

- The problems that policies are aimed to address should be clearly spelled out. The policy taken as whole, and in connection with other policies in the federal government, should respond to elements of the problem as defined.
- The policy should be internally consistent. Too often policies have been positive but contained inconsistent elements either within the program itself, in other parts of HUD, or in other federal departments. The non-compatible elements (often included to address a "political problem") undermine program implementation.
- The policy should reflect a realistic sense of what can or should be done by the federal government versus other sectors, including state and local government, the non-profit sector, private investors, and consumers. The expected role for each should be spelled out and appropriate incentive or outreach put in place.
- The policy should be within the resource constraints of the federal government and other parties involved. The scope of the policy intervention and the claims about its impact should match resources.
- There should be an explicit reference to the nonfiscal resources expected of local government and institutions and an encouragement of informal institutions.

Conclusion

We have made a case for greater attention in a national urban policy to families, institutions, and neighborhoods. We have argued less for specific urban policy interventions than for a process that makes the federal government act in support of local empowerment. The specific projects and program interventions would best come from local initiatives rather than from national policy. The federal government can contribute by providing financial resources and supporting strategic planning, collaborative initiatives, and impact assessments as ways of encouraging attention to how initiatives are framed at the local level and how resources of all types can be more effective. With this approach, there is a greater chance that modest federal programs in a new national urban policy can have great impact in local communities.

References

Bardach, Eugene. 1977. *The Implementation Game: What Happens after a Bill Be-comes Law* (Cambridge: MIT Press), pp. 65–148.

Boskof, Alvin. 1962. *The Sociology of Urban Regions* (New York: Meredith).

Dunlap, Eloise. 1992. "Impact of Drugs on Family Life and Kin Networks in the Inner City African-American Single-Parent Household," in A. Harrell and G. Peterson (eds.), *Drugs, Crime and Social Isolation: Barriers to Urban Opportunity* (Washington: The Urban Institute).

Espiritu, Yen, and Ivan Light. 1991. "The Changing Ethnic Shape of Contempo-rary Urban America," in M. Gottdiener and Christopher Pickvance (eds.), *Urban Life in Transition* (Newbury Park, CA: Sage), pp. 35–54.

Frieden, Bernard, and Kaplan, Marshall. 1975. *The Politics of Neglect: Urban Aid from Model Cities to Revenue Sharing* (Cambridge: MIT Press).

Goetze, Rolf. 1977. *Understanding Neighborhood Change: The Role of Expectations in Urban Revitalization* (Cambridge: Ballinger).

Hetzel, Otto. 1993. "Some Historical Lessons for Implementing Empowerment Zones and Enterprise Communities: Experiences from the Model Cities Program." Draft prepared for George Washington University Confer-ence (November).

Jencks, Christopher. 1992. *Rethinking Social Policy: Race, Poverty, and the Under-class* (New York: Harper Perennial).

Joint Center for Housing Studies of Harvard University. 1993. *The State of the Nation's Housing—1993* (Cambridge: The Joint Center for Housing Studies/Harvard University).

Karsarda, John. 1988. "Job Migration and Emerging Urban Mismatches," in McGreary et al. (1988), pp. 148–98.

_____. 1989. "Urban Industrial Transition and the Underclass," *The Annals of the American Academy of Political and Social Science,* 501 (January), pp. 26–47.

Keyes, Langley. 1992. *Strategies and Saints: Fighting Drugs in Subsidized Housing* (Washington: The Urban Institute).

Kirlin, John, and Dale Marshall. 1988. "Urban Governance: The New Politics of Entrepreneurship," in McGreary et al. (1988), 348–72.

Logan, John R., and Harvey Molotch. 1987. *Urban Fortunes: The Political Eco-nomic of Place* (Berkeley: University of California Press).

McGreary, Michael, et al. (eds.) 1988. *Urban Change and Poverty* (Washington: National Academy Press).

Rosenbaum, James. 1993. "Closing the Gap: Does Residential Integration Im-prove the Employment and Education of Low-Income Blacks?" in Lawrence Joseph (ed.), *Affordable Housing and Public Policy: Strategies for Metropolitan Chicago* (Chicago: The Chicago Assembly).

Rossi, Peter, and James Wright. 1989. "The Urban Homeless: A Portrait of Urban Dislocation," *The Annals of the American Academy of Political and Social Science,* 501 (January), 132–42.

Schorr, Lisbeth. 1988. *Within Our Reach: Breaking the Cycle of Disadvantage* (New York: Anchor Press, Doubleday).

Suttles, Gerald. 1968. *The Social Order of the Slum: Ethnicity and Territory in the Inner City* (Chicago: University of Chicago Press).

Warren, Donald. 1981. *Helping Networks: How People Cope with Problems in the Urban Community* (Notre Dame: Notre Dame University Press).

Warren, Roland. 1970. "The Good Community: What Is to Be Done?" *Journal of Community Development Research,* 1:1 (Spring), 14–23.

Wacquant, Loic, and William Wilson. 1989. "The Cost of Racial and Class Exclusion in the Inner City," *The Annals of the American Academy of Political and Social Science,* 501 (January), 8–25.

Wilson, James Q. 1971. *Varieties of Police Behavior: The Management of Law and Order in Eight Communities* (New York: Atheneum).

Wilson, William J. 1987. *The Truly Disadvantaged: The Inner City, the Underclass, and Public Policy* (Chicago: University of Chicago Press).

Yates, Douglas. 1982. *The Ungovernable City: The Politics of Urban Problems and Policy-Making* (Cambridge: MIT Press).

Commentary

Repairing the Community Fabric

Margaret Wilder

Phil Clay's paper addresses one of the most critical and fundamental issues confronting urban policymakers: restoring the basic institutions of urban life. As Clay asserts, a broad spectrum of institutions operate within such urban communities. Some of those institutions, (e.g. churches, schools, and community organizations) exist and function at a local scale. Other institutions such as the family or neighborhood are more personal in scope and influence. As Clay argues, much of the decline in the health of urban communities can be linked to the deterioration of functions that were traditionally carried out by these basic institutions. Moreover, federal policies have directly impacted these institutions, often in a negative or neglectful manner. Economic restructuring and demographic change within urban communities have exacerbated urban decline and created a formidable set of social and political barriers to the improvement of inner-city lives. Clay calls for more strategic federal funding of initiatives, which would strengthen local institutions generally, and specifically facilitate the activities of community-based organizations.

I find little to disagree with in Clay's discussion. However, I feel that certain distinctions must be made in our discussion of urban decline and the character and interactions of institutions, if we are to strategically design and implement better urban policy.

There is a need to differentiate changes in urban conditions. There is a general tendency to assume that urban conditions have worsened because past policy actions were ineffective or debilitating. This type of assessment is both seductive and comforting. The logical next step is to correct bad policy. In order to do so we must understand the nature of urban ills, and identify the ways in which policy has impacted urban communities. This is no small order as evidenced by the plethora of research and debate that occurs within academic and nonacademic policy arenas. There are as many perspectives and assessments as there are commentators and analysts.

The basic task I envision is one in which we distinguish between those urban conditions which are attributable to faulty planning and policy action, and those problems which have evolved due to economic and demographic/social change within society. We cannot set aside the myriad of changes in urban life that are not the result of federal action or inaction. We must engage the question: Have public policies failed, or have the problems become worse, or both?

There is an equally critical need to differentiate the roles and interrelationships of institutions. As Clay suggests, institutions are entities that "manage society's functions." I agree with this basic definition, but feel the need to distinguish *formal* from *informal* institutions. Formal institutions, particularly governments, play certain roles in the lives of urban residents. Those roles run the gamut from service provider to regulator. Informal institutions, (e.g. neighborhoods, families, churches, non-profit organizations) have assumed certain roles that are traditional and non-traditional. The parameters of the roles played by formal and informal institutions have shifted significantly over the past fifty years.

Two types of changes are important to acknowledge. First, informal institutions have undergone significant internal changes. One of the most fundamental institutions, the family or household, provides a good example. In urban areas, family and household composition characteristics have changed dramatically since 1950. Single-parent households have increased at such a rate that the traditional two-parent household is becoming less of a norm for the society.

The second type of change is found in the shifting nature of intergovernmental relations. After the Depression, the federal government's role as a social welfare provider experienced almost unrestricted growth. Under this expanded social role, the federal government became a kind of surrogate parent for states, localities, neighborhoods, and households. With the advent of new federalism under Nixon and Reagan, an effective assault by critics of the social welfare state was launched. The weaning process began with the increased shifting of fiscal responsibilities for social programs from federal to state and local governments. The dismantling of the welfare state has become both economically and politically preferred. However, the process of social policy retrenchment is occurring at the same time that urban communities in general, and inner-city households in particular, are vulnerable and debilitated.

Much attention has been focused on the lack of effectiveness of urban policy. The federal government in particular faces a basic paradox.

By assuming *explicit* responsibility for the well-being of urban areas (especially in the 1960s), the federal government gained support from urban constituencies, but simultaneously became the target of blame for the persistence of urban problems. Since the 1970s, declining urban conditions have been blamed on ineffectual policy at best and wasteful initiatives at worst.

This critique is overdrawn. The nature of urban ills suggests that formal and informal institutions have been affected by social change, economic restructuring, political and spatial reorganization, technological innovation, *and* past policies.

The social, economic, and political polarization identified by Clay and other urbanists results from both active policy trends and decidedly more exogenous factors (e.g. adjustments to a global economy).

Have institutions failed or been overwhelmed? In answering this question we must acknowledge that many of our traditional institutions, designed for one way of life and work, are being overwhelmed by social and economic changes. Most of us would agree with Phil Clay's assertion that urban policy should reenforce institutions. But to do so requires a revised understanding of the institutions and their respective roles.

Much of the ineffectiveness of urban policy results from faulty assumptions about local institutions and the nature of problems. We face a serious and profound dilemma. We may continue to assume that institutions must function in certain traditional modes, or revise substantially our assumptions and expectations. If we maintain traditional expectations, we are subject to having to reform those institutions. This raises at least three practical problems:

1. we do not necessarily know how best to reform them;
2. we lack adequate resources to reform them; and
3. some changes are irreversible.

If we dare to revise our expectations of certain fundamental institutions, then we enter a murky and disturbingly unknown landscape. However, we may also enter a new terrain of solutions. Experimentation and creativity are needed to redesign formal institutions. A new model of "help" must also evolve to ensure that informal institutions can survive and adapt to the changing landscape of urban life.

Appendix 1:
Contents of
National Urban Policy Legislation

Text of 1970 Legislation

Title VII—Urban Growth and New Community Development

Short Title and Statement of Purpose

Sec. 701. (a) This title may be cited as the "Urban Growth and New Community Development Act of 1970".

(b) It is the policy of the Congress and the purpose of this title to provide for the development of a national urban growth policy and to encourage the rational, orderly, efficient, and economic growth, development, and redevelopment of our States, metropolitan areas, cities, counties, towns, and communities in predominantly rural areas which demonstrate a special potential for accelerated growth; to encourage the prudent use and conservation of our natural resources; and to encourage and support development which will assure our communities of adequate tax bases, community services, job opportunities, and well-balanced neighborhoods in socially, economically, and physically attractive living environments.

Part A—Development of a National Urban Growth Policy

Findings and Declaration of Policy

Sec. 702. (a) The Congress finds that the rapid growth of urban population and uneven expansion of urban development in the United States, together with a decline in farm population, slower growth in rural areas, and migration to the cities, has created an imbalance between the Nation's needs and resources and seriously threatens our physical environment, and that the economic and social development of the Nation, the

proper conservation of our natural resources, and the achievement of satisfactory living standards depend upon the sound, orderly, and more balanced development of all areas of the Nation.

(b) The Congress further finds that Federal programs affect the
location of population, economic growth, and the character of urban development; that such programs frequently conflict and result in undesirable and costly patterns of urban development which adversely affect the
environment and wastefully use our natural resources; and that existing
and future programs must be interrelated and coordinated within a system
of orderly development and established priorities consistent with a national urban growth policy.

(c) To promote the general welfare and properly apply the resources of the Federal Government in strengthening the economic and
social health of all areas of the Nation and more adequately protect the
physical environment and conserve natural resources, the Congress declares that the Federal Government, consistent with the responsibilities of
State and local government and the private sector, must assume responsibility for the development of a national urban growth policy which shall
incorporate social, economic, and other appropriate factors. Such policy
shall serve as a guide in making specific decisions at the national level
which affect the pattern of urban growth and shall provide a framework
for development of interstate, State, and local growth and stabilization
policy.

(d) The Congress further declares that the national urban growth
policy should—

(1) favor patterns of urbanization and economic development
and stabilization which offer a range of alternative locations and encourage the wise and balanced use of physical
and human resources in metropolitan and urban regions as
well as in smaller urban places which have a potential for
accelerated growth;

(2) foster the continued economic strength of all parts of the
United States, including central cities, suburbs, smaller
communities, local neighborhoods, and rural areas;

(3) help reverse trends of migration and physical growth which
reinforce disparities among States, regions, and cities;

(4) treat comprehensively the problems of poverty and employment (including the erosion of tax bases, and the need
for better community services and job opportunities)
which are associated with disorderly urbanization and rural decline;

(5) develop means to encourage good housing for all Americans without regard to race or creed;

(6) refine the role of the Federal Government in revitalizing existing communities and encouraging planned, large-scale urban and new community development;

(7) strengthen the capacity of general governmental institutions to contribute to balanced urban growth and stabilization; and

(8) facilitate increased coordination in the administration of Federal programs so as to encourage desirable patterns of urban growth and stabilization, the prudent use of natural resources, and the protection of the physical environment.

Urban Growth Report

Sec. 703. (a) In order to assist in the development of a national urban growth policy, the President shall utilize the capacity of his office, adequately organized and staffed for the purpose, through an identified unit of the Domestic Council, and of the departments and agencies within the executive branch to collect, analyze, and evaluate such statistics, data, and other information (including demographic, economic, social, land use, environmental, and governmental information) as will enable him to transmit to the Congress, during the month of February in every even-numbered year beginning with 1972, a Report on Urban Growth for the preceding two calendar years which shall include—

(1) information and statistics describing characteristics of urban growth and stabilization and identifying significant trends and developments;

(2) a summary of significant problems facing the United States as a result of urban growth trends and developments;

(3) an evaluation of the progress and effectiveness of Federal efforts designed to meet such problems and to carry out the national urban growth policy;

(4) an assessment of the policies and structure of existing and proposed interstate planning and developments affecting such policy;

(5) a review of State, local, and private policies, plans, and programs relevant to such policy;

(6) current and foreseeable needs in the areas served by policies, plans, and programs designed to carry out such policy, and the steps being taken to meet such needs; and

(7) recommendations for programs and policies for carrying out such policy, including such legislation and administrative actions as may be deemed necessary and desirable.

(b) The President may transmit from time to time to the Congress supplementary reports on urban growth which shall include such supplementary and revised recommendations as may be appropriate.

(c) To assist in the preparation of the Report on Urban Growth and any supplementary reports, the President may establish an advisory board, or seek the advice from time to time of temporary advisory boards, the members of whom shall be drawn from among private citizens familiar with the problems of urban growth and from among Federal officials, Governors of States, mayors, county officials, members of State and local legislative bodies, and others qualified to assist in the preparation of such reports.

Text of 1977 Legislation as Amended

Title VII—National Urban Policy and New Community Development

Short Title and Statement of Purpose

Sec. 701. (a) This title may be cited as "National Urban Policy and New Community Development Act of 1970".

(b) It is the policy of the Congress and the purpose of this title to provide for the development of a national urban policy and to encourage the rational, orderly, efficient, and economic growth, development, and redevelopment of our States, metropolitan areas, cities, counties, towns, and communities in predominantly rural areas which demonstrate a special potential for accelerated growth; to encourage the prudent use and conservation of energy and our natural resources; and to encourage and support development which will assure our communities and their residents of adequate tax bases, community services, job opportunities, and good housing in well-balanced neighborhoods in socially, economically, and physically attractive living environments.

Part A—Development of a National Urban Policy

Findings and Declaration of Policy

Sec. 702 (a) The Congress finds that rapid changes in patterns of urban settlement, including change in population distribution and economic bases of urban areas, have crated an imbalance between the Nation's needs and resources and seriously threaten our physical and social environment, and the financial viability of our cities, and that the economic and social development of the Nation, the proper conservation of our energy and other natural resources, and the achievement of satisfactory living standards depend upon the sound, orderly, and more balanced development of all areas of the Nation.

(b) The Congress further finds that Federal programs affect the location of population, economic growth, and the character of urban development; that such programs frequently conflict and result in undesirable and costly patterns of urban development and redevelopment which adversely affect the environment and wastefully use energy and other natural resources; and that existing and future programs must be interrelated and coordinated within a system of orderly development and established priorities consistent with a national urban policy.

(c) To promote the general welfare and properly apply the resources of the Federal Government in strengthening the economic and social health of all areas of the Nation and more adequately protect the physical environment and conserve energy and other natural resources, the Congress declares that the Federal Government, consistent with the responsibilities of State and local government and the private sector, must assume responsibility for the development of a national urban policy which shall incorporate social, economic, and other appropriate factors. Such policy shall serve as a guide in making specific decisions at the national level which affect the pattern of urban development and redevelopment and shall provide a framework for development of interstate, State, and local urban policy.

(d) The Congress further declares that the national urban policy should—

(1) favor patterns of urbanization and economic development and stabilization which offer a range of alternative locations and encourage the wise and balanced use of physical and human resources in metropolitan and urban regions as well as in smaller urban places which have a potential for accelerated growth;

(2) foster the continued economic strength of all parts of the United States, including central cities, suburbs, smaller communities, local neighborhoods, and rural areas;

(3) encourage patterns of development and redevelopment which minimize disparities among States, regions, and cities;

(4) treat comprehensively the problems of poverty and employment (including the erosion of tax bases, and the need for better community services and job opportunities) which are associated with disorderly urbanization and rural decline;

(5) develop means to encourage good housing for all Americans without regard to race and creed;

(6) refine the role of the Federal Government in revitalizing existing communities and encouraging planned, large-scale urban and new community development;

(7) strengthen the capacity of general governmental institutions to contribute to balanced urban growth and stabilization; and

(8) facilitate increased coordination in the administration of Federal programs so as to encourage desirable patterns of urban development and redevelopment, encourage the prudent use of energy and other natural resources, and protect the physical environment.

National Urban Policy Report

Sec. 703 (a) The President shall transmit to Congress during February 1978, and during February of every even-numbered year thereafter, a Report on National Urban Policy which shall contribute to the formulation of such a policy and in addition shall include—

(1) information, statistics, and significant trends relating to the pattern of urban development for the preceding two years;

(2) a summary of significant problems facing the United States as a result of urban trends and developments affecting the well-being of urban areas;

(3) an examination of the housing and related community development problems experienced by cities undergoing a growth rate which equals or exceeds the national average;

(4) an evaluation of the progress and the effectiveness of Federal efforts designed to meet such problems and to carry out the national urban policy;

(5) an assessment of the policies and structure of existing and proposed interstate planning and developments affecting such policy;

(6) a review of State, local, and private policies, plans, and programs relevant to such policy;

(7) current and foreseeable needs in the areas served by policies, plans, and programs designed to carry out such policy, and the steps being taken to meet such needs; and

(8) recommendations for programs and policies for carrying out such policy, including such legislation and administrative actions as may be deemed necessary and desirable.

(b) The President may transmit from time to time to the Congress supplementary reports on urban growth which shall include such supplementary and revised recommendations as may be appropriate.

(c) To assist in the preparation of the National Urban Policy Report and any supplementary reports, the President may establish an advisory board, or seek the advice from time to time of temporary advisory boards, the members of whom shall be drawn from among private citizens familiar with the problems of urban areas, and from among Federal officials, Governors of States, mayors, county officials, members of State and local legislative bodies, and others qualified to assist in the preparation of such reports.

Sec. 921. Improved Coordination of Urban Policy

Title VII of the Housing and Urban Development Act of 1970 (42 U.S.C. 4501) et seq.) is amended—

(1) *in section 702(d), by striking paragraph (8) and inserting the following: "(8) increase coordination among Federal programs that seek to promote job opportunities and skills, decent and affordable housing, public safety, access to health care, educational opportunities, and fiscal soundness for urban communities and their residents";*

(2) *in section 703(a)—*

> *(A) by striking "during February 1978, and during February of every even-numbered year thereafter," and inserting ", not later than June 1, 1993, and not later than the first day of June of every odd-numbered year thereafter,"; and*

> *(B) in paragraph (8), by striking "such" and all that follows through the end of the sentence and inserting "legislative or administrative proposals—*

> *"(A) to promote coordination among Federal programs to assist urban areas;*

> *"(B) to enhance the fiscal capacity of fiscally distressed urban areas;*

> *"(C) to promote job opportunities in economically distressed urban areas and to enhance the job skills of residents of such areas;*

> *"(D) to generate decent and affordable housing;*

> *"(E) to reduce racial tensions and to combat racial and ethnic violence in urban areas;*

"(F) to combat urban drug abuse and drug-related crime and violence;

"(G) to promote the delivery of health care to low-income communities in urban areas;

"(H) to expand educational opportunities in urban areas; and

"(I) to achieve the goals of the national urban policy";

and

(3) by adding at the end of section 703 the following new subsection:

"(d) Referral.— The National Urban Policy Report shall, when transmitted to Congress, be referred in the Senate to the Committee on Banking, Housing, and Urban Affairs, and in the House of Representatives to the Committee on Banking, Finance and Urban Affairs."

Appendix 2:
Discussion Outline

Harold L. Wolman

and

William R. Barnes

I. Should the federal government have an explicit and articulated "urban policy"?

    A. Is "urban policy" an intellectually coherent and useful concept?

    B. Is "urban policy" a politically useful concept?

    C. Is there a political constitutency for urban policy and what is it?

II. What function (s) can/should a national urban policy report serve.

    A. Assist the government in formulating its own policies toward urban areas—in particular forcing it to bring together different agencies and viewing urban problems and policy responses as a whole rather than as separate and fragmented.

    B. Stimulate public discussion about urban problems, needs, and policies, including discussion of the administration's existing and proposed policies to deal with urban problems.

    C. Provide a summary and discussion of the state of research and knowledge on urban processes, problems, etc.

    D. Provide data on conditions and trends in urban American, i.e. perform a tracking and monitoring function.

    E. Assess and evaluate existing policy and programs in terms of their impact on urban America.

    F. Develop support for the administration's policies.

III. To what audience(s) should the report be addressed?

    A. Administration policy makers.

    B. Congress.

    C. Professional association and interest groups concerned with urban problems.

    D. The public.

    E. Academics and researchers.

IV. Who should prepare the report and through what processes?

    A. Department of Housing and Urban Development, as at present.

    B. The White House through its own policy apparatus or through an interagency task force.

    C. An independent entity (such as the National Academy of Sciences—although presumably this would not involve any presentation of the administration's preferred policy response to the nation's urban problems.

    D. A research organization (e.g., the Urban Institute, Brookings, Rand, etc.) on contract from HUD, at least for the part that does not involve administration policy recommendations.

V. How often should the report be issued and in what years (election years, off-year)?

VI. What should be the geographic focus of the report, i.e. what is meant by "urban"?

    A. Central cities
        1. All central cities
        2. Only large cities

    B. Metropolitan areas
        1. All MSAs
        2. Only large MSAs

    C. Metropolitan areas and their component parts (cities, suburbs) considered separately

    D. All urban places above a certain size (25,000?) of whether or not they are in an MSA.

VII. What level(s) of analysis should the report focus on?

1. Individuals who live in urban areas (people-based)

2. Governments in urban areas (jurisdiction-based)

3. The urban economy and labor markets (labor market-based)

4. The physical condition of urban areas (place-based)

VIII. What should the report cover (and should it cover the same items each time)?

1. Conditions and trends (i.e. monitoring urban areas)

2. Description and discussion of basic processes affecting urban areas

3. Identification of urban problems (from the administration's perspective)

4. Evaluation of federal (and other) programs and efforts as they affect urban areas and their residents

5. Presentation of the administration's strategy, approach, or focus for dealing with urban problems.

6. Presentation and discussion of the administration's specific policies and/or programs with respect to urban problems.

IX. How should the report be organized (and should the organization be similar for each report)?

A. By urban systems or function.
   1. Economic, social, and physical as in Reagan/Bush reports of the 1980s.
   2. Urban economy, individual well-being, social institutions, physical structure, and public sector as suggested by the organization of this conference.
   3. Other.

B. By urban problem or policy area (i.e. housing, community development, crime, education, poverty, etc.),

C. By salient issue as determined by the administration (e.g. the underclass, the fiscal crisis, racial discrimination, the appropriate role of the various levels of government, etc.).

D. By possible solution (e.g. community-based efforts, regional problem-solving, empowering individuals, stimulating the economy, expanded federal or state role, etc.).

X. How should the report be better disseminated and utilized (obviously depends upon responses to II. above).

    A. Congressional hearings.

    B. Responses by professional associations, interest groups.

    C. Academic conferences and symposia.

    D. Media coverage.

XI. Are there other vehicles or options that might better achieve the functions (see section 2) served by the national urban policy report rather than (or in addition to) the report?

XII. Should there be a national urban policy report and if so how should it be changed and improved?